THE GREAT
401(k) HOAX

Also by William Wolman and Anne Colamosca

The Judas Economy

THE GREAT
401(k) HOAX

Why Your Family's Financial Security
Is at Risk, and What You Can Do About It

WILLIAM WOLMAN
AND ANNE COLAMOSCA

PERSEUS
PUBLISHING

Copyright © 2002 by William Wolman and Anne Colamosca

Cataloging-in-Publication Data is available from the Library of Congress
ISBN 0-7382-0635-0

Perseus Publishing is a member of the Perseus Books Group.
Find us on the World Wide Web at http://www.perseuspublishing.com

Perseus Publishing books are available at special discounts for bulk purchases in the U.S. by corporations, institutions, and other organizations. For more information, please contact the Special Markets Department at the Perseus Books Group, 11 Cambridge Center, Cambridge, MA 02142, or call (800) 255-1514 or (617) 252-5298, or e-mail j.mccrary@perseusbooks.com.

Text design by Janice Tapia
Set in 11-point Berkeley Book by the Perseus Books Group

First printing, April 2002

1 2 3 4 5 6 7 8 9 10—04 03 02

Dedicated to Paul Chapman
Co-director of the Employment Project,
who has happily spent many years
helping American families
because he understood the issues
way ahead of everybody else

Contents

Acknowledgments

OVER THE YEARS we have benefited mightily by our interaction with the finance and economic staff of *BusinessWeek* magazine. Seymour Zucker, John Templeman, Michael J. Mandel, Jeffrey M. Laderman, Gary Weiss, and Bruce Nussbaum have been especially stimulating. We are grateful to Joan Danaher of *BusinessWeek* for help with our charts, and to Steve McCarthy for helping us with technical support.

We would like to thank the many people we have met through our contacts with the Employment Project. It wasn't just Paul Chapman who helped us to understand the real financial issues facing the American family. They saw the 1990s in a different way from most people, and we learned a lot from their unique perspective.

The work of two academicians, Robert J. Shiller of Yale University, and Jeremy Siegel of the University of Pennsylvania, has been invaluable to our understanding of the stock market. We are especially grateful to Professor Shiller for updating his critical data on the long-term performance of the stock market. The work of University of Notre Dame economist, Teresa Ghilarducci, helped us immeasurably in understanding how the private pension system in the United States came to be what it is.

Joe Spieler, our agent, did what an agent is supposed to do, and we thank him.

We are especially grateful to our editors at Perseus. Nick Philipson and Arlinda Shtuni both took great care with our manuscript and gave us their best critical judgment. They both spent many long hours helping us to shape the manuscript. Above all, Perseus allowed us to write the book that we wanted to write. For that, Elizabeth Carduff, executive vice president in charge of marketing at Perseus, also deserves our warm thanks for her support. Copy Editor Michele Wynn and Senior Project Editor Marietta Urban were extremely helpful. Nancy Van Itallie, veteran book editor and personal friend, read an early draft and made some useful suggestions.

Finally, the usual disclaimer. Those whose help we acknowledge do not necessarily agree with either our analysis or our conclusions. Nor are they responsible for any errors or omissions in this book.

PART ONE

STRADDLING TWO ERAS

EVENTS SINCE THE FIERY ATTACK on the World Trade Center pose critical financial problems for the American family that are still not widely understood. In the preceding decade, America's victory over communism in the Cold War had unleashed a wave of faith in the free market that was unparalleled. Everyone from a Democratic president, Bill Clinton, to a Russian president, Vladimir Putin, had declared that, to use Clinton's words, "the age of big government is over." And for a while, it all seemed wonderful. With a peace dividend in hand that the nation had not seen in almost fifty years, the American economy grew rapidly, particularly in the second half of the 1990s. And the stock market responded with a phenomenal rise, quintupling over the ten years of the 1990s.

The average American family got caught up in the free market frenzy of those prosperous years. Many had made some money in the stock market. The acceptance of the free market ideology became almost universal. Even the traditional defender of government intervention, the Democratic Party, began to look with favor on the symbols of a free market gone rampant; the biggest merger wave in history met little opposition, and cries for privatization of virtually everything from prisons to the retirement plans of solid working people swept the land. Waves of excessive faith in the free market had been seen before, notably in the years preceding the great stock market crash of 1929. And the consequences for the financial and economic health of the American economy, as we all know, have always been severe.

The great free market myth had been showing signs of unraveling prior to the attack. The record shows that the United States entered a recession in March 2001 that brought with it pared-down earnings and a wave of layoffs. It had been almost a year and a half since the stock market peaked in the spring of 2000. American families had lost hundreds of billions of dollars. And before September 11, average Americans began to sense that the stock market was not going to support most people, least of all make everybody rich in a hurry. Most disturbing to Americans who had held onto their jobs was the slide in the value of 401(k) plans, for just as the World Trade Center had become a physical icon of the power of the free market, so the 401(k) had become an unquestioned icon of the financial security and hope that had been promised by Wall Street.

Wall Street responded to the World Trade Center attack by wrapping itself in the American flag. Its message to the public was that since Osama bin Laden's aim was to undermine American capitalism, Americans should respond in a patriotic way and invest. True, the market fell between September 17, the day it reopened, and September 21. But then it seemed to respond to the patriotic message that was coupled with optimistic forecasts of economic recovery. After the attack, there was little talk emanating from the Street about the internal problems of the stock market. To Wall Street, it all seemed to hang on the need for Americans to fight the terrorist scourge together and support the market by buying stocks and the economy by maintaining normal spending patterns. And if they did, said Wall Street, everything would be fine. And for a time the message seemed to work. Stocks came off the bottom and a chorus of economists of all political and theoretical stripes professed to see an early end to recession.

But the Street's claque was dead wrong. Suddenly, and strangely, everything was turned upside down in the opening month of the palindromic year 2002. The mantra of the 1990s had been that anyone who was energetic, hardworking, and self-sufficient could make it. But the bankruptcy of Enron, coming as it did after a two-year slide in stocks, reinforced feelings that the economic security provided by a private sector run rampant is fragile at best. Nowhere was this more evident than in the vaporization of the 401(k) plans of Enron employees during a period in which the corporation's top executives realized over $1 billion from the sale of the company's stock.

In the immediate wake of the Enron debacle, the focus shifted to the possible political scandal resulting from the sinister collapse of the company that was the biggest fund-raiser for President George W. Bush's election campaign. But tantalizing though the appeal of a Republican Whitewater might have been to the Democrats and the media, the narrow political focus misses the main point. At bottom, the Enron debacle is unnerving because it provides vivid, if extreme, evidence of systemic problems in a society in which deregulation had gone too far, in which the cooking of corporate books had become endemic, and in which both accountants and securities analysts have laid waste to any notion that their responsibility is to the public as well as to the executives who are their direct clients.

The negative effects of the Enron scandal are substantial and are likely to place a burden on the economy that will persist for years to come. Particularly because of the involvement of Enron's accounting firm, Arthur Andersen, there will be a tendency to question the books of virtually every publicly traded company in the United States. The vast majority of corporations used "creative accounting" to make their revenues seem higher than they really were and their costs lower during the hectic period that led up to the stock market crash that began in the spring of 2000. This is in accord with what happened following earlier stock market bubbles, particularly the one that exploded in 1929. In the wake of the 1929 bubble, there were many congressional investigations of what went wrong. Indeed, "Sunny Jim" Mitchell, the chairman of First National City Bank, which was the predecessor of Citicorp, was put on trial. The effect of the endless series of hearings that were held in the early 1930s was to keep suspicions of inappropriate corporate behavior and accounting alive for four or five years.

The scale of malfeasance that surrounded the great stock market bubble of the late 1990s is not yet known. But it is relatively certain that it will keep alive public hesitation to invest in stocks and will therefore be a factor in contributing to an investment climate that will be at best stagnant.

But even more ominous is the likely impact of Enron on the willingness of business to invest. In the heady days of the 1990s, creative accounting allowed companies to keep their books in such a way that made their reported revenue growth look stronger than it really was and their costs lower than they really were. That obviously made the seeming return to capital investment higher than it otherwise would have been. Inevitably, the Enron debacle will force more realistic accounting on the corporate community. As this happens, the newly imposed conservative accounting will constrain the rate of return to new investment and therefore cause capital spending to be notably lower than it would have been if the Enron scandal had never occurred. The greatest corporate bankruptcy in American history will loom over the U.S. economy because it will constrain capital spending and therefore hinder economic growth.

And the downward pressure on the economy and the stock market would indeed have occurred, we believe, whether or not the Bush administration appears to have acted against the public interest in its handling of the Enron affair. The characters in the billion-dollar charade—endlessly upbeat stock market analysts, accountants dealing in fantasy figures, bankers who wanted to help jack up stock market prices—had all been put into place during the great globalized roar of the 1990s, when the Clinton administration held power. Anybody who looked too hard or asked questions about the great boom were at best patronized, ground down, or fired by those who were intent on keeping the Great Party going.

In thinking about the Enron debacle, the average investor began to be alarmed by the callous attitude of Washington toward the impact of the sudden and cataclysmic corporate bankruptcy on American families who were cynically induced by the corporation's top executives to keep their 401(k) money in Enron stock. On their side, the Republicans argued that they had done nothing wrong because they refused to help the company when it came to them in the fall of 2001. It is important to recognize, however, that the Bush administration did not do anything right, either. It did not move to protect Enron employees from the machinations of a group of executives who sold over a billion dollars' worth of stock after they knew that the company was heading for the rocks and while they were sending e-mails to employees assuring them that the company was in glowing health. Apparently, the Republicans and the Bush administration were much more concerned with keeping their collective noses as clean as possible than they were in preventing the average investor or Enron employee from going broke.

Taken together, terror at the World Trade Center and the financial folly of which Enron is a symbol have already led to a breathtaking reversal of public and private attitudes that existed in the 1990s. After September 11, for the first time since the days of John F. Kennedy and Lyndon B. Johnson, the entire country turned to Washington for help on what was essentially a domestic issue. The need was so great, the concern so overwhelming, that it had, finally, become difficult to go it alone anymore. In a speech that not even the most clued-in political commentator could ever have conjured up, Texas conservative President George W. Bush talked with approval about Eleanor Roosevelt, as his administration strove to reach out and reassure America's families in the midst of the fear. Eleanor's response, we believe, would have been that if President Bush wanted to use her language, he should also use her policies, meaning that America's families would need more than psychological reassurance. After the fall of the new economy, they would need a new New Deal to help keep them financially afloat in a dangerous world, which, like it or not, is all too reminiscent of the 1930s.

The financial future of the American family is precarious. We believe that prior to the attack, policy was headed in the wrong direction, focused as it was on schemes to privatize Social Security, supposedly because the Social Security system was threatened by bankruptcy. But "lockbox" and all, the financial future was at least being debated. The danger in the post–WTC crisis is that this entire debate will virtually disappear, leaving the United States exposed to an intergenerational crisis of unprecedented severity.

But the post–WTC, post-Enron world also brings new opportunities. A new sense of community has emerged as a response to the attack on America. And even more important, ordinary working Americans—policemen, firemen, and steelworkers—have emerged as the nation's real heroes. This could be an opening for much-needed social and political changes that would really put the needs of the average American family on the same level as those of the corporation.

Reform of the 401(k) is at the top of the agenda. We believe that our book points the way to the needed changes both in private behavior and public policy. But even if the 401(k) were reformed so that employees would never again be misled by management as they were at Enron or be "locked into" disastrous stock holdings that could bankrupt them, the long-term economic outlook raises serious questions about the adequacy of the 401(k) as the foundation stone of the American pension system.

The record of the 401(k) shows that it left most Americans grossly un-prepared for retirement after two decades of stock market boom. And the problem can only intensify as the population ages and many more people live into their eighties and nineties. Layoffs in the wake of the re-cession that started in March 2001 show that workers in their fifties and early sixties are highly vulnerable in the twenty-first-century job market. Even if older workers get new jobs, very often those jobs pay less and are sometimes temporary. Those who start their own businesses in late mid-dle-age also often have a hard time making a living for themselves. Americans who hit hard times when they are in their late fifties could face a thirty to thirty-five year period bereft of both substantial earnings and a decent pension. The cold fact is that the new century arrived after twenty years of stock market boom that left 85 percent of all stock own-ership in the United States concentrated in the top 10 percent of the population. As difficult as it is to think about, many in the other 90 per-cent may indeed have a difficult time putting together enough funds to support themselves as the years go on.

America's prior 100-year history of troubled pension policy based on an inconsistent mix of private and public plans has been dragged into the twenty-first century. In the other countries of the developed world, the two systems have been melded into one and the total pension tends to be a more adequate replacement for wages and salaries earned at work. In Germany, for example, retiring citizens receive between 75 and 85 percent of their salaries through a public retirement plan. In the United States, Social Security was passed in 1935 as a result of the crisis caused by the Great Depression. It was viewed by some as a supplement to private pen-sion plans. And though Social Security is still seen as "supplemental," less than 50 percent of those on retirement receive private pensions.

As the country shifts away from old-style "funded" retirement plans to 401(k)s, there are ample numbers around to demonstrate that many Americans either don't understand how their 401(k)s work or just don't have enough leftover money from their salaries every month to invest in these plans. Many Americans have alarmingly small amounts in their 401(k)s, and if the stock market stagnates for several years, as we believe it will, the growth in their retirement funds will be meager.

Depending on the 401(k) for retirement is inherently risky. Even if Congress does reform 401(k)s, these plans are likely to remain "voluntary." Companies that are not making large profits can decide they no longer want to contribute matching funds. Even if they continue to contribute the matching funds to lower-paid workers, they don't add up to much. They can also easily change employees over to temporary status whenever they feel like it—reneging on the promise to match employee contributions to the 401(k). None of these actions is illegal. No fraud is being committed. But as a result, many more Americans could continue to be left financially in the lurch.

Despite the furor over Enron and the growing momentum for campaign finance reform, we are not optimistic about the prospects for fundamental pension reform in the United States. Coupled with the prospect of a stagnant stock market for many years to come, the inadequacies of the pension system make straight thinking mandatory for those families whose financial fate is tied to the 401(k). This book is intended to guide your family through the needed thinking process. If anything has become clear in the opening years of the new millenium, it is that it can be disastrous to rely on employers, or Wall Street, or the politicians to do your thinking for you.

Chapter 1

Introduction

The occasions are rare. But there are times when an ugly combination of letters and numbers penetrates deeply into the American consciousness. There was a time when "4F" was one of the best-known expressions in the American language, connoting a young man who became exempt from the military draft because he had flunked the physical. *Catch-22*, the title of a book by Joseph Heller about a military snafu in the war against Japan, became famous as a description of a problem with no solution.

A similar fate awaits the combination that defined the hopes and dreams of American families as they celebrated the booming 1990s and looked forward to a new, exciting postmillennial decade: 401(k). Those four symbols had become an American icon, seeming to contain within them the promise that the average American family, neither rich nor poor but middle class, could stake a claim for its share in the prosperity created by the technological wonders that energized the American economy in the 1990s.

The vision of family wealth turned the 401(k) into a cultural icon celebrated in cartoons, fiction, television, magazines, and front-page stories in the nation's most famous newspapers. The 401(k) is a form of retirement plan in which employees are responsible for managing their own pensions and employers voluntarily contribute matching funds or stock. It differs from traditional defined benefit plans, which guarantee a monthly income to retirees. In a defined contribution plan such as the

401(k), the risk of the plan, especially if the stock market declines or the employer opts not to provide matching funds or company stock, is borne by the worker. The 401(k) seemed to be ideally suited to an age in which politicians refused to pay for high-priced government programs and "go it alone" endeavor ruled the day. The 401(k) was portable in a workplace where frequent job changes were fashionable and held to be desirable. It provided some scope for eligible employees to make their own decisions about how to invest their money in an era when investment information dominated the airwaves and Internet. It seemed ideally suited to a world in which it was cheaper and cheaper to trade stocks. And above all, it appeared as a device that made it easy for the average worker to participate in the greatest boom in history. It seemed that the 401(k) would be a perpetual wealth machine for each and every member of the great American middle class.

It felt great while it lasted. But the 401(k) will turn out to be the greatest systemic financial hoax ever perpetrated on an unsuspecting public. The danger inherent in the four characters is, as Vice President Dick Cheney would say, "big time." The problems with the 401(k) suddenly surfaced in late 2001, when a recession that was already underway was intensified by the attack on the World Trade Center. In quick succession, some leading corporations, including Daimler-Chrysler, Lucent, Bethlehem Steel, Wyndham International, and above all, Enron, scaled back their matching contributions to 401(k)s. And Enron and Lucent were shown to have forced their employees to hold company stock even against their will, with catastrophic consequences in a market where those stocks were plunging. Some 30 percent of assets held in 1.5 million 401(k) plans were in the stock of the company sponsoring the plan, putting many people at risk (see Chapter 8). In the wake of these revelations, employees around the country held their breath in case their 401(k)s should suffer a similar fate.

The financial threat of a 401(k) system gone sour goes beyond anything that has yet been seen. By comparison, the Dutch tulip mania of 1637 was a rose tournament in Portland, Oregon; the South Sea Bubble of 1720, a tempest in a backyard swimming pool; the gold rush of 1849, a treasure hunt at an eight-year-old's birthday party; the Great Crash of 1929, the production of an off–Off Broadway play. Protecting the American family from the potential ravages of the 401(k) will require radical changes in both private finances and public policy.

The new approach to retirement offered the family a share of ownership in the great American corporations that dominate the global economy, indeed, in the stock of any company traded on the New York, American, and Nasdaq exchanges. To make it easy, those shares could be gradually acquired on what felt like an installment plan: easy monthly paycheck deductions. A big feature of most 401(k)s was partially matching contributions from employers. And the Internal Revenue Service kicked in, too: The money put into the 401(k) is a deduction from the family's taxable income. The government only gets its money later, after employees retire and begin to live off the stocks that they had so patiently accumulated.

The 401(k) ushered in a revolution in the way Americans were able to think about their financial prospects as they grew older. And as with all revolutions, the 401(k) created serious new risks. In America's traditional pension plans, spanning most of the twentieth century, employees were promised a monthly check by their employers after they reached retirement age. The responsibility for making sure that this all-important check would not bounce rested with companies. And since the size of the check was fixed, the traditional retirement plans came to be known as defined benefit plans. Employers were made liable and assumed the risk that the investments that funded defined benefit plans would be successful enough to guarantee the retirement income of all workers who participated.

The retirement revolution took the risks inherent in investing away from the corporation and put them squarely on the backs of employees. The 401(k) came to be known as a defined contribution pension plan. Theoretically, it left employees free to choose from a menu of their own investments, with the caveat that any risk that investments would turn sour would be the responsibility of workers.

In effect, 401(k)s ask American workers to ape the investment behavior of the rich, even though they obviously do not have the resources to ride out bad markets of the kind that we believe will prevail for the next decade. By law, working Americans own the money in their 401(k) plans and are free to invest it as they will. But in reality, most companies do not include an adequate range of investment choices to safeguard savings in volatile markets. At their core, the choices available in most 401(k)s represent a sometimes subtle, and sometimes not so subtle, implication that the employee would do best by investing in stocks.

The 401(k) is, of course, not the only defined contribution retirement program that is "tax advantaged"—given a favored tax status—by the Internal Revenue Service. It is only the best-known member of a family of defined contribution pension plans. We chose to use it in the title of our book because it is an icon of the public culture and also represents similar private-sector programs: all forms of profit-sharing plans, stock bonus plans, employee stock ownership plans (ESOPs), employee Keogh plans, and simplified employee pensions (SEEPs). There are also 403(b) plans, similar to 401(k)s, which cover schools, churches, and other tax-exempt organizations.

By mid-February 2002, American investors had lost $5 trillion or 30 percent of their stock wealth since the spring of 2000. Yet Wall Street's propaganda in favor of the family market continued to be backed by gobs of advertising dollars and millions in campaign contributions and lobbying, along with brokers and analysts hired to promote stocks day after day, no matter how bad things got. Andrew Smithers, the brilliant British financial analyst, once told the authors that he could make a lot more money by being a bull and being wrong than by being a bear and being right.

The same cannot be said of those who depend on their 401(k) programs. The American public has been hoodwinked by political and corporate forces into relying on the 401(k) as the primary long-term investment mechanism. In doing so, the stock market has been put at center stage in providing for a comfortable retirement for the average American. The 401(k) represents an implicit promise to middle-class Americans that they can live off the income that they receive from stock ownership, just like the rich do. It is a promise that is impossible to fulfill: It is the great 401(k) hoax.

Income from stocks comes in two forms. The most basic is dividends. This is money paid to stockholders after a company has met its business expenses, paid taxes, and made investments needed to keep the company solvent. The other component of the income from stocks is, of course, capital gains, realized by those who can sell their stocks for more than they paid for them.

As a source of income for the average middle-class American retiree, dividends are a dog that won't hunt. In 1999, a boom year, the total dividends paid out to stockholders came out to a puny 364 billion. And judging by the proportion of stocks owned, some Americans are far more equal than others. Data compiled by New York University economist Edward N.

Wolff shows that the top 1 percent of the population owns just under 50 percent of the stock outstanding; the top 10 percent of the population owns 85 percent. Dividends are roughly proportional to the amount of stock owned, so if you subtract the share of the top 10 percent from total dividends, the amount available to the rest of the population is a scant $55 billion. That is roughly $225 per person. That is not per week, per month, but *per year.* The monthly figure is $18.75 per person.

The numbers look better if you just look at the dividends available for distribution to those age sixty-five and over, above the traditional retirement age. The income available from dividends looks better than that for the population as a whole, of course. But it only amounts to $1,618 per year, or $135 per month, less than the average monthly Social Security check, worth $804 in 1999. It is a jarring number, raising profound questions about Wall Street's view of an adequate retirement income for the average American.

A warning of the gross inadequacies of the 401(k) was already apparent even at the end of the booming 1990s, when stock prices had quintupled. At the height of its hold on the American imagination, the average 401(k) was puny as compared to the long-term financial needs of the American family. The average 401(k) account shrank to $49,024 in 2000, down from $55,502 in 1999, according to the Employment Benefit Research Institute. And this number looks a lot better than it really is because it averages in the 401(k)s of the top earners. A much more realistic figure is the median 401(k) account (half American families below, half above), which at the end of 2000 was only $13,493, down from $15,246 in 1999. And even these numbers give a generous interpretation to how the nation's families fared during the boom, because "old-fashioned" pensions—defined benefit plans—were fading from the scene and Social Security was under political attack, particularly from the right wing of the Republican Party.

Taken by themselves, the small size of 401(k) plans point to a looming retirement crisis in the United States. But they are far from the end of the story. Adjusted for inflation, the amount of money that the average American family had set aside for retirement did not increase in the 15 years between 1983 and 1998, despite the stock market boom and the supposed benefits of the 401(k). It will come as a surprise to most Americans who have been lulled into complacency by Wall Street's advertising barrage. But New York University economist Wolff has analyzed the data and compared what he calls the retirement wealth of people in comparable age groups in 1998 with what it was in 1983. His numbers show that in 1998, 65 percent of all American households headed by a person between 47 and 64 had either the same or less pension wealth in 1998 than they had 15 years earlier. For the household right in the middle—the median—retirement wealth fell by 13 percent over the 15 years. The most important reason, of course, is that pension contributions are tied to wages that, for most Americans, grew painfully slowly in the 1980s and the first half of the 1990s.

As might be expected in an era of growing inequality, the well-to-do did better than average families. But you had to be close to the top to really make out. For the top 20 percent, pension wealth grew by 19 percent over 15 years; not bad, but probably less than they would have guessed. It was only the rich that made out. The pension wealth of the top 5 percent increased by 176 percent.

The inability of the average American family to build a retirement nest egg during a stock market boom implies that the capital gains game envisioned by 401(k) proponents has all the makings of a Ponzi scheme. The chain letter phenomenon central to the machinations of the famed Bostonian, Charles Ponzi, was a fraud, pure and simple. Victims could, and did, call the cops, and the original improper Bostonian ended up in the bastille.

No such easy outcome is open to those depending on the 401(k). As Yale University economist Robert J. Shiller has observed, the unrealistic expectations that were built up about the financial returns promised by the 401(k) represent what is in effect an innocent fraud, the product of "a naturally occurring Ponzi process." The fraud was perpetrated in a period when Wall Street came close to convincing the American public that its economic and political system, rooted as it was in the free market, could do no wrong. It was a period in which the belief that a new and vibrant technology, particularly in information processing, could perpetuate rapid economic growth into an indefinite future.

How We Will Make Our Case

"One page of history is worth volumes of analysis." These are the words of the famed Supreme Court justice Louis D. Brandeis. Although it is forgotten these days, the wording in the title of Justice Brandeis's most famous book, *Other People's Money*, reflects his expert knowledge of Wall Street behavior. Our book describes what we believe to be the underlying historical forces, including inadequate social and economic policies that are designed for failure in protecting an American family. This means that working Americans will be forced to deal with the ominous consequences of Wall Street's great hoax on their own.

We begin by analyzing the anatomy of the great 401(k) hoax (Chapter 2). In defense of this hoax, Wall Street relies on an "analysis" of the earnings prospects for particular companies and an assessment of the growth of profits in the economy as a whole. Wall Street's approach as to whether the price of stocks is too high, too low, or just about right is based on projections of an essentially unknowable future.

We, by contrast, turn to the lesson of history: Excess faith in the corporation and in the profits it earns will plague the coming decade. There is simply no way in which corporate profits will be large enough to meet the financial needs of older Americans.

The history of stock prices goes all the way back to 1803, when stock trading started under the Buttonwood Tree in Lower Manhattan. That history shows that stock prices move up and down in long, persistent waves. Particularly pertinent is the history surrounding the twentieth century, which shows that stocks were driven to unsustainable highs three times: in 1901, 1929, and 1966. Each of these flights into a valuation fantasy was followed by more than a decade in which stock prices stagnated or declined. That does not mean that there were no rallies in these periods, but the fact is, the stock market could not, and did not, go on to new highs.

The great danger in the opening decade of the new century is that the average investor will ignore this lesson. In large measure, this danger is the result of social, political, and economic trends that allowed Wall Street to emerge as the real victor in the great social debates of the 1990s and capture "family values" for itself and for the corporations in whose stocks it trades (Chapter 3).

The lessons of history go far beyond the patterns traced by the stock market itself. Even more important perhaps is an historical view of the implications of broad economic, cultural, and political trends. And here the most useful lessons can be seen in a comparison of the 1920s and 1930s with the 1990s and the postmillennial decade (Chapters 4, 5, and 6).

The conclusions one must draw from such a comparison are disturbing. And history also shows that the family will get little help from the political and corporate establishments in preparing for a difficult decade. It was an uphill battle throughout the twentieth century. It took a real crisis, the Great Depression of the 1930s, to pass Social Security, the only nationwide government program the middle class could depend on, since it offered all Americans financial support when they could no longer work. Equivalent and usually superior programs were in place in Europe decades earlier. And in the 1990s, corporations and Wall Street combined to promote plans to at least partially privatize the Social Security system (Chapter 7). This opposition to public programs continued throughout the twentieth century, even though history shows that private-sector pension plans were grossly inadequate, subject to sudden termination, and riddled with other flaws (Chapter 8).

We believe that there is a way for the family to survive and perhaps even flourish in the difficult years that lie ahead. The path to financial success must begin with a journey of escape from the thrall of Wall Street. That requires drowning out the noise that comes from the Street on financial television, in the business press, and via the reports from the Street itself, all of which inundate current and potential customers for stocks. Years of experience has taught the brokerage houses how to lure customers into dubious investment (Chapter 9).

When Wall Street's message is cast aside, a new set of rules for investing in a low-growth environment emerges from the lessons of this book. We call these rules "stillwater investing" (Chapter 10). In sum, we believe that pension reforms must be made and the American family has to be involved in making them (Chapter 11).

Chapter 2

The Anatomy of a Hoax

"Madness!" uttered the stunned medical officer upon seeing his commander, played by Alec Guinness, attempt to prevent an allied commando force from demolishing the bridge on the River Kwai. It had been built by the men in his British brigade while they were held captive in a remote Japanese prisoner-of-war camp inside Burma during World War II. Guinness had become so proud of the quality of his brigade's work that he could not bear to see it destroyed, even though it was to be used against the Allies.

Yes. It's perfectly possible for well-organized, hard working, normally prudent people like those in Alec Guinness's model British brigade to take leave of their senses and commit acts of self-destruction. That in fact was what was happening to the average American family as the twentieth century was coming to a close. The United States had enjoyed a string of spectacular successes—victory in the Cold War in the late 1980s, a booming economy in the 1990s, and the information technology revolution that spanned both decades. As a consequence, Americans entered the twenty-first century with an inflated notion of what even the world's most powerful economy could accomplish for its average citizen. That is the "madness" that will be hard to dislodge from the American psyche and will dominate economic life in the opening decades of the twenty-first century.

The "madness" is primarily a financial madness. There have been many episodes of financial delusion before. The great stock market boom of the late 1920s is only the most famous example.

But nothing that happened in the past was nearly as all-encompassing as the great American stock market boom of the late twentieth century. Not only did it drive stock market valuations to unprecedented heights but the "madness" did not recede even after the initial bubble burst on March 18, 2000, slashing the wealth of many families by more than 25 percent. Despite plunging corporate profits, a paltry growth for gross domestic product (GDP), and a slew of overseas financial troubles, many investors clung to the idea that the shimmering days of the late 1990s would soon reemerge.

Most Americans seemed to need Wall Street's illusions because Main Street life was becoming harder and harder to sustain. For the average American, the real long-term legacy of the 1990s was a huge "flexible" workforce. It seemed to appear and disappear as obediently as the conscientious bird in a cuckoo clock. Yet increasingly, it seemed sinister. Even the executive class had tied its income to gains on stock options that were becoming more and more illusory. Without continued belief in the promise of stocks, the reality of a financially anchorless existence was too much for the winners of the Cold War to bear.

As the United States moved into the twenty-first century, its financial psyche was in the grip of four delusions that created the great 401(k) hoax: (1) It's *always* a good time to invest in stocks; (2) mass participation in the market will keep stock prices rising; (3) baby boomers guarantee rising stock prices; (4) stock market "perks" to workers, especially the 401(k), will more than compensate over the long haul for "damped-down" wages. Our purpose in writing this book is not primarily to debunk conventional financial wisdom, though it richly deserves ridicule. Rather, it is to expose the fantasies and lay bare the real trends that will affect the returns to investment and to equip the average investor with the tools needed to navigate the opening decades of the new century.

Delusion 1: It's Always a Good Time to Buy Stocks

The most common delusion is that it's always a good time to buy stocks. Wall Street asks the investor to accept its projections for the future, instead of relying on a realistic reading of the history of stock market trends. Wall Street insists that the investor is always better off to invest

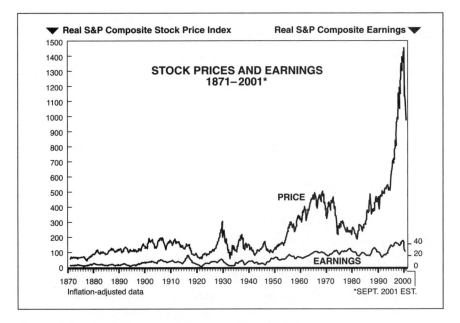

Figure 2.1   Stock Prices and Earnings 1871–2001.
Source: Robert J. Shiller, Yale University

for the long term by buying stocks rather than any other investment, including bonds.

There is a sense in which Wall Street's mantra worships a true god. The statistical record of the American stock markets extends all the way back to 1803 when stocks were traded under the Buttonwood Tree on Wall Street. That record does show that over two centuries, stocks have indeed outperformed other forms of investment.

But it must clearly be understood that this very long record provides scant comfort to anyone who is saving through stocks in the opening decade of the twenty-first century. There is one figure that shows why. It should be burned into everyone's mind.

Figure 2.1 shows that since the beginning of the twentieth century, there were four periods when stock market bubbles raised prices into the stratosphere: those ending in 1901, 1929, and 1966, and one probably ending in the year 2000. The most spectacular rise is the most recent one; it was only that of 1929 that came remotely close.

And as Figure 2.2 shows, stock market bubbles undermine realistic measures of stock market valuation, such as the price-earnings ratio, in a fundamental way.

What can only be called stock market depressions followed the first three bubbles. In each case, it took at least twenty years for the market to surpass the highs of the bubble years. In the twenty years following the 1901 peak, the inflation-adjusted return to stocks, including dividends, averaged –0.2 percent. It averaged 0.4 percent a year for the twenty years following 1929 and averaged 1.9 percent for the twenty years following 1966. And those returns include not only capital gains but also dividends. These are not rates of return that would provide the American family with a comfortable means of retirement in the years ahead. Yet it is highly unlikely that the stock market will provide better returns than in earlier periods that followed stock market bubbles.

It's hardly a matter of rocket science to conclude that by far the greatest proportion of twentieth-century stock market gains were compressed into forty years. In the other sixty of the hundred years of the twentieth century, stocks languished. In those sixty years, the stock market was hardly a place where the average investor could compound for a comfortable retirement, or accumulate money to educate children. Indeed, the returns over these years were lower than the much-reviled 2 percent inflation-adjusted annual return that is promised by the Social Security system, which contains a cost-of-living allowance. It is also far below the 4 percent return that is guaranteed by the newly created inflation-indexed Treasury bonds.

The record of post-bubble stock markets has enormous implications for the American family. One relatively easy way to grasp these implications is to compare the return to systematic stock market investing promised by Wall Street with the returns that history suggests are far more realistic. In its most somber and serious moments, Wall Street tells the American family that it can rely on earning an inflation-adjusted rate of return of 7 percent on its money with a long term stock-savings plan. Reality, on the contrary, suggests that a return of fewer than 2 percent is a far more realistic outlook for a period that extends well past the end of the first decade of the twentieth century.

The difference between what Wall Street promises and what history suggests is the difference between comfort and virtual penury. This can be seen by comparing buildup of savings at alternative rates of return.

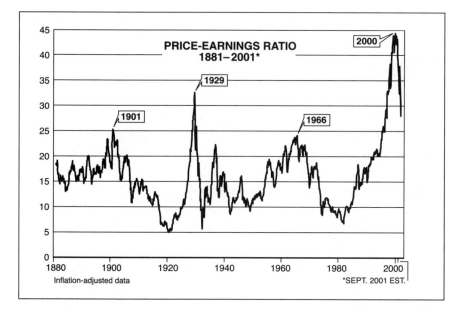

Figure 2.2   Price-Earnings Ratio 1881–2001.
Source: Robert J. Shiller, Yale University

That comparison is at the base of our investment recommendation discussed in detail in Chapter 10. If the real rate of return to savings is 7 percent, which is in effect Wall Street's minimum promised number, a systematic program to save $1,000 a year for twenty years would build a fund of $43,873 at the end of twenty years. The investment would amount to $20,000, the profits to $23,873. A $5,000-per-year investment would grow to $219,365; a $10,000 annual investment to $438,730. The vision provided for a $10,000 annual investment, at a 7 percent real annual rate of return, is a purchasing power equivalent to what $30,711 a year, or $2,559 a month would buy in today's purchasing power. In themselves, these numbers are not large. But combined with Social Security and the possibility of generating income from the home that the retiree owns, they do suggest comfort.

In reality, however, history suggests that the rate of return to systematic stock savings will be far lower than the 7 percent figure. We optimistically assume that the 1.9 percent real rate of return to stocks that prevailed after the 1966 market peak is the likely outlook for the opening decades of the twenty-first century. Under these conditions, each $1,000 invested annually for twenty years would result in the accumulation of a portfolio worth $24,506; each $5,000, a portfolio worth $122,530; each $10,000, a portfolio worth $245,060. If investors get an annual rate of return of 1.9 percent on their money at the end of the accumulation period, their annual income from investment would be $4,656 at the end of the accumulation period; and their monthly income, $388 in today's purchasing power. No matter how this sum is sliced or supplemented, it provides the opposite of a comfort zone for retirement. The stock market can be a treacherous place, and history shows this to be true not only in the short run, but also in such longer periods as the first twenty-nine years of the century as a whole.

We believe that the 1.9 scenario is the most realistic benchmark for the next twenty years. But it is hardly a worst-case scenario. If the total real returns to stock over the next twenty years approximated the –0.2 percent of the two decades following the 1901 market peak or the 0.4 percent real rate of return of the years following 1929, the results will obviously be far worse.

By far the most important cause of stock market bubbles is a flight from reality that has its roots in economic, cultural, and political trends that produce a grossly overvalued market. Figure 2.2 depicts the history of the most basic measure of stock market valuation, the price-earnings ratio that is conventionally compressed into the famed "p/e." The p/e ratio equals the price of the stock divided by the company's earnings (profits) per share. If a company has profits of $5 per share, and each share sells for $50, then the p/e ratio is 10. P/e's come in two flavors, one plain vanilla, the other a fancy concoction and possibly fake. The earnings figure used to calculate the real p/e is a matter of history. It deals with what Wall Street calls "trailing earnings," with the figure based on what the company actually earned in the most recent twelve-month period for which figures are available. The possibly fake p/e is based on what some analyst or group of analysts project as earnings per share over the coming year, a number that could just as easily be wildly off base as correct. P/e's are also calculated for the popular averages, like the Dow Jones Industrial Average and the popular indexes like the Standard & Poor's 500 Index. It should be obvious that we have a preference for the real historical figures, and they are the ones that we use in this book, unless we warn you otherwise.

The p/e ratio is probably the most useful measure of the state of investor confidence in a company. When the p/e ratio is high, it means that investors believe that the rate of profit growth will increase, perhaps rapidly. A low p/e indicates a lack of confidence that earnings can be sustained or increased. By comparing the p/e's that prevail at a given moment in time with their historic levels, it is possible to form a judgment as to whether stocks are expensive, cheap, or priced about right.

A long-term comparison of stock prices (Figure 2.1) and price-earnings ratios (Figure 2.2) shows that they reach peaks at about the same time. This means that stock market bubbles are, in the words of Alice in Wonderland, "a grin without a cat," a psychological phenomenon. And the flight from reality can persist for a long time. It was at the end of December 1996, when the Dow Jones Industrial Average was at 6700, that Federal Reserve Board chairman Alan Greenspan first warned of "irrational exuberance" in the stock market. At that time the price earnings ratio on the Dow was 25. Five years later, despite a weak market in 2000 and 2001, the p/e on the Dow was 30. Apparently, market psychology had not eroded as rapidly as the market itself. As a benchmark, throughout its history the average p/e on the Dow has been 15.

A comparison of the state of the stock market and the state of the economy in the opening years of the new millennium therefore strongly suggests that the dream of continued 7 percent return on stock market investing is a hoax on the American public rather than a realistic appraisal of the future. This is a critical fact in an economy in which pension plans have increasingly been geared to stock market returns. Defined contribution plans that are stock market dependent have overwhelmingly replaced plans in which companies promise fixed, reliable benefits to retired employees. Under Ronald Reagan, George Herbert Walker Bush, and William Jefferson Clinton, many pension plans turned into 401(k) plans—profitable during the boom years. And the mantra of the 401(k) continues to flourish under George W. Bush and his Republican and Democratic centrist allies, despite the 401(k)'s potentially catastrophic consequences, especially for those employees who entered the market too late to accumulate boom-time savings. Along with shrinking overall benefits for most workers, this threat to long-term economic security will prove to be deeply troublesome for workers in the twenty-first century.

In fact, it is our belief that the financial markets are headed for extended trouble. Our analysis strongly suggests that the great bull market that saw the Dow Jones Industrial Average quintuple between the end of the Cold War in the summer of 1989 and mid-July of 1999 will be followed by a stock market slump that could last for two decades and could financially devastate the unprepared family. That is what history suggests.

One possible scenario for the next two decades will be a chilling repeat of the Japanese experience that saw a grinding 60 percent decline in the stock market in the ten years following 1989. No, the tech wreck that led to a startling 60 percent decline in America's Nasdaq between March 2000 and April 2001 is not the forerunner of a similar steep decline in the United States. Instead, the likely scenario for stocks in the United States is for a period of stagnant prices that could grind on for an entire decade or even longer.

Delusion 2: Mass Participation in the Market Virtually Guarantees Rising Stock Prices

It's not only a history showing prolonged periods of stock market misery that concerns us. Deeply troublesome as that history is, the emergence of mass participation in the markets could easily result in an environment where stocks will actually perform worse than the historical record suggests. The two-century-old history lesson drawn from the Street refers back to a time when stock investment was essentially the playground of the rich, not the financial crutch of the average man. Although the market always had a fringe of two-bit players that expanded in size during bull markets like the one of the 1920s, public participation in the market has been essentially narrow. The statistical estimates are obviously squishy, but even at the height of the Roaring Twenties, it is likely that no more than 2 million Americans had tied their future to the market favorites of those years—stocks related to radio, telephone, autos, and the like. If you're a baby boomer, that was your grandfather's market, or, more probably, the market he couldn't afford to get into.

Few economists—the stress is on the word *few*—have recognized the dangers in a family-dominated stock market. America's first Nobel laureate in economics, Paul A. Samuelson of MIT, did issue an implicit warning about the instability of the family market fairly early in the game. That warning, ironically, appeared in the form of "advance praise" on the back cover of the first edition of the famed book by the Wharton School of Business's Jeremy Siegel, *Stocks for the Long Run,* published in 1994. Siegel's numbers do not deny that gains in stock prices are compressed into relatively short periods like forty of the 100 years of the twentieth century. But his figures showed that if held long enough, stocks were indeed the best of all possible long-term investments. However, the long run that Siegel talked about may have been the one that John Maynard Keynes described as the one "in which we are all dead." No one could dispute Siegel's numbers, which span two centuries. And we will make no attempt to try.

But the amazing record documented by Siegel was compiled in a far different market than the one that prevailed at the end of the 1990s. And that is the difference that will end by compounding trouble for American families. Samuelson's warning of the possible trouble is couched as a left-handed compliment to Professor Siegel's work: "Jeremy Siegel makes a persuasive case for a long run buy-and-hold stock investment strategy. Read it. Profit from it. And when short-run storms rock your ship, sleep well from a rational conviction that you have done the prudent thing. And if you are a practitioner of economic science like me, ponder as to when this new philosophy of prudence will self-destruct after Siegel's readers come someday to be universally imitated."

And imitated they were. According to NYU's Wolff, the number of households that held stock (including IRAs, Keogh plans, and 401[k]s), rose from 31.7 percent in 1989 to 48.2 percent in 1998.

Samuelson's comment was dropped from the book jacket for the 1998 second edition of *Stocks for the Long Run,* but the basis for Samuelson's concern may well lie in the workings of a phenomenon that economists call the "fallacy of composition," a concept that was popularized in all twelve editions of the Nobel laureate's textbook, *Economics.* The fallacy of composition rests on the idea that mass action can often frustrate the goals of individual action. That phenomenon explains why a strategy that works for an individual or a relatively small group of individuals goes awry if there is a bandwagon effect huge enough to involve a majority of the population. This is the question that Siegel and virtually every other conventional stock market commentator has failed to address. And the answer implies that the United States could face a stock market catastrophe, worse than that of the 1930s.

Is it possible that a mass rush by Americans into the stock market will drive returns so low as to spoil the fun? That is surely the way in which the real world often works. Those who find an enticing new beach or an excellent new restaurant often say, "Let's keep it a secret or the crowds will spoil it." At the racetrack, a sudden rush of money on a particular horse will drive the odds so low that what had been a good bet for a single individual suddenly becomes a bad bet. The desire of more and more American families to see the nation's national parks has led to more crowding and more restrictions on access to the most important sites, so as to often spoil the fun of seeing Glacier or Yellowstone.

Why does the fallacy of composition threaten the stock market and therefore the future of the middle-class American family? The answer lies in the role of profits in a world where the stock market becomes the playground of the masses. The simple fact is that the amount of profits earned by American corporations as a whole is so small that there is simply no reasonable way that stock ownership can provide an adequate retirement income for the mass of Americans.

The threat that inadequate profits poses to the investing public becomes clear in the link between profits and stock. Stripped to its essential, a share of stock is a claim on the profits of the company that issues the stock. One critical point about profits is that over the very long run, they grow at about the same rate as the economy as a whole. Importantly, there is a long-term historical relationship between GDP and profits, sometimes referred to as the "iron law" of profits. Data on the profits generated in the American economy show that over the past two centuries, corporate earnings have averaged about 10 percent of GDP before taxes. So, if GDP growth averages about 2 percent a year, then overall corporate profit growth usually averages around 2 percent also. The "iron law" of profits, which is seldom made clear to investors by Wall Street, limits the amount of money that's available to distribute to those who own stocks, a fact that is particularly hard on small investors.

The 1990s were one of the strongest decades in America's economic history. Yet in 1999, a fat year for the corporation, profits generated by the corporate sector of the U.S. economy totaled $711.6 billion. After all the tax collectors, Uncle Sam, and the 14,000 units of state and local government (who are his nephews and cousins) got their share, the profits figure shrank to $455.7 billion. The $455.7 billion that remained may sound like a lot, but in fact it was exactly $1,669 for each of the 273 million Americans living that year. And that number is not per day ($4.57), per week ($32.10), or per month ($139.08). It is $1,669 per year. If each American were to have to live solely on an equal share of the profits generated in the nation, he or she would be living way below the poverty line. Yes, those are the numbers. They show that corporate profits are thin gruel indeed if they are viewed as a way to support the entire American population. We have stressed this point because most public opinion surveys show that the average American has a grossly inflated opinion of the share of profits in America's national income.

Wall Street can and will argue that any analysis of the ability of profits to support families that stresses the entire population grossly misses the mark. What the Street is talking about in all its advertising and personal sales pitches is the ability of profits to support the retired population and to provide income to families who are sending their children to college.

On this basis, profits look a lot plumper as a source of income, at least at first blush. In 1999, there were a little over 34.5 million Americans who were sixty-five or older, some 20 million women and 14 million men. The $455.7 billion in after-tax corporate profits came to $13,403 per year for each of these Americans, or $1,117 per month and $258 per week. These numbers, though not princely, are clearly a better basis for retirement than the figures for the population as a whole suggests. And they are also about 40 percent higher than the Social Security check received in that year by the average member of the Social Security system. They indeed seem to make Wall Street's story about the virtues for stock retirement a lot more plausible.

Yet these numbers too are a vast exaggeration. Consider, to begin with, that Wall Street promotes stock investment, not only to finance retirement but also to finance education, at least at the college level. In 1999, there were about 18.9 million Americans of college age. That, in effect, means that the profits pool would have to have financed the expenses of 53.4 million Americans, not just the 34 million on retirement. The annual income of these stock-supported people would have been $8,598 per year, or $717 per month and $165 per week.

Modest though these numbers may be, they still vastly overstate the degree to which Americans can count on the corporate sector to finance education and retirement through stock purchases. We have so far only considered one claim on profits that eats into the amount left for the average American. That claim was taxes that must be paid by corporations. But there are two other claims on profits that must be met before the average family can claim its seat at the corporate feast. The first is the need of the corporation to reinvest a goodly share of its profits in new plant, equipment, and research needed to keep the business growing. The second is, of course, the dividends that must be paid to existing stockholders if they are to continue to hold shares in an existing corporation. In 1999, corporations retained $103 billion, or about 18 percent, of their earnings to finance the spending needed for growth.

And they paid out $328.9 billion in dividends. Those dividends may seem to be a pool of monies available to meet the needs of the average family. But nothing could be further from the truth: Profits tend to be highly unequally distributed throughout society, with huge shares flowing into the hands of relatively few people. Those people become the heroes of their age—J. P. Morgan, John D. Rockefeller, and Andrew Carnegie in the 1890s, Henry Ford, Alfred P. Sloan of General Motors in the 1920s, and Bill Gates and Michael Dell in the 1990s. Blended in with these heroes are, of course, the names of famed antihero operatives who also became famous in great stock market booms; Jay Gould in the 1890s, "Sunny Jim" Mitchell in the 1920s, Michael Milken and Ivan Boesky in the leveraged buyout fiasco of the 1980s. These names are only at the top of the list, but each wave of innovation tends to have within it thousands who do indeed emerge as very rich, as well as hundreds who have fed off shady operations and ended up in the bastille.

Everyone is aware that income is unequally distributed in the United States, and we will show in this book that distribution tends to become even more unequal in stock booms. The reason, of course, is that profits are even more unequally distributed than are other shares of income. Far more unequally distributed. Yes, F. Scott Fitzgerald was right. The rich are different from you and me. But Ernest Hemingway was also right: "Yes. They have more money."

The reason that profits are unequally distributed is about as straightforward as things can get. It is simply that stock ownership—which represents the claim on the profits that an economy generates—is highly concentrated in the hands of the few. In 1999, the top 1 percent of the population owned 49.6 percent of all stocks, and the top 10 percent, 86.3 percent. This distribution highlights the problem that the average American family will have if it expects to finance its college costs and its retirement out of stock ownership. In effect, the calculation that each American's share of annual profits comes to only $1,885 a year is based on the assumption that all Americans own the same amount of stock.

But if a soupçon of realism is introduced into the calculation, the average person is not nearly that well off. Exclude the top 10 percent, and there were 246 million Americans in 1999. Since claims on profits and dividends are roughly proportional to stock ownership, the implications of wealth inequality are startling. In 1999, the top 1 percent of the American population came to about 273,000 people. They had a claim on $226 billion in after-tax profits, or $827,838 per year! The top 10 percent of the population had a claim on $393.2 billion in profits and $283 billion in dividends. Their annual claim was $14,555 in profits and $10,481 in dividends.

That obviously left precious little over for everyone else. Indeed, in 1999, the bottom 90 percent of Americans had a claim on $82 billion in profits and $45.9 billion in dividends. Putting these numbers on a per capita basis can only be described as a jarring experience. Each of the 246 million Americans in the bottom 90 percent had a claim on $333 per year in profits or $186 per year in dividends. For the retired population, the numbers obviously look somewhat better. Each of the 34.5 million people who were sixty-five or over in 1999 had a claim on $2,177 per year in profits and $1,387 per year in dividends. But again, the numbers are jarring.

Disturbing as these numbers may be, they are clearly in accord with the experience of American families over the past two decades. In the millennial year 2000, the typical American family with a 401(k) found itself with just over $49,000 accumulated toward retirement. As that family examined its records, it discovered that the dividend yield on its stocks at the end of 2000 was 1.2 percent. This, of course, means that this typical family was having some $588 in annual dividend income added to its 401(k) account in 2000. The numbers are far smaller for those families who first were enrolled in a 401(k) toward the end of the 1990s. Indeed, about half of all 401(k) accounts were under $14,000 at the end of 2000.

Some investors may ask: What has this got to do with me? Sure, they may say, corporate profits as a whole might not be growing very fast, but if I had put a thousand dollars into Microsoft at the end of 1991, it would have grown to $26,500 by the end of 2001, and I would have plenty of protection. A thousand dollars invested in Oracle at the same time would have been worth $10,623 at the end of 2001. A thousand dollars invested in Cisco would have been worth $34,126. Sure, the investor may say, the crash in the Nasdaq may have knocked those numbers down, but they're still big money.

Stellar stock market gains scored in the 1980s and 1990s do give rise to stock market stories that show huge gains for individual stocks. But they are not, as we have seen, stories about the growth of the pool of profits over the long haul. That is what is available to support future retirees, many of whom did not get around to actually investing in stocks until the mid-1990s.

And since the pool of profits, as we have seen, is finite, than it must be true that if Microsoft's profits grew extremely rapidly, its percentage share of the total profits pool grew as well. That must mean that the percentage share of some other companies declined. An old-line company, Whirlpool, for example, enjoyed rising profits in the 1990s, but because its profits grew more slowly than those of Microsoft, Whirlpool's share of the total profits pool nevertheless declined.

Microsoft, Oracle, and Intel were shining examples of new economy companies of the 1990s; and as we will see in Chapter 6, in the dual economy of that decade, the 20 percent of companies in the new economy accounted for a staggering 75 percent of the total growth of profits. Over the same period, the 80 percent of companies in the old economy accounted for only 25 percent of total profits growth. In those days, tech-stock dazzle was offset by old economy stock blues. Old economy companies may stage a relative profits comeback in the current decade. But that will be negated by profit problems in the new economy, which in all probability, will take a number of years to recover. The "iron law" that profits as a whole grow at about the same rate as the economy as a whole will prevail, and the odds are that economic growth will be lower, perhaps substantially lower, in the coming years.

Wall Street trumpeted the rise in profits at the top of its lungs in the 1990s. To listen to the Street was to believe that owning stock meant that the average American could buy into a meaningful share of the profits boom. Yet despite the broadening of stock ownership and the great rise in stock prices during the great bull market of the late twentieth century, the stock market remained, at its core, very much a rich man's game. That was underlined in the heyday of Microsoft at about the time that the Nasdaq peaked at over 5000 in March 2000. At that point in history, Bill Gates was worth $50 billion, a sum equal to the wealth of the bottom 120 million Americans.

The Gates-versus-the-poor comparison represents an extreme case. But it signals an important point about the family market that does have ominous implications: Despite the emergence of the average family in the market, there is no evidence that the share of profits going to the rich has declined. The market game is still one that the father of President John F. Kennedy, Joseph Kennedy, who was a stock market operator in the 1920s, would have understood.

In the kind of calculus that was used by the truly smart operators of his day, the market is divided into periods when people like Joe Kennedy buy stocks from the average "Joe" at low prices, and sell them back at higher prices. Surely, the Kennedy patriarch would have viewed the wild markets of the late 1990s and early 2000 as a perfect time to sell stock to a public in the grip of a zeitgeist of the times. If this turns out to characterize the millennial market, average Americans have been the victim of a particularly cruel aspect of the 401(k) hoax. After all, they were not lured into the market by any decision made solely on their own. They got their feet wet on Wall Street because their employers' defined benefit pension plans had disappeared or had been skinned back and the 401(k) had become the only viable option.

Despite its supposed egalitarian tradition, the distribution of wealth in the United States became more, rather than less, unequal during both the 1920s and the 1990s. Again, research by Wolff shows that the relative fortunes of the top 1 percent improve dramatically in booms. Wolff's numbers show that the rich man's share increases mainly because of stock market gains.

The "Bill Gates" effect enriched only those who already owned mountains of stock. But especially in the 1990s, lesser executives also became major players in the inequity. The reason is that business, especially new economy companies, generously issued large blocks of stock options at low prices to key employees who became wealthy as the stocks in their companies catapulted upward. Clearly, the optioned classes experienced a far greater increase in wealth than the ordinary investor. None of this is meant to criticize the great entrepreneurs and innovators of the new economy, but merely illustrates that their efforts did nothing to increase the proportion of stock market wealth owned by the average investor and available to finance retirement. On the contrary, it reduced the proportion of the profits pool to which average investors could lay claim.

Delusion 3: The Baby Boomers Guarantee Rising Stock Prices

Of the delusions foisted on the average investor by Wall Street, the most familiar is demographic. This instance of financial "madness" lies in the belief that the demographics of the baby-boomer generation alone virtually foreordain a rising stock market at least until 2012, when the leading edge of the post–World War II generation reaches retirement age. Therefore, worries about the likes of dividends and high p/e's are concerns that pertain to a far-gone past—impossibly old-fashioned and irrelevant in the postmillennial years.

Romancing the baby boomers was at the center of Wall Street's advertising message throughout the 1990s and has shown no signs of abating in the postmillennial decade. Not since the days when the Reverend Thomas Robert Malthus wrongly predicted that population would grow far faster than the food supply way back in the late eighteenth century has any demographic trend received more attention. And not since the days of Malthus, has any prediction based on demographics been more certain to be wrong.

That the boomer generation guarantees rising stock prices is part of the Holy Writ of Wall Street, for it seems to offer a promise that the boomers will always have people around who are willing to buy their stocks. These people are of course younger boomers. The first boomers were born in 1946. The final members of the boomer generation were born in 1964. The important thing, says Wall Street, is that boomers will continue to reach retirement until 2029. These financial "fellow travelers" through the age profile will continue to grow in number, says Wall Street, assuring that boomers will have a ready-made and growing market for their stock, which they will be able to sell at higher and higher prices—not unlike those who purchased land in Florida during that great boom in the 1920s.

At bottom, the role of stocks in meeting the retirement needs of the baby boomers shifts the "fallacy of composition" inherent in the supposed beneficence of the mass market into hyperdrive. If anything, "Boomernomics" amplifies the dangers of the mass market. The percentage of boomers who have invested in the market is higher than the percentage of nonboomers. Therefore, when they begin to retire in large population chunks over the next decade, it will bring laserlike clarity to the inadequacy of the profits pool. And to top it off, the boomers are a financially voracious generation used to living well. The odds are they will need money for a long period of time simply because longevity is likely to increase. In this important sense, the glaring inadequacy of the profits pool is at the heart of the "innocent" Ponzi scheme that has driven price-earnings ratios to unrealistic levels, therefore making the hope that capital gains will finance retirement more and more unrealistic.

The argument that the demographic consequences of the baby-boomer generation will keep the stock market moving higher and higher represents a reading of history that is 180 degrees off the mark. The true consequences of the aging of the boomers and its impact on the growth of the economy as a whole, and on the growth of profits, is at the heart of the argument. An aging population leads to a slowdown in economic growth.

The United States unquestionably grew more rapidly in the 1990s than both Western Europe and Japan. With new economy advocates, particularly business consulting firms that could see a bonanza in the argument, acting as cheerleaders, the American public was induced to believe that strong American growth could be explained by the vigor of its managers and the ingenuity of its technology. And in making the argument for the existence of a new economy, its advocates conveniently ignored what was probably the real reason for America's growth advantage: the simple fact that the American population profile was younger than that of either Europe or Japan.

A country or region's age profile has a huge impact on its growth rate. The older a nation's population, the slower its growth rate. And if that is

true, the statistics surely suggest that the aging of the American population will slow economic growth no matter how the retirement of older
Americans is financed.

By itself, of course, this demographic argument undermines the notion that stock investment is the answer to the retirement problem.
Indeed, it may make it more severe simply because an aging population
foreordains slower, not faster, growth for the profits pool.

Witness what has happened to Japan, where the population is aging
more rapidly than in the United States and where economic growth has
slumped. The population of Europe is also aging more rapidly than in
the United States and growth has been slower. In fact, the demographic
argument for higher stock prices, as we will show in this book, is seriously flawed.

Delusion 4: Stock Market "Perks" for Workers Will More Than Compensate in the Long Haul for Damped-Down Wages

In the 1980s and 1990s, wages grew much more slowly than stock prices.
That, of course, means that a dollar's worth of wages would have given
workers a claim on an even tinier sliver of the profits pool at the end of the
period than at the beginning. Indeed, the main impact of worker stock
market participation was to increase the value of the stock already in the
hands of the upper income brackets. The ironic effect of the 401(k) was to
make wealth more, not less, unequally distributed. This means that average hardworking Americans whose companies put them in a position of
having to invest in the stock market rather than getting higher wages had
to pay higher and higher prices for stocks and therefore got a smaller share
of the corporate profits pool for each dollar they spent.

While the average wage earner in the 1990s often had many job
choices, he or she also worked longer hours at a more harried pace in an
environment that was increasingly described as "multi-tasked." All of
these trade-offs were supposedly worth it because of the excitement of
the limitless prospects of the "new economy." The hard-driven, increasingly globalized work world, characterized by endless mergers and a
"flexible workforce," occurred at a time when both political parties were

paying pious obeisance to the importance of "family values." That family values were a winner in the great marketing drives of the booming 1990s was not lost on Wall Street.

The long-term consequences of Wall Street's version of family values has yet to be played out. This version implies that in the slow growth economy that looms ahead, profits can be maintained only by suppressing wage growth even further. The typical American already settles for a lower salary in the hope of later making up the difference with a 401(k) plan or some other source of income that depends on converting a share of the company's profits into cash by selling the stock at higher and higher prices than the worker paid for them. At the same time, especially as the economy slows and corporate profit sheets erode, there is an even stronger need to keep consumer spending going. Average Americans then, are put in an untenable position. In order to keep their stocks growing, they must accept lower annual wage gains. At the same time, they will be told to keep their spending growing. That is a long-term variant of the "Shop 'til bin Laden drops" argument that business and political leaders were using to convince hard-pressed Americans threatened by the biggest layoffs in a quarter of a century.

This, then, is where the American family finds itself in the opening years of the postmillennial decade. It has been asked to buy into the innocent Ponzi scheme that lies at the heart of 401(k) plans to assure its financial future. To a large extent, the family has responded to the Ponzi invitation because the erosion of traditional pension plans has left it with no choice. Americans have long struggled over the entire twentieth century to deal with private pension plans that have suddenly disappeared when the economy has gone bad, and a nationalized pension plan— Social Security—that was never really designed to meet the overall pension needs of those growing older. The troubles that emerged in the 401(k) in the recession of 2001 are unfortunately only the most recent example of the tendency for private pension plans to shrink, or entirely disappear, when the going gets tough for the corporation. The family has been under enormous pressure to accept Wall Street's view of the steps that are needed to provide for a secure future.

The Wall Street view became the conventional view during the great stock market boom of the 1990s, and its power has persisted throughout the market decline of the early years of the postmillennial decade. But it is possible to succeed financially in the coming years by beating the Street at its own game. To do so, the journey to financial independence must begin with an understanding of the forces that allowed the Street to capture the American family in the first place.

Chapter 3

───── ⬥ ─────

"Family Values":
How the Hoax Was Perpetrated

I looked the man in the eye. I found him to be very
straightforward and trustworthy. I was able to get a sense
of his soul. I share many values with him. He is a family
man who loves his wife and children.

—President George W. Bush,
speaking of Russian president Vladimir Putin
after their first meeting in Slovenia, June 14, 2001

The 2000 election witnessed much talk of faith as being central to American society, but, in truth, it was not the God of our fathers, but the god of Wall Street, that had long since moved to the center of the American psyche as the fit subject for serious worship. The stock market had been sold throughout the 1990s as the one "sure" way that the American family could control its financial and ultimately its psychological future, at the same time most other things in their lives—schools, corporations, job security—were reeling out of control.

It was a triumph of marketing. Wall Street worked hard, and for a long time successfully, to convince the American family that stock certificates, a currency they never really saw, were the only assurance of long-term financial and therefore family stability. It was, as we have seen, a deeply flawed message. But for the last two decades of the twentieth century, the entire society seemed to conspire to help Wall Street emerge as the one institution that could be trusted above all others. Millions of Americans who had rebelled against traditional marriages, medicine, religion, and diets throughout the latter part of the twentieth century rallied together as traditional "true believers" in the stock market, even though the salvation it was selling was as phony as that of Sinclair Lewis's lustful evangelist, Elmer Gantry.

After his selection as president by the Supreme Court, George W. Bush put tax cuts at the top of his agenda, assuring the public that the economic slowdown and the tumble on Wall Street were temporary and would soon be ended. The Street, he implied, was at least as trustworthy as Vladimir Putin and would soon prove it, if only incentives would be reinforced by lower taxes for all Americans, but especially for the rich, who would get the lion's share of the gains.

Bush's embrace of the free market was rhetorically more intense than that of his predecessor. But there should be no mistake. He was not departing from the message of the Clinton administration, merely reinforcing it. The Arkansan's eight years in office saw a steady increase in the influence of Wall Street on Washington. Indeed, by the time Clinton left office, the American family had been delivered into Wall Street's hands. In 1999, Congress repealed the famous Glass-Steagall Banking Act, passed in 1933, that had separated investment banking, insurance, and commercial banking. Under Glass-Steagall, financial companies had to confine their business to just one of these three activities. Glass-Steagall was passed because the Great Crash of 1929 had shown that severe conflicts of interest had undermined the American financial system in the years leading up to that debacle. With Congress lubricated by generous campaign contributions, the financial service industry argued that it was being hampered by legislation that prevented its companies from competing across the board, by simultaneously offering investment banking, insurance, and commercial banking. If the barriers between these three activities were not struck down, said its lobbyists, American finance would be unable to compete effectively with the financial giants of Europe and presumably, Japan, where there were no such barriers. That left the road wide open to vast changes that were actually underway before Glass-Steagall was repealed. So confident had the financial industry become in the second half of the 1990s that two financial giants,

Citibank and Travelers Insurance, actually merged in early 1998, in effect challenging Washington to either undo the merger or change the law. By changing the law, Washington had decided to take the easy way out rather than challenging the two financial powers that had defiantly merged into a superpower.

The new atmosphere in Washington had ridden roughshod over traditional American suspicion of strong, nationwide banking monopolies. Huge interstate banking companies were changing the financial map all the way through the second half of the 1990s. And the new financial behemoths well understood how they could sell their growing monopoly power. On April 14, 1998—exactly one week after what was up to that point the largest financial merger ever announced, between Citibank and Travelers—David Coulter, then the CEO of Bank of America, claimed that his bank would merge with Nation's Bank "for the nation's families." Coulter's comment merely underlined the mass advertising by brokerages and other financial houses warmly sentimentalizing Wall Street's deepening affection for the American family.

The great financial mergers linked the fate of the American family to the movement of the stock ticker in the brokerage houses and banks of the nation. Wall Street's capture of family values was the real outcome of the torture inflicted on the nation by the scandal-ridden politics of the late 1990s that culminated in the impeachment of then President Clinton. Many of the impeachees were at least as vulnerable as the impeached, including Newt Gingrich, his would-be successor, Robert Livingston, and the congressman whom the Republicans had treated as though he were on the verge of sainthood, Henry Hyde. In the uncertainty and confusion, hopes centered on the gods of finance, Secretary of the Treasury Robert Rubin and Federal Reserve chairman Alan Greenspan. It was the adoration of Wall Street by many Americans that turned the anger and mayhem in Washington into what seemed like a sideshow. And it was fascination with the big money made in tech stocks that drew attention away from the stagnation in the standard of living of the typical American family.

The main tent was occupied by the dancing figures on the giant stock market scoreboards that had come to dominate Times Square by the end of the 1990s. The Street's capture of the Great White Way was facilitated by a decade of preparation by Wall Street's main organs of communication, advertising agencies, and the all-day financial channels that had appeared on cable television, mainly CNBC, but also CNNfn and Bloomberg. It was a spectacular result of Wall Street's decision to market its wares alongside those pushed by Betty Crocker, Colonel Sanders, and Ronald McDonald.

How Family Values Became "Family Values"

In an era in which a Democratic president had announced that "the age of big government is over," it was almost inevitable that the public would come to believe that it desperately needed the ministrations of the prime capitalist institution—Wall Street—to assure its future. Wall Street's decision to court the public was part and parcel of the same scenario that made the public feel the need to depend on its promises. So it was almost a "no-brainer" for Wall Street to usurp the real yearning for old-fashioned "family values," turning it into a boom time for itself.

The Republican Party had paid continuous lip service to social conservatism, but its practical policies were focused on economic conservatism, the extension of the free market, and the limitation of the role of government. During President Ronald Reagan's two terms in office, his essential argument was that the family would benefit the most from keeping more of its income, and his policy therefore focused on tax cuts. There is no indication that the average American family flourished during that period. It was the great age of restructuring for American business. Layoffs became common, company benefits were cut back, and, to make ends meet, the two-worker household became more and more common. Yet the real inflation-adjusted income of the average American family fell.

Reagan was popular, but particularly in the hands of his successor, George Herbert Walker Bush, Republican domestic policies were not. The public was unhappy with the elder Bush because economic growth was painfully slow. It threw him out in 1992 and put in his place a Democrat dedicated to the free market, despite the ravages it had exacted on the real wage of the typical American. It was "the economy, stupid" that won the presidency for William Jefferson Clinton. But he did nothing serious to provide major benefits for the American family. In the opening years of his administration, Clinton's most obvious mistake was to underestimate the power of vested interests to bury his medical system reforms. And the defeat of those reforms had the impact of creating a political environment in which the Democrats could not hold onto power in Congress. In 1994, when the Republican revolutionaries triumphed, Newt Gingrich's tough talk on Social Security and Medicare, coupled with his threats to shut down the government, scared many voters. This gave Bill Clinton a new opening.

His response was to brilliantly hijack the family values theme and again make the Democrats competitive on the issues surrounding the family. Gone were anti-abortion and school prayer. Bill Clinton began supporting welfare reform, tax credits for working parents, and a dozen other conservative demands. He went on to win the 1996 election and, at least for the first two years of his second administration, to become one of the century's most popular presidents. Many Americans who were not Democrats voted for Bill Clinton in 1996 because of his "family values" agenda, which was couched in much less strident, less frightening litany than that of Newt Gingrich. But that didn't mean that he did much for the family. The well-known academics Sylvia Ann Hewlett and Cornel West, in their best-selling 1998 book, *The War Against Parents,* commented, "Child poverty rates are up and SAT scores are down, teen suicide rates have doubled since the 1970s, and child homicide rates have quadrupled since the mid-1980s. In the words of one blue-ribbon commission, 'never before has one generation of American children been less healthy, less cared for, or less prepared for life than their parents were at the same age.'"

And it was not only children who were hurt. The decay of policies that really supported family values created new opportunities for Wall Street. As workers compliantly turned themselves from stable employees into walking portfolios of skills, they seemed to have no choice but to follow Wall Street's cheerleaders, applauding the latest mergers in the hope that their 401(k)s would benefit from higher stock prices. So it's not surprising that although unemployment rates were down, the workforce became more anxious, had more memory loss, more depression, more incontinence, more infertility, and the big bonanza disorder of all, more impotence, than it had ever had before, this time in demographically enhanced baby-boomer fits. And in the powerful spin cycle of the dual Clintonian–Wall Street world, the most fantastic thing happened! All these physical hiccups—no matter how unpleasant—were turned into a potential bonanza for Wall Street and its extended national investment family! Viagra alone, to help impotence, which had exploded to large portions of the male population during the 1990s, was expected to net a cool $11 billion a year, according to some optimistic analysts.

The economic stress on men created limitless possibilities for the Street in the late 1990s. The spin cycle spun just right! "It's kind of a cultural phenomenon," crowed Pfizer chief William C. Steere Jr. about Viagra. An elated public poured another river of money into high tech and pharmaceutical stocks. And as the money came gushing into the market by the billions, it became crystal clear that the United States put its deepest trust not in the power of government and churches to deal with the impact of stress—but in the Street.

For his part, President Clinton concentrated on keeping the market up. It mattered little that a record merger wave had transformed the American economy by the end of 1999. The general position of the Clinton administration was that as long as consumer prices were not rising as a result of the mergers, it had no problem with what was going on, thus signaling that the market and corporate world should not be afraid to do more mergers. Clinton suggested that investing in the market in a long-term way was intrinsically a good idea and in doing so, deepened the compact between himself and the Street.

Bill Clinton has to be seen as one of the most useful people that Wall Street has ever found. It would be hard to imagine a more favorable event for the financial community than the Clinton scandals. With his personal life in shambles and his moral leadership in question, the Democratic president had, in effect, been forced to ask the average family to judge itself, not by the moral standards ordinarily applied but by a set of financial criteria. And heavily supported by the Wall Street advertising barrage, the deflection of interest worked. Thus, the great saying of early 1998 that "America is more interested in Dow Jones than in Paula Jones" missed the point. In their influence on America's psyche, the two Joneses were locked in an embrace that President Clinton well understood.

Clinton had no choice but to do everything possible to make Wall Street happy. For having asked the American family to judge him by the economy's performance, he knew his presidency would stand or fall on the performance of the stock market. And indeed, after President Clinton "confessed" about his affair with Monica Lewinsky on August 17, 1998, there was widespread speculation in media circles about how big a drop in the Dow would be needed to force Clinton to resign or to force Congress to impeach him. But that didn't happen. After a deep swoon, the stock market suddenly recovered almost all of its lost 1,500 points. And when the president actually was impeached on December 19 of that same year, investors didn't flinch. After all, wasn't Alan Greenspan really their "main" man?

That the stock market was Clinton's savior was underscored six months later when the highly respected former cochairman of Goldman Sachs, Robert Rubin, decided to step down as treasury secretary. In interviews granted to any TV network that cared to stop by his office, Rubin stressed Clinton's ability to focus on the economic issues no matter how much trouble he was having on other fronts.

Good Shepherd Wall Street

Wall Street has always been brilliant in catching the scent of money. The pursuit of the average family required a major change in the culture of the Street. But with billions and maybe even trillions at stake if Social Security were to be partially privatized, the Street, at least publicly, quickly shed its historical disdain for the average man and learned to love "family values."

There had always, so to speak, been a "caring" side to the Street, but that "care" had been confined to families of the upper income brackets, the customers for whom the houses on the Street and the great banks had set up "personal banking departments." Wall Street knew, and still knows, these people very well. Herman Roseman, a colorful money manager who worked in the 1970s for Argus Research Corporation, a Wall Street firm, always described his money management job as "social work for the rich."

But to the rest of the world, the Street's upper echelons had chosen to operate behind a wall protecting the great inside operators who only had time for the biggest clients, the biggest deals, and the biggest transactions. The public, for whatever its business was worth, was to be left in the hands of the so-called wire houses—brokers who dealt mainly with relatively small investors—many of which, like Bache & Co., had been left in the dust. Some of these did continue to survive, and in the case of Merrill Lynch, Pierce, Fenner & Beane, streamlined in 1954 into plain

Merrill Lynch, to flourish. It wasn't exactly that Merrill was doing business with the average man, mind you. The firm had become highly involved with the elite of middle America, the leading insurance men, accountants, lawyers, doctors, and small business owners in America's midsized towns and prosperous suburbs. In the Midwest, many clients called Merrill "The Bank." And they still do. But even so, not even Merrill Lynch presented itself to the average American as "family."

The expression of a tender solicitude for the family that emerged in the 1980s and especially the 1990s was something new for Wall Street, the product of an era that had made the 401(k) into an icon. Traditionally, Wall Street had viewed small investors as suckers. They were expected to appear in the market only when bull runs were reaching their top. Wall Street, perhaps far more realistic than it is now, tended to view markets as divided in the accumulation phases, when the smart people bought stocks at low prices, and the distribution phases, when the smart people sold stocks at high prices to the gullible. Typical family breadwinners were not viewed, as they are today, as customers to be courted with seductive advertising campaigns and told that "the quality of their lives depended on the quality of their investments." The individual investor was perceived as a convenient "fringe" in the bull phase of the market, not as a central character in the Street's long-term plans to make money.

The image was of remote figures reaping huge rewards playing shadowy games to which the public was not invited, and at whose nature they could barely guess. There were those who operated in shadows, Jessie Livermore and the pool operators of the 1890s, and Joe Kennedy, the great short seller just before the crash of 1929. And more recently, the maestro of insider trading, Ivan Boesky, who was rumored to leave his office to go to a pay phone and talk to inside sources, but never to you. And there was Michael Milken, who held those predators' balls to which you were never invited.

Then there was the "white shoe set," which operated in the sun, at the center of a club to which ordinary mortals could not aspire. Morgan Stanley, heir of J. P. Morgan himself; Salomon Brothers, ruler of the inner sanctum of the government bond market; Goldman Sachs, the legendary German-Jewish investment bank and trading house whose former co-head, Robert Rubin, had become secretary of the treasury. Just try to get a minute with those guys!

Yet by the time the United States had reached the late 1990s, nothing could be further from the image that the Street was presenting to the public. The market heroes were no longer the Ivan Boeskys and Michael Milkens, who, even before they were indicted for illegal market practices, were widely known to have made their money in a sharp way. They were, instead, reassuring, comforting presences, epitomized by the 1990s Wall Street icon, the plain-tailored, pleasant-looking Abby Joseph Cohen. The media fell in love with the Beardstown ladies, a cheerful group of elderly Midwestern women who had stitched together a successful investment club during the same period (although it was later revealed they had fudged their profits to make them more media-friendly). Nor were the reassurances confined to the market's soft, feminine side. A string of avuncular male figures regularly appeared on the market's captive news media, CNBC, and the financial programs running on CNN including the then host of *Money Line*, Lou Dobbs and such putative Wall Street gurus as the longtime bull, Ralph Acampura. These were relatively new voices added to the steady flow of upbeat comment from public television's pioneer of investment reassurance, Louis Rukeyser, whose "authoritative" words could not be doubted, because, as was said in the television industry, he looked like George Washington.

And then, of course, we have the advertising, the hundreds of millions spent by financial houses each year, to promote stocks as the ideal long-term investment vehicle to achieve family goals, replete with gatherings around cozy kitchen tables with sentimental background music; inviting leafy gardens where well-shod successful investors quietly wiled away their free time; reassuring pictures of babies; graduating college seniors; couples moving into financially well-lubricated retirement; and of course, grandmas and granddads.

401(k) "Magic"

Whether the economy's performance in the 1990s would rescue Clinton's long-term legacy remained very much to be seen. What did seem certain however was that it was the main factor that allowed him to hang onto his job after his impeachment by the House of Representatives. Call it 401(k) magic! At the end of a decade in which stocks had quintupled, the homely 401(k) plan set up by many corporations in the 1980s to save their financial rear ends suddenly emerged as a surefire way to wealth, capturing the imaginations of Americans who earned their living from work.

Nothing is more important to the American family than to understand the true origin of 401(k) plans. It was the slow-growth period in the American economy, the years from the beginning of the OPEC oil embargo in 1973, to the mid-1990s that undermined the old pension system. The 401(k) became the new model for pensions, not during a period when American capitalism was enjoying great economic success but rather when the great corporations were having a tough time making money. First under the impact of OPEC, then under the assault of stiff competition from Germany and Japan, American industry went through a tough twenty-year period.

That slowdown was traumatic. It began with the shrinkage of some of the nation's most prosperous and best-paying industries, notably steel and autos, and then turned much of industrial America into a rust belt. It continued with a discovery that the middle managers of the prosperous 1950s and 1960s—the organization men in gray flannel suits—were no longer vital, needed, long-term employees of the great corporations.

Of the many consequences of that great slowdown, the ones most important to the evolution of what was to become the new relationship between the Street and the family was the burning desire of corporate America to get out from under its long-term commitments to its employees. And if this meant chopping away at the employees' social safety net, so be it.

It wasn't the current cost of pension plans that most frightened corporate America. The real financial trauma was the implication of these obligations for the future of corporate balance sheets. Long-term pension liabilities were showing up as virtual black holes. In the corporate gloom of those slow-growth days, companies were forced to report that they had underfunded pension liabilities on their books. Great corporations from General Motors to Caterpillar to International Paper and even IBM came under severe pressure. The result was not only a loss of executive dignity. The stock prices of many companies fell, and their ability to raise capital on Wall Street was impaired.

The upshot was a frantic hunt for ways in which corporations could get out from under. And the solution that emerged was simple: Design a pension system that depended not on defined benefits for employees but rather on defined contributions made mainly by employees. If a corporation could meet its pension obligations by allowing workers to voluntarily contribute a part of their earnings toward 401(k)s, the dreaded unfunded liabilities would simply not exist. Companies were also given tax incentives to "match" worker contributions either with stock or with cash. In effect, the corporation told its workers: "You are now the owner of your own investment fund. But we are not responsible for whether it will be enough to provide a decent pension. That depends on you." That's why the 401(k) was, in effect, the major tool used by Wall Street to capture family values.

Nothing worked more certainly to provide fuel for Wall Street's massive drive to capture the public's resources. For years Wall Street had been hawking mutual funds as a solution to the long-term financial problems of the family and had done reasonably well. In the twenty years prior to 1984, the number of families whose financial future was tied to stocks grew gradually. But, as we have already seen in Chapter 2, it was the 401(k) plan that really tied the long-term financial future of the family to the stock market.

As ferociously as the political far right had worked to sell the nation its version of family values or as diligently as the Clinton wonks and the Gingrich revolutionaries daily proclaimed their versions of family values, no "sell" ever began to click or take hold of the popular imagination the way Wall Street's version did in the mid-1990s. Hands down, it was a winner. Labor halls, libraries, banks, university buildings, restaurants, and grocery stores relentlessly tuned their TVs to financial news throughout the day for their many customers bent on keeping up with the market. And "family values" as defined by the Street became embedded in the psyche of the United States.

Tying the fate of the American family to the level of the Dow Jones represented a radical restructuring of America's pension system. Through most of the nation's economic history, including the rapid growth days of the late nineteenth and early twentieth century, employers offered their workers no system of benefits to allow them to meet their health needs, educate their children, or provide for some kind of income after they became too old to work. Family security was overwhelmingly viewed as something that a ruthless capitalist system on the rise could not afford to provide for its workers.

As the United States became more prosperous, the attitude of business toward family security and retirement began to change. It is perhaps fitting that the first major post–World War I pension insurance plan was introduced by one of the nation's leading retailers, Montgomery Ward. That plan, modest though it was, provided workers, when they retired, with a fixed annual income or annuity. Eventually, it evolved into what is now called a "defined benefit plan."

"A great burst of pension formation activity occurred between 1911 and 1915, and an even greater number of plans were established by smaller companies between 1916 and 1920," according to University of Notre Dame pension expert Teresa Ghilarducci. But private pension funds like Montgomery Ward's fell considerably during the 1920s, and some went belly up during the 1930s. Defined benefit plans were the goal of most corporations in the so-called Golden Age of the American economy, the prosperous quarter of a century that followed the end of World War II. In those years, partly under the pressure of a vigorous union movement, of which United Auto Workers' Walter Reuther was the seminal figure, defined benefit pension plans became more widespread. Yet even by 1980, less than half the civilian labor force was covered by old-fashioned defined benefit plans. The growth in these plans slowed dramatically. The number of people covered increased by a lethargic 3 million—to 41 million Americans—between 1980 and 1996. By contrast, the number of workers participating in defined contribution plans ballooned from just under 20 million in 1980 to over 50 million in 1996.

Defined benefit plans did represent a certain commitment by American companies to their workers. Nevertheless, the monthly pension checks of many old-fashioned plans were, in fact, quite small. Even so, they were better than not getting a check at all every month. Under the pressure of ongoing pension reforms, responsible companies had to set aside monies each year—called pension reserves—adequate to meet their financial commitments to their retirees. These pensions were, and still are, protected under federal law, and represent real, ongoing payments that older workers know will not disappear.

The Groves of Academe and the "Oni"

The great bull market of the 1990s occurred not just because of Wall Street's campaign to capture the savings of the average family, or even the emergence of the 401(k). Those alone would not have been enough. Wall Street had a critical ally in convincing the American family of the superiority of stock market investment as the best way to build family nest eggs: the university. Americans were deluged with mountains of information and reams of statistics coming from the seemingly objective source of academic research demonstrating that stock investments, patiently made over the years, were a safe source of investment yields superior to those that could be earned from other forms of investment, including bonds, gold, real estate, or anything else that you could think of. The reason, said the academics, was that stocks are the way an average family can reap its share of the rewards for creativity and enterprise that flowed so freely from the abundance created by American capitalism. The allure of this approach was that it seemed to insulate the process of wealth creation from all the vicissitudes of America's cynical political system, instability in the global economy, and the normal ups and downs of financial markets. If patience is all that is needed to make money grow, surely the mutual fund and the 401(k) are a source of peace in a turbulent world. Business life in the global economy may be difficult, but the promise of a serene retirement and an ability to pay educational expenses seemed to be virtually guaranteed.

It is Professor Jeremy Siegel of the University of Pennsylvania's Wharton School who is probably the most respected guru of the virtues of long-term investment in stocks. Among those in the know, he is far more influential than anyone whose hands have been sullied by actually taking a job on the Street. "The bull market since 1982," he wrote in the 1998 edition of *Stocks for the Long Run,* "has been fueled by investor recognition of the superior long-term returns that are found in equities." Nothing obviously pleased Siegel more than public acceptance of the virtues of long-term stock investment.

There is no doubt that Siegel is a numbers whiz. But there are fundamental questions about whether his work fully reflects what really happens on the Street. Business, including that conducted by major financial institutions, is not merely a skein of market relationships; it is also a system of power. The most vivid description of that fact and its consequences that the authors of this book have ever come across is not a profound analysis of the American business system. It is, rather, a simple Japanese folk tale that is well worth telling to those who are certain of the virtues of long-term investment.

"Long, long ago," that tale begins, "there was a funny old woman, who liked to laugh and to make dumplings of rice-flour." This was how she fed herself.

"One day, while she was preparing some dumplings for dinner, she let one fall; and it rolled into a hole in the earthen floor of her little kitchen and disappeared. The old woman tried to reach it by putting her hand down the hole, and all at once the earth gave way, and the old woman fell in."

"She fell quite a distance, but was not a bit hurt; and when she got up on her feet again, she saw that she was standing on a road, just like the road before her house. It was quite light down there; and she could see plenty of rice-fields, but no one in them." She ran along the road crying: "My dumpling, my dumpling! Where is that dumpling of mine?"

An Oni—a Japanese "wise guy"—spied her, noted her worry, and took her into his house, which had a huge kitchen. Giving the old woman a small wooden rice-paddle, he said: "You must always put only one grain into the pot, and when you stir that one grain of rice in the water with this paddle, the grain will multiply until the pot is full." Every time she moved the magic paddle, the rice increased in quantity; and in a few minutes the great pot was full. This, as we shall see, is not where the story ends. But the beginning of this wonderful Japanese folk tale goes to the heart of the reasoning that caused the American family to fall in love with Wall Street in the second half of the 1990s.

The notion that wealth can grow infinitely and indefinitely through the process described by compounding interest is deeply ingrained not only in Oriental folklore but also in that of the West. There is, for example, the story of the king who placed a chessboard before a young man. Imagine, the king said, if you started with one grain of rice at the top left of the board, and that the number of grains doubled as you moved through its sixty-four squares until you reached the square at the bottom right-hand corner. By the time you reached this final square, you would have more rice than existed in the entire world.

Change rice to money and transform the old Japanese woman into the American family and the story is the same as the one told by Professor Siegel in the most influential stock market book written in the 1990s. It was not a book emanating from a brokerage house seeking to add to its customer base, although such a book, *Grow Rich Slowly: The Merrill Lynch Guide to Retirement Planning* does exist. Nor was it a book by a money manager prospecting for new clients, although that kind of book, *Dow 40,000*, written by David Elias, also exists. Rather, it was a book wrapped in the mantle of a great temple of higher business learning.

No academic utterance was more influential in the electric financial atmosphere of the late 1990s. The tale that is told, coming out of real financial data—not merely a folk tradition—would warm the hearts of both the Japanese Oni in the Eastern folk tale and the king in the Western fable. *Stocks for the Long Run* "proves" that compound interest is indeed magic, especially magical, in fact, if the substance that is multiplying is not some prosaic commodity like rice, but rather the value of stocks issued by America's largest and most powerful companies. It is, after all, Commodore Vanderbilt, E. H. Harriman, John D. Rockefeller, J. P. Morgan, Henry Ford, and Bill Gates that Siegel is talking about, not an old Japanese woman.

Siegel's canvas is American financial history. He traces the returns to stocks all the way back to the founding of the American stock market back in 1802. His basic point is that the total returns to stocks far exceeded those earned by investing in any other financial asset—bonds, short-term Treasury bills, or gold. Siegel's numbers show that gold was by far the worst performer, seeming to indicate that old-fashioned attachment to a supposedly highly safe investment can be extremely naive.

The secret of financial success, says Siegel, is simple. One must invest for the long run, holding stock through thick and thin, no matter what is going on in the market. Taken to its logical conclusion, Siegel's advice is to live as austerely as possible and put all your money into the stock market. To Siegel, the root of financial failure lies in a lack of patience and an unwillingness to save adequately. It is a question of individual behavior, not of the way in which society as a totality works. To him, a failure to grow rich is an individual failure. "It is rare," he writes "for anyone to accumulate wealth for long periods of time without consuming his or her return . . . The stock market has the power to turn a single dollar into millions by . . . forbearance . . . but few will have the patience or desire to let this happen."

Siegel's individualist message that the failure to acquire wealth results from a lack of willpower resonates in many societies, including that of the United States, a capitalist country that is heavily Protestant in its religion and that professes to have lost faith in the effectiveness of collective action undertaken by government. As has been shown by two great scholars—R. H. Tawney, the famed English economic historian in his *Religion and the Rise of Capitalism,* and Max Weber, the great German sociologist, in his *The Protestant Ethic and the Spirit of Capitalism*—there is an intimate link between the capitalist system and religion that places great stress on the individual. Indeed, one of the main findings of both Tawney and Weber is the close bond between the rise of capitalism and the Calvinist doctrine that worldly success is a sign that God has elected those who have amassed wealth to the higher realms of heaven. This idea in fact reflected the political interests of the merchant classes, the great short-term beneficiaries of the rise of capitalism in the sixteenth and seventeenth centuries. It is therefore no surprise that the two leading countries in the early stages of capitalism, Holland and England, were centers of the Protestant Reformation. That, indeed, is what Tawney's and Weber's books are all about.

Siegel's celebration of traditional Calvinist virtues seemed to be totally justified by the huge returns reaped by those who followed his individualistic advice in the great bull market of the 1990s. But the effect was to nakedly expose the financial fortunes of the average American family to the instabilities of the global economy. By 1999, American households had more of their assets invested in the stock market than at any time in history. From 1990 through 1997 alone, the portion of household wealth in stock more than doubled, and for the first time ever, stocks represented a higher percentage of assets for the average American household than real estate, or owning a home, which had always been the most prized financial asset in the United States. The shift into stocks came as stocks gained 30 percent annually between 1995 and mid-1998, a Shangri-la of profits that had rarely existed before. And never had the gains from a roaring stock market appeared to be so widely shared by so many families.

Where Is the Full Rice Bowl?

There is however a severe problem with the way in which Siegel's paean of praise to savings plays out in the real world. There was a best-selling book floating around in the late 1990s called *The Millionaire Next Door,* purporting to show that it was fairly easy to get rich, essentially by following Siegel's advice to be frugal and save. That was a theme that would have met with a similar welcome in the 1920s. But the truth of the matter was that where income distribution is concerned, the average family has never achieved, and certainly never hung onto, great wealth. The system never worked that way in the past and did not work that way in the 1980s and 1990s. Data from NYU's Wolff show that America's top 20 percent of families owned 83 percent of total household wealth in 1998, compared to just under 52 percent in 1982. In fact, the wealth disparities in the United States were greater than they had been since the great boom of the 1920s. Indeed, the trend in wealth distribution in the 1990s was not toward more equal wealth distribution but rather toward greater inequality.

And for much of the American population, accumulating wealth is an impossible dream. In *Nickel and Dimed: On (Not) Getting By in America,* social critic Barbara Ehrenreich points out that close to a whopping one-third of all working Americans spent the late 1990s grinding away for wages of $8 an hour or less, living in inadequate housing with no unemployment benefits, let alone pension benefits, yet they didn't seem to be on the radar screen of anyone, whether New Democrats or Republicans. These folks could barely put a roof over their heads, let alone invest in the stock market or spend evenings hunched over computers worrying about 401(k) plans, despite the unrelenting din by the media and the politicians that the age of prosperity had changed the nation.

It wasn't until after March 2000, when the economy began to turn sour for some middle-class Americans, that reality struck—far from everybody in the nation was living the good life. We've seen that the corporate trauma of the 1970s and 1980s signaled an end to the growth of defined benefit plans. Another prolonged slowdown in the economy of the kind we think is likely for the remainder of this decade could similarly knock the 401(k) for a loop. The real destroyer of the dream of great wealth for the average individual shows up in both the Japanese folk tale and the performance of Japan's own stock market in the years since 1989.

The folk tale does not end with the magic paddle and the ever-full rice pot. It goes on to say that the Oni kept the old woman in the kitchen compulsively making dumplings for him and his friends many hours every day. Wanting to control her own life again, she plotted a way to escape and go back to her own small kitchen. But for a long time, the Oni managed to keep her chained to the stove, stirring the magic pot. Although the Oni and his friends appeared to be kind to her, they did everything they could to keep her from leaving, because she was, in effect, needed to keep the system that fed them going.

Could this be a parable that explains Wall Street's solicitude for the American family, its relentless advertising, designed to attract their savings? Does it explain the huge profits reaped from family investment in the 1990s? Were these profits used to benefit the family or to expand the power of America's merchants of stock—the financial service industries—through a spectacular wave of mergers aimed at forming giant companies that would be even more effective in sopping up the savings of American families? The answers are obvious.

What might be less obvious, and what was certainly ignored in the financial euphoria of the time, is that the savings economy of the kind that has emerged in the United States has within it the seeds of compound disaster that will work even more surely than the compound interest process itself.

This time, our canvas shows us what happened in Japan in the 1990s. Personal industry and good savings habits, like the old woman's, were not enough to ensure that she would accumulate wealth, or even feed herself adequately. There is no doubt that the Japanese are models of industry and thrift. The reason an addiction to saving is common in some countries on the Asian side of the Pacific Rim lies deep in the cultural traditions of Buddhist and Confucian devotion to the importance of family. No one is more relentless or patient in savings habits than the Japanese families who were the beneficiaries of that country's great post–World War II revival. Even during the 1990s, a deeply troubled decade in Japan, that country's personal savings rate averaged some 20 percent, far higher than it was in the United States. Surely no nationality was a more devout follower of Siegel's rules for achieving riches than the Japanese.

Yet no advanced country experienced so dramatic a decline in wealth. The Japanese stock market plunged by over 50 percent between 1989 and 1998. There was no better sign of the erosion of Japanese wealth in the face of high savings than the announcement by the company that controls the diamond trade, De Beers, in late April 1998, that its diamond sales fell by 50 percent in just one year, attributing most of the decline to a falloff in Japanese demand for polished diamonds. Fabulous fortunes are apparently very hard to find in Japan these days.

Nor is Japan unique in this respect. The number of countries in which the average individual has achieved great wealth and kept it over a sustained period of time can easily be counted on the fingers of no hands. Apparently, there is much more to the sustained increase in wealth than the patience and good savings habits of which the Japanese have been exemplars in recent decades. Despite whatever the results of Siegel's research may be or what Wall Street may be telling the average family, relentless savings do not necessarily lead to ever-full rice pots.

It is important to remember that through most of the 1980s, Japan seemed on the verge of ruling the economic world, and American executives were making best-sellers out of books on Zen management. But some people knew better. At the time that Japan seemed unbeatable, the authors can remember a conversation in Rome with an official of the Banca d'Italia, Italy's central bank, an institution that was then, as it is now, a center of economic wisdom in that underrated economy. (The standard of living in Northern Italy may be the highest in the world, despite what the published numbers may show.) When asked whether the Japanese would assume world economic leadership, an outcome that was widely expected at that time, he replied: "No. I do not quite know how you say it in English, but the *radichi* of American economic strength are far healthier than those of Japan." *Radichi*, as we quickly found out, means "roots." And concerning how the world economy would evolve over the next twenty years, the Italian banker's forecast turned out to be far more accurate than most contemporary predictions in American executive circles, which generally extolled the virtues of Zen management.

It is not just relentless savings that are important but also what is done with those savings by the financial institutions that are entrusted with their care and feeding. This apparently matters just as much, and perhaps even more. What Wall Street is doing with America's family savings is not in the least reassuring. There is now ample evidence that America's savings were being wasted just as were those of the average Japanese family. There are signs of a wasteful use of capital in a rapacious merger wave, corruption, and what Walter Bagehot, the first editor of the *Economist*, and perhaps the greatest financial journalist of all time, called just plain stupidity: "Much has been written about panics and manias . . . but one thing is certain, that at particular times a great deal of stupid people have a great deal of stupid money. . . . the money of these people—the blind capital, as we call it, of the country—is particularly large and craving; it seeks for someone to devour it, and there is a 'plethora'; it finds someone, and there is 'speculation'; it is devoured, and there is 'panic.'"

Bagehot's warning talks not of Japan but of lessons drawn from virtually the entire history of the consequences of late phases of bull markets. His critique should serve as a warning that Wall Street is unlikely to prove immune from the kinds of disasters that have occurred in the past.

What is new, of course, is the extent of involvement of American families in the bull market of the late 1990s. It may be that Wall Street is smarter or luckier than those exchanges that have been the scene of past disasters. But if it isn't, the new financial and emotional commitment of American families to the stock market make it certain that the consequences of a market decline will not be a ripple but a powerful, long-lasting flood. That is particularly so since there are disturbing similarities between the way the global economy evolved in the 1990s and the way it behaved in the 1920s.

That would be so even if the market were still mainly the playground of the rich. The unique problem of the next decade, however, is the fall-out from a family market.

PART TWO

THE LESSONS OF HISTORY

THE 1920S HAVE A UNIQUE place in the American mind as the last time that the United States took leave of its senses and centered its hopes and dreams on a grossly overvalued stock market. That reputation is undeserved. Even at the end of the fateful year 2001, which had witnessed a terrorist attack on a bastion of capitalism and a severe recession, price-earnings ratios on the major stock market indexes were still higher than their 1929 peaks. That is so even though at least one newspaper headline screamed, "Its Official: Gatsby Economy Ends."

But the truth is that the market mythology that created the great boom of the 1990s is still very much alive at the time of this writing, in early February 2002. The 401(k) has elevated the stock market to a much more important role in the American psyche than it ever achieved during the Roaring Twenties, and the illusion that stocks promise unimagined wealth is stronger than ever. It is an environment in which the dangers posed by the stock market will, in a fundamental sense, be greater in the next decade than at any time in the past.

We make our case by following the advice of Justice Louis D. Brandeis: "One page of history is worth volumes of analysis." We first compare the economy of the 1990s with the economy of the 1920s. Both were, of course, periods of great technological achievement and rapid economic growth. The problem in both cases was that the United States turned a record of which it could be proud into a form of what might be called "American triumphalism," the notion that the economy could do no wrong and that rapid growth and a booming stock market were fore-ordained to continue. That triumphalism was visible in the 1920s, but faith in the U.S. economy was even stronger in the 1990s and by the end of that decade had risen to a level where it posed even greater dangers to the chances of dealing realistically with what is still likely to come.

But economic fantasy does not exist in a vacuum. It requires cultural and political forces that make the aberrant and excessive seem common-place and normal. These forces were clearly at work in the 1920s. However, in the 1990s, they were compounded by President Clinton's desperate attempt to use prosperity to prevent his impeachment, which led to an exaggeration of the strength of the economy, an exaggeration reinforced by Republican right-wing arguments about the miracles that could be expected from the spread of the free market around the world. The political need to point to economic miracles produced a culture that valued individualism above all and that worked to sever the all-too-fragile safety net that the New Deal had painfully woven to protect the American family from the vicissitudes of a free market economy. Collective bargaining was weakened, government regulation was cas-trated, and Americans found themselves spinning in the wake of the hugest merger wave that had ever been seen, the devastating fallout from which will only become clear later in the postmillennial decade.

The economic, political, and cultural excesses of the 1990s have cre-ated the conditions for an extremely difficult postmillennial decade, just as the excesses of the 1920s created the conditions for the difficulties of the 1930s. The current outlook is for the brave new world's version of the Great Depression. Government action will limit the depth of the eco-nomic chasm. But economic growth is nevertheless likely to be painfully slow in a period when American society will have to make provisions for supporting a population that is growing older. That means that the American family will be very much on its own in fighting off the ravages of the difficult decade that is to come.

To see why economic growth is likely to slow and the stock market is likely to stagnate, it is necessary to compare the 1990s to the 1920s in some detail and to consider the political and cultural milieu as well as economic performance. That will set the stage for an analysis of the likely course of both the economy and the stock market in the coming decade, just as the Roaring Twenties set the scene for the troubled 1930s.

That is not to say that we expect a rerun of the Great Depression; the role of government is now large enough to prevent that. But we do expect the coming decade to pose frightening difficulties for the American family, whose fortunes are far more tied to movements in the stock ticker than at any time in the past.

Chapter 4

Rhyming the 1990s with the 1920s: Politics and Culture

History does not repeat, but it rhymes.

—Mark Twain

Market manias are not phenomena that appear in an economic vacuum. As noted above, political and cultural factors must also converge to produce an environment in which the aberrant and excessive appear to be commonplace and normal. What is not widely understood is that these forces were far more powerful in the 1990s than they were in the 1920s and became even more deeply embedded in the American psyche.

Just four months after the 1990s ended, in that "cruelest" month of April 2000, the Nasdaq began a decline that was to slice 60 percent off its value. It was at this exact time that New York City's favorite film critic, David Denby of the *New Yorker*, "confessed" in an amazing ten-page magazine piece that he watched endless hours of CNBC every week because he was in the midst of separating from his wife and badly needed a million dollars to keep his comfortable West End Avenue apartment in Manhattan. "I am amazed at myself," Denby wrote, "amazed that a writer with no business experience would place in jeopardy his substance and his peace and would risk falling among the rotting railroad ties and worthless certificates of a dozen schemes gone bust. But, like many Americans, I have begun to wonder if risk is now something I can afford to avoid, and if the usual grim historical lesson—the cautionary tale of euphoria, panic and collapse—has any power over me."

Extreme though it was, Denby's soul-baring dilemma was hardly unique. The American family had become hostage to the stock market, not its master. And there was no certainty that it could find any help in an environment where both Democrats and Republicans were beholden to special interests. "The culture of money dominates Washington as never before; money now rivals or even exceeds power as the preeminent goal . . . it has transformed politics . . . and has subverted values," wrote one of Washington's most respected veteran reporters, Elizabeth Drew.

Though Drew wrote these lines before the Enron debacle came to light, she was dead on in her analysis. The passage of the Private Securities Litigation Reform Act of 1995, pushed through Congress as part of Newt Gingrich's Contract with America, shielded corporate executives and accounting firms from liability for making dubious financial projections. "It was the ultimate in special-interest legislation," James D. Cox, professor of corporate law and securities regulation at Duke University, told the *New York Times*. Perhaps the greatest folly though was the "fox guarding the chicken coop" cast of the congressional investigations that took place in early February of 2002. Some of the same key figures involved in getting the 1995 bill through Congress originally—Democratic senator Christopher J. Dodd, and Republican representatives Billy Tauzin of Louisiana and Michael G. Oxley of Ohio, were all recipients of large political donations from the accounting industry. They were also central on investigating committees looking at the Enron scandal.

The triumph of money politics in the 1990s was at root a license for private power to capture the allegiance of the family. All government programs up to and including Social Security were painted as a thinly veiled form of the kind of socialism that had proved ineffectual. The phrasing of Francis Fukuyama's book title, *The End of History*, proclaimed America's victory in the Cold War, meaning, of course, that the free market had triumphed once and for all.

It was this sense of free market victory that dominated the 1990s. The ethos of proceeding periods—the disaffection of the 1960s, the economic stagnation of the 1970s, Ronald Reagan's economics that weakened the labor unions and unleashed a wave of job-destroying leveraged buyouts in the 1980s—all contributed to defining the 1990s. But it was the end of the Cold War that was the principal factor in setting the stage for this new zeitgeist, the German word for the spirit of the times. The war that ended in 1989 may have been "cold," but the entire ethos of the decade—not merely its economics and finance—rhymed very closely with the post–World War I 1920s. The chief difference was that the victory of business interests, the use of cheap labor around the world to hike up profits, and the free market mood that seemed to legitimize these strategies was even more overwhelming than it had been in the 1920s. Whether achieved in hot or cold war, geopolitical triumph changes the zeitgeist surely and decisively.

Politics: How the Free Market Trumped Its Opposition

An ideology tends to triumph when it co-opts or captures its opposition. In that sense, the parallel between the 1920s and the 1990s is astonishing. The free market was given free reign in the 1990s because Bill Clinton turned his back on the progressive wing of his party. What is forgotten is that the extreme pro-business climate of the 1920s involved a similar change in the Republican Party. First Warren Harding, then Calvin Coolidge, and finally Herbert Hoover presided over a decade in which the Republican Party turned its back on a progressive, Bull Moose tradition, the legacy of President Theodore Roosevelt. "The 1920s were an era when great traditions and ideals were repudiated or forgotten, when the American people, propelled by a crass materialism in their scramble for wealth, uttered a curse on twenty-five years of reform endeavor," wrote historian Arthur S. Link. "As a result," Link continued, Republican "progressives were stunned and everywhere in retreat along the entire political front."

President William Jefferson Clinton engineered a similar maneuver in the 1990s. Under the influence of successive secretaries of the treasury, Texas conservative Democrat Lloyd Bentsen, and Goldman Sachs executive Robert Rubin, Clinton suppressed the progressive tendencies of the Democratic Party and ended up delivering the White House to Wall Street.

In his 2001 book, David Halberstam reports that Clinton's labor secretary Robert Reich, who had been a fellow Rhodes scholar at Oxford, made the connection between the Republican White House of the 1920s and the Democratic White House of the 1990s. "'Deficit, deficit, deficit, deficit, deficit,' a frustrated Reich wrote about the first few weeks of the Clinton team's economic discussions. 'We have to cut it. By how much? That's all we talk about in the Roosevelt Room.'" Halberstam reports that it struck Reich as unfair that Wall Street was able to exact the kind of leverage against a liberal Democratic president that it never felt the need to exercise with Ronald Reagan and George H.W. Bush, conservative Republicans who normally represented its wishes. In a memo Reich wrote to the president, he warned that newspaper accounts of the president's economic plans made Bill Clinton sound like Calvin Coolidge.

Indeed, from the outset of his administration, Clinton decided to make cooperation with Federal Reserve Board chairman Alan Greenspan, a Reagan appointee and an avowed follower of Ayn Rand's "superman" brand of conservatism, the basis of his economic program. The symbolic apogee of this collaboration came in February of 1993 during Clinton's first State of the Union address, when Hillary Clinton invited Greenspan to sit next to her in the House gallery. Former Fed governor John LaWare said that Greenspan was "personally embarrassed" afterward, since the network television cameras showed him throughout the evening sitting in between Hillary Clinton and Tipper Gore. Every time President Clinton made a dramatic point, the two women clapped for the crowds, and he was caught in the national limelight. But there was in fact a close relationship between Clinton's Treasury Department and Greenspan, and indeed, it represented something new, certainly for a Democrat.

An obvious comparison could be made between President Warren Harding, the earlier Republican president in 1920, and Bill Clinton. Harding was the most popular, outgoing, cigar-smoking, golf-playing chief executive the United States had ever seen. Like Clinton, Harding's reputation as a womanizer was well documented and well known. He had at least one mistress who was regularly smuggled in and out of the White House during times his wife, Florence, was not around. But this "match" with Bill Clinton is far too easy. Reich had nailed it early on. It was the thrifty, taciturn Vermonter, Calvin Coolidge, who came to be Clinton's stealth political twin. And this was because it was Dow Jones, not Paula Jones, that was the barometer of the times and came to characterize what his presidency was all about.

Wall Street fueled both presidencies. Presidents Coolidge and Clinton insisted almost daily in public that the American economy had never been better. They displayed patterns of integrative public behavior that pretty much denied any bad news, and both held office during periods of frenzied, speculative prosperity. Yet it is also important that neither ever hinted that Wall Street had perhaps become too powerful. And President Clinton never seemed to worry that there could be a dark downside to the "flexible economy," which became a hallmark of his two administrations, in which companies constantly shed workers as easily as head-cold victims threw away Kleenex, at the mere hint of a profit downturn. What a contrast to John F. Kennedy, who laid down the gauntlet to steel industry executives so that prices would not rise in 1962 by telling the press that "all steelmen are sons of bitches." One could be sure that neither the taciturn Calvin Coolidge nor the loquacious Bill Clinton would be caught dead making a similar statement.

"The chief business of the American people is business," Coolidge famously announced. Like Bill Clinton, he was careful to do nothing that would interfere with the upward climb of the stock market. The "Coolidge Prosperity" had not been misnamed. "By . . . statement and inaction, the President had greatly encouraged business to expand," wrote Coolidge biographer Donald R. McCoy. "The results were temporarily magnificent . . . Yet it will forever be held against him that he did not see further and more clearly than his fellow Americans, and with some justice, for he had qualms and failed to act on them."

Coolidge, like Clinton, was extremely popular with the public. The Washington old-boy network, though, never thought of Coolidge as one of them—the same attitude they had toward Bill Clinton. The Teapot Dome Scandal—a rancorous affair during the Harding administration—still smoldered. Many Coolidge critics felt that though he had been Harding's vice president, he had somehow managed to slide out of the whole scandal all too easily. Newspapers snidely reported that three times a day, Coolidge rode a mechanical horse installed inside the White House. Reports were that the president came to enjoy his artificial horse rides, even to the point of whoopeeing like a cowboy while astride the electrically operated mount. One congressman wrote a mocking poem entitled "Cal's Hobbyhorse," which, McCoy writes, "mock[ed] the President as

Presidents had not often been mocked in Congress," an attitude with which Bill Clinton could surely identify in the late 1990s.

It is, however, well worth noting that Coolidge felt in his bones that the good times were coming to an end, and he did not want to be in charge when the bottom fell out of the bull market. Coolidge's economic advisers and Coolidge himself seemed to be aware that the economic boom would not last. The Vermont native himself was probably betting that the market would unravel, perhaps sooner rather than later, prompting his wife, Grace, to remark, "Poppa says there's a depression coming." Yet he carefully avoided mentioning this fear publicly. Instead, he bailed out of the presidency in the 1928 election, with nary a word about the stock market mania that made him uncomfortable. Coolidge, the president of masterly inactivity, was not about to try and figure out how to fend it off.

Clinton may not have felt there was a depression coming, but with price-earnings ratios in orbit, and with a brilliant friend—one of the savviest market analysts in the world, Treasury Secretary Robert Rubin— just down the street, it seems unlikely the two never shared private moments about the likelihood of a stock market blowout. It may indeed be why Rubin decided to quit in July 1999 when he was well ahead of the game. Even if he had private doubts, Clinton's main concern had to be keeping the bubble aloft; otherwise, he would have been politically strangled by Monica's thong. With his presidency in shambles after his impeachment in January 1999, he could not afford to raise doubts about the wonders of the American stock market. The public too was watching the ascending value of 401(k)s. That's what kept him in office.

Although it is not the job of the president to comment directly on the workings of the stock market, it is his job to help safeguard the well-being of his constituents. We cannot help wondering what would have happened had the United States had a president without a thong problem, a president who quietly reminded the country that historically, stock markets do get too rich and bubbles do burst. Suppose he had bravely said, "Folks, be a bit careful. I don't want anything to happen to any of you." Especially since during most of the mid- to late 1990s, more than two-thirds of 401(k) pension plan balances were in the stock market. As Yale economist Robert J. Shiller points out, "401(k) and similar plans are designed to give ordinary people economic security in retirement by encouraging them to mimic the portfolio strategies long pursued by the wealthy. But little attention is usually paid to the fact that the wealthy, because of the overall level of their assets, have less reason to worry about losing substantial amounts in a market decline."

American Hubris

Americans weren't much worried, though, about the Dow Jones effect on the presidency in the 1990s. Many of them were excitedly reading about and learning the ins-and-outs of global technology funds, developing world closed-end country funds, and yes, even dabbling in foreign market derivatives. Investment gurus such as Mark Mobius of the Templeton Funds, and CNBC's Jimmy Rogers, who rode around the world on his motorcycle investigating obscure investment opportunities in exotic places, gripped much of the public's imagination. Investing in the hinterlands of a newly privatizing Russia, China, or Turkey beat thinking or worrying about Clinton and his wall of worries in Washington.

In important ways, a period is always defined by the psyche of the generation "coming of age" during that time. In the 1990s, bright college graduates marched off to Goldman Sachs and Morgan Stanley, dreaming of the fortunes to be made as investment bankers. Business school enrollments boomed. And zeal to make at a bare minimum, a million dollars, flourished. But it is also important to look at those in their twenties because it provides clues about what will happen when the prosperity runs out. Although the environmental and antiglobalization protests were visible in the mid- to late 1990s, they were largely ignored and marginalized by most of American society. But the protests are fated to become an important part of the postmillennium era, a forerunner of a new period of political activism that will parallel the 1930s.

Both the probusiness ethos of the 1990s and the reaction against it were the product of an American hubris that took the form of a conviction that the American economy was performing feats that had never been seen before and would continue to grow at a breakneck pace. Not only had the United States bested the Soviet Union, it had also sprung ahead of Germany and Japan, which had put it to shame in the 1970s and 1980s. Indeed, the United States seemed more confident of its future in the 1990s than even in the Roaring Twenties.

The victory of its ideology was important in explaining a level of hubris that had never before been seen, even in an America that was traditionally optimistic about its economic future. The American presidency under Harding, Coolidge, and Hoover ardently promoted free market capitalism, and each president, in his own way, was an apologist for the system. The faith in capitalism survived Harding's Teapot Dome Scandal, was more fervently embraced than ever under Coolidge, and lasted for the first three years of the depression under Hoover. But as compared to the 1990s, the free market ideology of the 1920s never achieved anything resembling a complete victory: Free market capitalism was challenged around the world, not just in the Soviet Union. All of Western Europe had powerful Socialist movements. Although they seldom achieved power, there were brief intervals of genuine Socialist governments in France and Britain.

Outside the United States, the left of the 1920s was a real left. In Germany, the Social Democrat Friedrich Ebert was not as accepting of the virtues of the free market as was Germany's preeminent post–World War II leader Social Democrat Helmut Schmidt. In Great Britain, the Labor Party of the 1920s hardly embraced the market with the fervor of the Labor prime minister of the late 1990s, Tony Blair. Indeed, throughout the world, intellectuals and politicians, even when not Communists or doctrinaire Socialists, were genuinely skeptical of the capitalist system. But in the early 1990s, by contrast, belief in the market swept through the intelligentsia abroad.

That is not to say that the United States did not revel in its global economic power in that decade. Although the United States is usually described as "isolationist" in that decade, the isolationism was political, not economic. After World War I, the United States came into its own and, really for the first time, was recognized as the most powerful capitalist power in the world. "It was Europe that had suffered the war," wrote literary critic Alfred Kazin, "where Americans had merely participated in it; it was Europe that now lay paralytic after four shattering years, where Americans were merely disillusioned by the aftermath; and most significantly . . . America now emerged completely as a dominant World Power . . . although to most people it merely appeared as richer and more comfortable, if less naive, than the world of 1914." If Kazin had said "world economic power," he would have had it exactly right.

Exhausted by World War I, Europe had difficulty in competing with the United States. In particular, European manufacturers were hard put to compete with the new American methods of mass production. American corporations in the 1920s crept under national barriers by buying or building factories in desired marketing areas, and their combined expertise in research, design, and production techniques made them almost unbeatable. The leading American companies of those days were alarmingly like the innovative, high-octane American technology companies of the 1990s that blew their global competitors away for most of the same reasons. But nothing that the American corporation had accomplished in the 1920s equipped it to cope with the problems of the 1930s.

It is likely that it will be even more difficult for American families to capitalize on the past successes of the American corporation in the post-millennial decade than it was in the 1930s. The geopolitics produced by the free market ideology have knocked down tariffs and other limits to free trade to an unprecedented degree. As the American economy slows and pressures on profits increase, the American corporation will have more incentive than ever to move production abroad, and foreign corporations will face few impediments to exporting to the United States. The integration of the world economy is likely to wreak havoc on workers in those countries that pay high wages, the United States among them, especially in a slow-growth decade where productivity is rising and fewer people are needed to do the same amount of work. With the idea of the "flexible workforce" firmly embedded in the American economy during the 1990s, high-salaried white-collar jobs had long since begun moving abroad, alongside their blue-collar counterparts. In the postmillennial era, computer services are likely to move to India and China, auto production to Korea and Brazil, personal computer manufacture to Taiwan and other countries in Southeast Asia at an increased pace. And because of the Internet, white-collar jobs in the infrastructure of a vast array of service industries will migrate around the world, costing large numbers of jobs in the United States. The integration of the global economy will impose heavy costs on working families in the coming decade, both by putting downward pressure on wages and by creating huge job losses. And to complicate matters, the United States has been behind other industrial countries in providing homeland security against terrorism. Paying for increased expenditures on security that are the consequence of the

World Trade Center tragedy will therefore impose greater burdens on American business than on corporations in the other advanced industrial countries. These are not forces that those pinning their hopes on the 401(k) can afford to ignore.

The Cultural Spirit

Like the geopolitics, the cultural spirit of the 1990s was heavily influenced by America's victory in the Cold War. And as in the 1920s, the lifting of the burden of war from the shoulders of the United States turned its citizens inward, away from social concerns and toward a cult of individualism.

As with the fiction of the 1990s, the writing of the 1920s was deeply apolitical. F. Scott Fitzgerald recorded the emotional color of his seminal decade. His narrative often reveals a sudden flash of truth in the most casual of comments. "America was going on the greatest, gaudiest spree in history and there was going to be plenty to tell about it . . . The whole golden boom was in the air—its splendid generosities, its outrageous corruptions. . . . All the stories that came into my head had a touch of disaster in them." And it is, indeed, the work of F. Scott Fitzgerald, particularly *The Great Gatsby,* that for many still most vividly evokes the 1920s.

Overwhelmingly, both decades were permeated by celebrity cults. In the 1920s, the newly prosperous country entertained itself with radio, tabloid newspapers, and the newly created *Time* magazine, which wrote about Charles Lindbergh and Henry Ford ad nauseum, as it did about O. J. Simpson and Bill Gates in the 1990s. And surprisingly, along with the new economy, *Time* reemerged as a national media favorite. As Frank Rich wrote in the *New York Times* after the much-covered seventy-fifth anniversary bash of *Time,* when guests included everyone from Joe DiMaggio and Louis Farrakhan to Anita Hill and Imelda Marcos, it was "celebrity über alles, indeed, as in Luce journalism, star-sized personalities guaranteed entrée more than intellectual or moral attainment."

American literature of the 1990s had no Fitzgerald, but it did survive with the help of Amazon.com and Oprah Winfrey. Just as Fitzgerald wrote about the corrosive effects of the hunt for money and the narcissism that gripped the part of society he was writing about, Kurt Andersen's *Turn of the Century,* Mary Gordon's *Spending,* and Tama

Janowitz's *A Certain Age* all dealt with the shallowness of life in the 1990s. Whereas the great 1920s classic *The Great Gatsby* has lasted because of its poetic language and powerful metaphors, most 1990s fiction about empty and superficial characters is basically also empty and superficial. "As *A Certain Age* builds to its mordant conclusion," wrote Henry Alford, "we can't help feeling that were Florence's superficiality and sense of expedience leavened by some less noxious trait, Janowitz's tale might be more moving, more cautionary." In the 1990s, the narcissism was greater than ever, and the fascination with the ways of the wealthy and famous more engrossing than ever. Indeed, the entire culture was even more conducive to the celebration of Wall Street's values than it was in the 1920s. Such was the cost to the United States of defining literature downward.

Social critic David Brooks takes hilarious aim at the 1990s business bourgeoisie in *Bobos in Paradise: The New Upper Class and How They Got There*. He writes that the countercultural 1960s and the achieving 1980s, defying expectations and maybe logic, have been combined into one social ethos during the 1990s. By now, we're all familiar with modern-day executives who have moved from SDS to CEO, from LSD to IPO. But the serious and apt criticism by the talented Brooks is that at the heart of Bobo culture—whether Republican or Democratic—serious compromises were made that deeply affected the United States of the 1990s. Bobo politicians—both liberal and conservative—adopt policy suggestions while somehow sucking the real essence out of them. Yet Brooks falls short when he suggests that "today's . . . intellectuals have a foot in the world of 401(k) plans . . . and so have more immediate experience with life as it is lived by most of their countrymen." His assumption that this makes them superior to old-fashioned bohemians who lived without 401(k)s is false. Today's "bobo" intellectuals had been so involved in keeping track of their own personal profits on the Internet that they never took time out to critique some of the possible pitfalls of the plan.

Similarly, H. L. Mencken, editor of the literary magazine the *American Mercury* in the 1920s, is especially remembered for barbs that he aimed at the business middle classes, which he called the "booboisie." But Mencken never really critiqued the economic system itself that produced the behavior that so offended him. His favorite young author, Sinclair Lewis, from Sauk Centre, Minnesota, who was to win the Nobel Prize for literature in 1930, like Mencken, worked hard to define what he saw as the psychological cast, language, and mores of America's "booboisies," most notably those in the Midwest. *Main Street, Babbitt,* and *Dodsworth,* describe, for the most part, an upper middle class from the prosperous Midwest that is often psychologically at war with, and often bored by, its own comfortable, conforming existence, but not with the system that produced it.

Yet as original and exuberant as it was and still is, the American literature of the 1920s also left intact the gigantic myth created by the business and political establishments of the time that the Roaring Twenties in the United States was a period of unparalleled prosperity for almost everyone. And when the Great Depression hit, Mencken's circle lost much of its popularity, and he personally came to be thoroughly hated by some of the public because of his sweeping derision of American life, his endless Roosevelt-baiting and deep cynicism about government at a time when desperate Americans—even those of the middle classes—began turning to Washington for survival.

In the 1920s, Willa Cather may have underlined the ethos of the literary establishment the most clearly in an essay called "The Novel Demeuble." In it she pleaded for a movement to throw the "furniture" out of the novel. "Are the banking system and the Stock Exchange worth being written about at all?" Willa Cather asked, and she replied that they were not. Along with the factory, she felt they had no place in modern literature. But at some level, abstract money of the kind that Wall Street worships remained very much alive in the novel. F. Scott Fitzgerald's *Great Gatsby,* of course, is the prime example. As literary critic Elizabeth Hardwick has pointed out, "Gatsby has devised a name for himself, imagined an eloquent background of situations and accomplishments. The money he has made is . . . unreal and subject to disappearance, like a ghost vanishing at dawn." This is a sentiment that the supposedly heroic entrepreneurs of the great dot-com bubble that burst in 2000 must surely understand.

David Brooks's "bobos" were not a purely American species. In some profound ways, the love affair with what Hardwick called "unreal" money had a worldwide dimension in the 1990s. Indian politician N. Chandrabubu Naidu, a former soap opera hunk, became a multibillion-dollar software deal maker. So great was his reputation in the 1990s that he became prime minister of Andrha Pradesh and was rumored to be the next prime minister of all of India. India had long been in love with its version of Hollywood, and a man who had succeeded in the nation's other middle-class passion—software—could not be resisted. This combination of talents could indeed have made him the developing world's sexiest man if the exuberance of the period had carried on. Not even Bill Clinton had managed to wrap all that into one! The authors, who were lured by a public-relations barrage into meeting with Naidu, are at a total loss to explain his popularity.

It is only fair, however, to recognize that globalization did work real literary magic. Some critics convincingly argue that in the 1990s, some of the most original fiction came from fresh non-Western voices. Asian writers such as the Pen- and Hemingway-award-winning Chinese writer Ha Jin impacted the international literary community, as did an immensely talented group of young Indian writers, including the 2000 Pulitzer Prize–winning author Jhumpa Lahiri, author of *Interpreter of Maladies.* They were joined by two Jamaican writers, Zadie Smith, author of *White Teeth,* and Margaret Cezair-Thompson, who wrote *The True History of Paradise.* These writers exploded onto the international literary landscape in much the same way that American writers dislodged Europeans in the 1920s, because they had discovered exhilarating new ways of using language and reinventing traditional storytelling. As expatriates, they represented a new generation of writers dealing with a complex world of multiracialism.

It may well be that these non-Western writers developed a style and a set of interests for what will be the American literature of the postmillennial decade, a decade that will have to confront new economic difficulties. These writers may in fact have played the same role in the 1990s that a native American writer, Theodore Dreiser, filled in the 1920s.

Although he was hardly a great stylist, it was left to Theodore Dreiser to drag Cather's "furniture" into 1920s fiction. An Indiana native, Dreiser was the son of a crippled German-American factory worker and a Mennonite mother who made her living as a Christian evangelist. Together, the two raised twelve children, most of whom ended up hustling for a living throughout the Midwest. Dreiser, well into his middle-aged years, retained enough of an old-fashioned European sensibility to understand the darker side of the 1920s in the United States. Yet the unfashionable Hoosier was derided by the smart literary set of that decade as being an anachronism because of his sometimes graceless, rather heavy-handed, fatalistic style. As Alfred Kazin wrote, "Dreiser was the primitive, the man from the abyss, the stranger who had grown up outside the Anglo-Saxon middle-class Protestant morality and so had no need to accept its sanctions . . . he stood in no-man's land, pushed ahead like a dumb ox."

More than any other major writer of the 1920s, Dreiser's work dug away at the economic infrastructure of the United States—it described the pliant, eager, and frighteningly vulnerable new immigrant labor pool; the great energy, color, and imagination of a newly great nation on the move; and the gritty underbelly of an economic giant rolling forward along with, or often over, those who couldn't cut it. Dreiser's America, the America that he had lived and worked in, was one that the often insulated and sometimes supercilious H. L. Mencken never saw.

In working the backstreets, manufacturing plants, and meatpacking districts of cities across the Midwest and East Coast, it was Dreiser who inevitably captured the rough world of laissez-faire America going through a technological revolution that made some rich. Those who weren't lucky enough, smart enough, or physically tough enough were simply ground under, and it is this America that Dreiser chronicled. Dreiser inevitably acted as an invaluable and realistic literary bridge— from the "feel-good" 1920s to an America reeling under the depression. In *An American Tragedy,* the middle-aged Dreiser chronicled the lower-class journey to "make it in America" in a way that no other writer in the 1920s, or in the 1990s, has ever done.

There were few fiction writers in the United States during the 1990s with the powers of Theodore Dreiser or the instinct of F. Scott Fitzgerald to guide the way into the next decade. But William Finnegan, a journalist of the first order who writes for the *New Yorker*, explores some of the same psychological terrain in the 1990s as Dreiser did in the 1920s and earlier, in his nonfiction work, *Cold New World: Growing Up in a Harder Country.* Finnegan's riveting, poetic account about the people living in the backstreets of New Haven, Connecticut, East Texas and Yakima Valley, Washington is evocative of the Dreiserian tradition, and writers such as James Agee.

Finnegan asserts, at the beginning of his book, "While the national economy has been growing, the economic prospects of most Americans have been dimming . . . A new American class structure is being born—

one that is harsher, in many ways, than the one it is replacing . . . What the triumphalism of most American business writing ignores is a frightening growth in the number of low-wage jobs."

In 2001, Barbara Ehrenreich's *Nickel and Dimed* chronicled firsthand just what those jobs are like. Ehrenreich's witty but ultimately angry account of trying to make ends meet as a home health-care attendant, waitress, and cleaning lady for $6 and $7 an hour brought home the fact like no other book had that close to one-third of Americans had been living under the economic radar screen in the buoyant 1990s, and still do. Yet the longtime social critic has a hard time explaining to skeptical friends, convinced that all of the United States lived as well as they did, about her sojourn among the working poor in the late 1990s. "[I]t is alarming, upon returning to the upper middle class . . . to find the rabbit hole close suddenly and completely behind me. You were where, doing what? Some odd optical property of our highly polarized and unequal society makes the poor almost invisible to their economic superiors."

The Culture of the Workplace

"The whole upper tenth of a nation" said Fitzgerald, writing about the 1920s, "was living with the insouciance of a grand duc and the casualness of a chorus girl." But as became apparent in the 1930s, the glitter masked as much as it revealed about ominous changes that were taking place in American society.

For the vast majority of Americans, the cultural changes that really matter do not occur in the tony clubs and restaurants of New York and Los Angeles. Rather, they center in a much more prosaic locale: the workplace.

In this sense, the accession of George W. Bush to the presidency in the 2000 election set the stage for a rerun of the end of the 1920s. Just as Clinton resembled Coolidge in unexpected ways, George W. Bush is likely to emerge as an unlikely Hoover. Bush's early history hardly mirrored that of Hoover, the pious, hard-working Quaker who had coordinated war relief efforts after World War I in Belgium. Bush's high moral tone emerged far later in his career. But, like Hoover, Bush ran on a program focused on bringing high-mindedness, moral reform, and efficiency back to Washington.

Hoover's high-mindedness was fixed on the notion that business can be made to serve social ends. Before the roof fell in on Wall Street, Hoover worked hard to put a smile on corporate efforts to promote harmony. To prove that unions were unnecessary, many "enlightened corporations" in the 1920s sold the idea that the highly profitable "new technology" companies could easily give workers what they needed. Many corporations were quite ready to promote employee welfare, provided it was not forced upon them. Factories, restaurants, social centers, and hospitals were built, and contributions were made to community chests and to other community efforts. And, though many were fated to come to no good end, private retirement programs were expanded. It was clear that a movement toward "welfare capitalism" was under way. Hoover's approach did hamper the resurgence of a union movement that had not recovered from brutal police attacks in the early 1920s, when New York union members in particular were often deported or imprisoned for being Communist sympathizers in the aftermath of the 1919 Russian Revolution. It was no accident that as the decade wore on, Samuel Gompers, head of the AFL, was dubbed "Tame as a tabby cat," by H. L. Mencken.

If pressed, George W. Bush's policy team would say that Hoover was a closet liberal. To the majority of Republican idea men of the postmillennial decade, the responsibility of business to its employees ends with what is in effect a check that gives employees some money to pay for their benefits. That is the role of the 401(k). That is the idea behind schemes to privatize Social Security and to establish medical savings accounts as a partial substitute for Medicare. It is indeed clear that George W. Bush is far more willing to trust the future of the American family to the market than Herbert Hoover ever was. And the prospect is that the postmillennial decade will witness an unprecedented degree of free market extremism that calls to mind the title of Thomas Frank's insightful book, *One Market Under God*.

The exposure of the American family to the unregulated dictates of the market became a feature of the American economic scene well before the accession of George W. Bush to the White House. Clearly, the business community, heavily represented in the Bush cabinet, was the big winner of election 2000. Its wedges into the Bush administration, if it needed any, were Vice President Cheney, who had been CEO of

Halliburton, and Treasury Secretary Paul O'Neill, former chairman of Alcoa. And though none of the stars of Wall Street would deign to join the cabinet, it could still find plenty of reasons to cheer.

A devotion to corporate interests had of course emerged as a feature of the Clintonian 1990s, well before Bush took over. Throughout the Clinton years, every trade treaty signed by the United States insisted on guarantees of intellectual property rights that protected business patents but contained few environmental or labor standards for American workers. And in 1998, the Clinton administration reacted to the first appearance of a surplus in the federal budget by vastly increasing its spending on pork-barrel projects designed to benefit the business supporters of congressmen, especially Republican congressmen who controlled the flow of legislation.

The effect, of course, was to expose American workers to a set of forces working to shift what were good paying jobs abroad. As in the 1920s, the proportion of workers who were unionized fell in the 1990s. But in a sense, the attack on employment security was even more pronounced in the 1990s. Constant reengineering and a move to hire "permanent" temporary workers—from high-priced software engineers to janitorial help—fed insecurity. The bottom line for workers: No matter how strong the economy, many of them would not become permanent employees with retirement benefits and perhaps even stock options. Instead, they would remain on part-time status.

Despite its strong ties to labor, the Clinton administration basically never addressed the breakdown of a social contract that had evolved in the United States between labor and management during the 1950s and 1960s and was based on the notion that labor and management were both part of the same community. In the 1980s, this pact began to crumble when President Ronald Reagan essentially broke the unions by intervening against the union during the air controllers' strike, at a time when union membership was sliding anyway. By Clinton's second term, it had become crystal clear that business could do pretty much whatever it wished with workers (as long as it didn't employ children) and it would hear no complaint from 1600 Pennsylvania Avenue. The phenomenal success of the 1990s bull market had kept the Arkansan high in the polls. It was a given that President Clinton would never risk his strong ties with Wall Street to deal with the real key issue of the late 1990s—

the staggering loss of any real power or control by those in the workforce who were rejiggered and fired even when profits rose—whether they were white or blue collar. "The labor force is not organized enough to get any real wage hikes even though the labor market is tight," said one shrewd analyst on CNBC in August 1999. "Management has very little to fear." There seemed to be few limits to Clinton and Treasury Secretary Robert Rubin's efforts to keep Wall Street happy.

In *The Corruption of Politics,* Elizabeth Drew argued that Clinton's presidency was a lost opportunity. Even before he was trapped in the sex scandal that blew up in January 1998, she wrote: "His formidable political skills and exceptional brain went more to self-preservation than to leadership. . . . At a time of unparalleled prosperity, and even into his second term, Clinton had given the country no sense of direction . . . Exceptional prosperity had given him an opportunity to resolve two long-range and politically difficult problems: assuring the soundness of the Social Security and Medicare programs, about to be flooded by the 'baby boomers.'" But in both cases, she says, Clinton did nothing.

Followed as it was by the Bush administration's right-wing policies, Clinton's failure to address the real problems facing the family could lead to a political explosion as the postmillennial decade moves on. The reason is simply that the love affair of Fitzgerald's "grand ducs" of the upper tenth of the population is not shared by the other 90 percent. As long as the economy continued to grow strongly, the American public was willing to tolerate worship of the gods of the free market. But it was apparently uneasy with the notion that it could fully trust its fate to the corporation.

There was in fact a latent anger aimed at corporate power even in the heyday of the 1990s that could easily explode as the economy stagnates in the coming decade. That anger showed up in two critical opinion surveys. One was the Worker Representation and Participation Survey of 1998, the most comprehensive survey of worker attitudes ever conducted in the United States. The results are reported in *What Workers Want,* by Harvard economist Richard B. Freeman and University of Wisconsin economist Joel Rogers. They show little evidence that American workers trust the corporation to protect their interests.

To begin with, the survey shows that the 14 percent of the American workforce that was unionized strongly supported their unions, particularly at the local level. And more important, the survey reveals that a full one-third of the workforce that was not unionized would have voted for union representation if they had been give the chance. Adding the two figures together brings home the conclusion that if the American workers had had their way, some 44 percent of the entire U.S. workforce would be unionized. The conclusion in *What Workers Want* is that the level of unionization is kept low and in decline because business aggressively fights unionizing drives with every weapon at its command. One business that clearly flourished in the 1990s, mainly under a Democratic administration, was that part of the consulting fraternity that specialized in teaching companies how to prevent unionization.

The study reveals that workers want unions not only to bargain with management on the traditional battlegrounds of wages, hours, and working conditions. Rather, workers were interested in having their views represented in management decisions. They overwhelmingly felt that their jobs could be made more meaningful, more rewarding, and more productive if they could influence how the workplace—where they obviously spent so many hours—is organized. They most resented that despite the lip service that was paid to worker participation, there was enormous resistance to any encroachment on what management saw as its prerogatives. It would therefore seem that despite the tight labor markets of the late 1990s, workers were far from happy with the workplace in which they found themselves.

A second survey conducted by the Harris organization for *BusinessWeek* magazine in the week after Vice President Gore's "populist" acceptance speech at the Democratic Convention of 2000, shows that some 62 percent of the American public as a whole agreed with the statement that "corporations have too much power." And that, of course, was before the corporate hold on power was consolidated after the younger Bush became president in 2000.

There were even some signs of discontent with the corporate system in the comfortable middle class able to pay for Broadway theater tickets: A wrenching Broadway revival of Arthur Miller's *Death of a Salesman* seemed to strike deep at the heart of New York. The revival was dominated by the large, vulnerable figure of Brian Dennehy, playing Willy Loman. No one seemed able to explain why sophisticated New Yorkers were not only responding to the play but sobbing uncontrollably at

Loman's blighted life, as the *New York Times* pointed out in a page-one story. Could it have been that some of the people they had seen around them in the bubbly 1990s were suffering the way Willy had, but there was no emotional outlet for their sympathy, save in the *Dilbert* cartoon strip?

These discontents do not bode well for public attitudes toward the fundamental institutions of capitalism, including the stock market, should things begin to really go wrong. Public discontent with the system makes it vulnerable to political attack. The outcome of the 2000 election has already exposed severe divisions in society. And though the bin Laden attack on the World Trade Center did produce an aura of national unity, if the recession deepens and unemployment grows, the reaction could be bitter indeed.

Chapter 5

Rhyming the 1990s with the 1920s: Economic Comparisons

Dangerous bull markets do not begin with an immediate denial of reality. On the contrary, the denial only takes place some years later, after a society, from its leaders to its ordinary citizens, comes to believe that it is witnessing some kind of economic "miracle" never before seen. Usually, miracles are proclaimed some years after the emergence of a new generation of technology that is believed to unlock the keys to growth both in productivity and in the economy as a whole.

The problem lies in a phenomenon that might be called an excess of "techno-optimism." In their enthusiasm over the real benefits of the introduction of a new technology, nations have a way of forgetting that technological progress does not proceed in straight lines, but rather occurs in waves that have a small beginning, a fat and prosperous middle, and often a harrowing end that produces recession followed by slow economic growth, with devastating consequences for investment in the stock market. The United States entered a tech slump in the spring of 2000. And because the preceding boom produced an excess of this sort of optimism, recovery from the slump will be slow and painful.

Too Good to Be True

The early phases of waves of techno-optimism are invariably rooted in a good, plausible story. The run-up in markets that led to the panic of

1847 had its basis in a great canal-building boom that unquestionably increased the productivity of American agriculture by sharply reducing the costs of bringing agricultural products to market. Both the crash of 1873 and the crisis of 1893 followed high phases of the railroad revolution that opened a continent to the low-cost exchange of goods produced by agriculture and an emerging manufacturing industry. The soaring markets of the 1920s had a solid basis in the automobile, the electric utility, the telephone, and the radio. In each case, there was, as John Kenneth Galbraith graphically described in *The Great Crash,* "that indispensable element of fact," on which "men and women had proceeded to build a world of speculative make-believe."

The economic story of the 1990s unquestionably contains that "indispensable element." The economic performance was grade A while it lasted. There are many sideshows in assessing the economic performance of the advanced industrial countries, of which the United States surely is one. But the big tent is occupied by two sets of numbers, those on real growth and those on the rate of inflation. For decades, part of the cardinal wisdom of economics maintained that rapid real growth could only be bought at the expense of rising inflation. But that is not what happened in the second half of the 1990s. Between 1994 and 1999, the average growth rate of the U.S. economy was 3.9 percent, an extremely rapid expansion by historical standards. Yet inflation continued low, with the broadest measure of inflation, the GDP deflator, hovering just above 1 percent.

Behold a "new economy!" The improvement in growth and the absence of inflation were widely held to have been caused by the technological revolution in information processing, the computer, new software, and the Internet. The wonder of this revolution was held to be a marvelous tendency for costs to fall as technological progress advanced. Between 1988 and 1999, the consumer price index for information processing equipment—basic home computers—declined by 72 percentage points per year, and at the same time, the government's measure of productivity took off. Between 1995 and 1999, output per man-hour in the private business sector advanced at an average annual rate of 2.7 percent, a stellar rate of increase by historical standards.

Remembering that historical comparisons are inexact and that history rhymes rather than repeats, there are remarkable resemblances between the 1920s and the 1990s, in economic performance, economic policy, and economic attitudes. The 1990s witnessed greater extremes. But like the 1990s, the 1920s benefited from a seemingly magical combination of low inflation and rapid economic growth. In the seven years between 1923 and 1929, the American economy grew at an astounding 4.7 percent annual rate, and inflation was nonexistent: The growth rate was even higher than the 3.9 percent of the second half of the 1990s.

During the 1920s, it was, of course, innovation in the auto industry, electric utilities, and the telephone system that were the technological holy grails. Buoyed by these industries, and in a similarly benign economic environment—the Federal Reserve was held to be at least as wise in the 1920s as it had been in the 1990s. It was said that the benefit of this growth could be directly seen in the behavior of the economy.

In and of themselves, waves of technological innovation of the kind that occurred in the 1920s and the 1990s are indeed the key to economic growth and rising standards of living; it is technology that is responsible for the remarkable progress of the advanced industrial economies. The problems occur because of the existence of what Robert J. Shiller calls "amplification mechanisms" that turn a good story into a story that is too good to be true.

There were four groups of players in the amplification game. As we have already seen, the Clintonians, who needed a good economic story to extricate their leader from the consequences of Monica's thong, made up the first group. The other three groups included a chorus of Wall Street analysts, an unlikely band of academic economists, and last and perhaps most important, the Federal Reserve Board itself. As each group played a role to maximize its own interests, it would eventually lead to an overall environment of such extreme excess that the financial fortunes of the average American family would be badly damaged. As we analyze the impact of each bloc of all-important actors in the roar of the 1990s economy, we can see the seeds of disturbing trouble ahead. The Clintonians obsessed on success and exaggerated it greatly in the last half of its final year of administration; the Wall Street analysts indulged in their usual game of finding reasons the public should buy stocks; economists felt a need to repent for forecasting mistakes that led them to underestimate the strength of the economy in the 1990s by becoming over-optimistic about the prospects for the postmillennial decade; and at the Federal Reserve, Chairman Greenspan lent the weight of his authority to the belief that the United States was indeed benefiting from a "new economy" that would enjoy unprecedented gains in productivity and would ensure rapid growth far into the future.

The tendency of Wall Street analysts to amplify a good story is the easiest to explain and, indeed, barely deserves explanation. Wall Street is always in search of seemingly sophisticated stories that provide reasons to buy stocks. That is what explains why such gurus of perpetual prosperity as Abby Joseph Cohen of Goldman Sachs, Edward Yardeni of Deutschebank, Ralph Acampora of Prudential Securities, and Joe Battapaglia of Gruntal & Company enjoyed a period in the sun in the late 1990s.

The male members of this cast faded fast when the market began to falter in mid-2000. But Abby Joseph Cohen who was made a partner at Goldman Sachs and had become the most influential market strategist in the country, continued to be influential for a time. In recognition of the market's spectacular gains in the final two years of the twentieth century, she had granted at the beginning of the year that 2000 would show more modest returns, with the Standard & Poor's 500 Index rising to 1575 by the end of the year, a modest gain over 1999. As it turned out, the S&P 500 declined by 9 percent, the Nasdaq index by 46 percent from its March 2000 high, while the Dow went down by 6 percent.

Nothing, of course, damps excessive optimism on the part of Wall Street analysts. Instead of admitting their forecasting error, Wall Street's seers, ignoring the losses that their clients had already sustained, were busy hailing the 2000 declines as a return to sanity on Wall Street, a needed cleansing, and the building of a bottom for a new advance. Cohen forecast an S&P of 1375 by the end of 2001, a figure not too different from the Wall Street consensus. There was no change in the basic psychology of the Street anywhere in sight. When the year ended, the S&P 500 stood at 1148. As far as Wall Street's analysts were concerned, the 2000 decline in the market did not reflect any basic change in the economy and had no implications for how the investor should view the market beyond recognizing that Mr. Clean, Scrubbing Bubbles, and Lysol had been applied, readying stocks for another advance. Irrational exuberance had been conquered, said the analysts, and a rational realism had again become the order of the day. For the record however, it should be noted that the decline in the market continued in 2001 and that it was tech stocks that led the way down. It is also worth mentioning that most of the decline happened before the attack on the World Trade Center could be used as an excuse.

Excess optimism was of course also a feature of the Street in the late 1920s. Those too were days when the Street liked to wrap itself in the mantle of academia. "It was a golden age for professors" says John Kenneth Galbraith: "The American Founders Group, an awe-inspiring family of investment trusts, had as a director Professor Edwin W. Kemmerer, the famous Princeton money expert. . . . Still another great combine was advised by Dr. David Friday, who had come to Wall Street from the University of Michigan. Friday's reputation for both insight and foresight was breathtaking. A Michigan trust had three college professors—Irving Fisher of Yale, Joseph S. Davis of Stanford and Edmund E. Day then of Michigan—to advise on its policies."

Yet the academic contribution to the "amplification mechanism" was both louder and more pervasive in the 1990s than in the 1920s. The 1990s was a period when the business schools worshiped the market in a way that the Vatican's pontifical institutes worshiped the holy texts. They were, after all, the years in which the doctrine of "rational expectations" was highly popular in the academies of commerce. "Rational expectations" theory holds that the prices of stocks on any particular day are the best possible guide to the true value of the underlying companies because they embody all the information that is pertinent to the future, except inside information. The validity of rational expectation analysis is a controversial issue in the business schools. But to those who believe in it, the stock ticker itself is the only reliable guide to truth about the value of the market.

The conversion of the economics profession to the "new economy" view can best be understood as a process of burying past mistakes. Because the American economy had grown painfully slowly for almost twenty years following the OPEC oil embargo of 1973, the economics profession was busy finding reasons for slowing growth and was making projections that slow growth and chronic underperformance would last, and last, and last.

When economic growth began to rise in the second half of the 1990s, MIT economist Robert Solow, who had won a Nobel Prize for his studies of economic growth, expressed skepticism about what was taken by many as the possible wellspring of a new growth surge. The wonders of the computer, he said contemptuously, could be found everywhere except in the productivity statistics.

Solow is a Democrat. But pessimism was an equal opportunity sentiment crossing party and ideological lines with ease. In the wake of President Clinton's barely successful 1994 legislative drive to reduce the federal deficit mainly by extracting funds from the American rich—an initiative that passed the Senate by one vote, that of Vice President Gore—gloom and doom became the coin of the conservative realm. Predictions of disaster were widespread on the American right as well as on the left.

As it turned out, the experts, whose reputations based on a life of study were at least partly deserved, were wrong about the second half of the 1990s. And that, of course, paved the way for the dominance of "new economy" thinking, to which Wall Street quickly subscribed.

But the cinching argument for the new economy view emanated from America's supposed cathedral of economic prudence and sobriety, the Federal Reserve. In July 1997, BusinessWeek, in a cover story about the Fed's chairman, reported that Alan Greenspan, who had denounced what he called "irrational exuberance" only seven months earlier, had been converted to the "new economy" view that the new technology of the information revolution had raised productivity growth to a new and higher plateau, a view he has consistently espoused ever since. According to Yale's Shiller, it was only after Greenspan espoused new economy thinking that it became widely accepted and was clearly an influence in causing the great stock market surge of 1998 and 1999.

Remembering again that historical comparisons are inexact and that history rhymes rather than repeats, there are remarkable resemblances between the "new economy" thinking of the 1990s and the "new era" thinking of the 1920s. During the 1920s, it was, of course, innovation in the auto industry, electric utilities, and the telephone system that were the technological holy grails. Business spent heavily to take advantage of the burst of innovation in these industries. That capital investment was responsible for the inflation-free prosperity of the 1920s.

Despite the determined hosannas raised to the stock market by many American economists who should have known better, it should be clear that just as the surge of the late 1990s came as a surprise to many careful thinkers like Lester Thurow and Robert Solow, the successes of the 1920s also came as a surprise to the famous British economist John Maynard Keynes and those who were affected by his enormously influential book, *The Economic Consequences of the Peace*. In that slim volume, Keynes made a cogent argument that the peace terms agreed to at the Versailles Peace Conference, vividly described in his book, were so onerous as to doom defeated Germany to a grim economic future. In the short run, Keynes, of course, was wrong. The Dawes Plan of 1924 promoted large capital inflows into the Weimar Republic and were an essential prop to the booming markets of the late 1920s. But the fundamental system was unsound, as was shown by the disasters of the 1930s that almost destroyed the Western world, and capitalism with it.

But such concerns were obviously far from the minds on Wall Street during the 1920s, as well as in the 1990s. It is remarkable, indeed, that not just the performance of the market but the performance of individual stocks ran parallel in both periods. In the 1990s, it was, of course, the likes of Microsoft, Sun Microsystems, and Dell that showed an amazing tendency to multiply. In the 1920s, it was also new forms of communication—the information revolution surrounding the telephone, in the guise of American Telephone and Telegraph, and radio, in the guise of Radio Corporation of America.

Call it the law of equivalent exuberance! The 1920s had their share of Microsoft and Cisco equivalents. Government-sponsored research created computer languages and invented the Internet during the Cold War. Similarly, research and development done as a result of World War I made the 1920s a period of ongoing and exciting new products produced by companies like DuPont. Rayon became so significant that DuPont's breakthroughs were celebrated by the markets. Early forms of plastic production created a virtual DuPont monopoly on cellophane wrappings and even new and sexy cellulose sausage casings. Metallurgy at big steel created new alloys for springs and cheaper filaments for radio tubes. Nonshatterable glass at Corning made automobile driving safer and lessened danger from fire. New paints, dyes, and fabrics multiplied as advances in chemistry created a whole new host of innovative companies for Wall Street to worship.

But boom-bust cycles are not a phenomenon of the past. Periods that have preceded great stock market slumps are extremely similar no matter when those slumps have occurred. They have indeed been alive and well during the 1980s and 1990s, as a study conducted by economists at the Hong Kong and Shanghai Bank clearly shows. In a brilliant analysis done with the cooperation of the Oxford Economic Institute, HSBC studied the defining characteristics of the stock market bubbles that preceded the severe slumps that have occurred since 1985. These recent bubbles—throughout the international economy—were more numerous than is perhaps widely recognized, totaling eight. They were also perhaps more widespread, including the surge in Japan, March 1986–December 1989; in Britain, August 1986–April 1989; in Spain, October 1985–September 1989; in Mexico, April 1989–November 1994; in Sweden, January 1986–December 1990; in Norway, October 1985–August 1990; in Finland, August 1985–May 1989; and in Thailand, July 1986–June 1996.

The upswing of each of these bouts of irrational exuberance was followed by periods of market turbulence and slow economic growth in the affected countries. Each was based on a story that turned out to be too good to be true. And each was followed by painful economic adjustments.

But none was as all encompassing as the great Wall Street boom of the late 1990s. And none led to global distortions even remotely resembling what is already shaping up for the postmillennial decade. The problem is, the milieu of the late 1990s turned America's eyes away from a series of serious economic dislocations that will haunt the coming decade.

"Trickle-Down"

Viewing the economy through the "new economy" lens leads to other kinds of distortions as well. One important characteristic of a stock market–dominated culture is the dangerous habit of perceiving the way a society distributes income purely in terms of the supposed impact on shareholder values. It was the "fallacy of composition" carried to ludicrous heights. If only one company squeezes the wages of its employees to the nth degree, its shareholders are the clear beneficiaries. But if all companies are equally callous, the purchasing power of the masses declines and most companies suffer from a fall in their sales that ends up by hurting the economy as a whole, as well as the majority of stockholders.

In the Reagan and Bush years of the 1980s and early 1990s, the kind of mindset that hates wage increases and worships profits was called "trickle-down" economics, a term meaning that "lean and mean" corporate policies stressing profits at any cost would produce greater overall societal wealth; the "trickle-down" effect would make everyone profit in the end. And after the 1992 election, with the Clintonians at the helm, the New Democrats continued to be unconcerned about unfairness in the distribution of income between a corporation's major executives and stockholders, on the one hand, and its employees, on the other. Particularly after the Monica Lewinsky affair, the White House was reluctant to admit that there was anything wrong in the American economy.

Clinton's New Democrat wing of the Democratic Party in the 1990s did preside over the creation of 22 million new jobs. Yet his administration rarely mentioned the dramatic income disparity in 1990s America—even more severe than it had been during the days of Ronald Reagan. As John E. Schwarz pointed out in the *Atlantic Monthly*, "just as the buoyant Reagan economy of the 1980s masked seas of red ink, so the booming Clinton economy of the 1990s masks bad news particularly on income distribution." And on this front, the performance of the economy under William Jefferson Clinton and his Republican Congress was truly horrendous.

The final years of the 1990s saw a shift in income that goes well beyond what happened in 1928 and 1929. An analysis by the Center on Budget and Policy Priorities, based on data from the Congressional Budget Office, presents a startling picture of the growth of inequality in just the final two years of the 1990s. The numbers indicate that in 1999, the gap between rich and poor grew into an economic chasm so wide that the richest 2.7 million Americans—the top 2.7 million, or the top 1 percent—had as many after-tax dollars to spend as the bottom 100 million. The change in the short two-year interval between 1997 and 1999 was so large as to almost defy the imagination. Between 1997 and 1999, the average after-tax income of the top 1 percent of the population increased by 119.7 percent, from $234,700 to $515,600. Over the same period, the income of the bottom fifth, perhaps under the impact of "welfare reform," declined from $10,000 in 1997 to $8,800 in 1999, a decline of 12 percent. But it was not only the poorest who lost out to the rich. It was also the middle of the middle class. The income of the middle one-fifth of Americans declined from $32,400 to $31,400, or by 3.1 percent.

The worship of "trickle-down" was also a characteristic of the 1920s. It was not just coincidental that it also characterized the "Coolidge Prosperity" and the "flapper era." The general aura of prosperity in the 1920s often covered up the unequal distribution of income in the 1920s: 5 percent of the country's families received one-third of all income. After the crash, "when the wealthy cut their consumption and corporations retrenched to weather their losses, together they contributed to falling consumer demand, decreasing production, and increasing unemployment, a process repeated in a downward spiral."

Indifference to trends in income distribution could easily turn out to be one of the big mistakes in the economic history of the 1990s, just as it was in the 1920s. Historian Lynn Dumenil writes, "5 percent of the country's families received a third of all income . . . average Americans . . . did not share enough in the prosperity of the country to keep buying the goods that rolled off America's productive assembly lines." The 1920s provides much evidence that periods in which the distribution of income shifts toward the rich end up in economic difficulty.

A Sea of Red Ink

Spending by the American consumer turned economics on its head in the second half of the 1990s and prevented the economy from moving swiftly into recession in 2000 and 2001. For as long as the statistics had been kept, they showed that the savings rate of the American consumer tended to rise during business upswings. But in the prosperity of the late 1990s, Americans changed their ways and took on more and more debt. As a consequence, the savings rate began a relentless decline. And by the first half of 1999, Americans were spending more than they were earning, and the personal savings rate actually went negative for the first time since the desperate days of the Great Depression, when American families had to dip into what savings they had to keep food on the table.

And the savings dearth continued even after the economy began to slow in 2000. The savings rate fell in 2000 and reached a post–World War II low in 2001. Yet before September 11 of that year, many economists could still be heard saying that the condition of the consumer had never been better; unemployment was low; and real income was rising rapidly.

Americans had become exponents of the "shop till you drop" philosophy long before the onset of the 1990s. But it was in that decade that American consumerism took on a wholly new dimension. "The new consumerism is . . . built on a relentless ratcheting up of standards," writes Harvard economist Juliet B. Schor. "If you haven't been to Europe, the presumption is that you will get there, because you deserve to get there . . . The proliferation of new products (computers, cell phones, faxes, and other microelectronics) [must be constantly upgraded] . . . Oddly . . . many of us feel we're just making it, barely able to stay even."

It is likely in fact that the consumerism of the 1990s was more intense, perhaps more neurotic—considering all the consumer debt that was being piled up—than ever. America's feeling that it must spend took on a global dimension. Schor's view is that this consumerism is different from the "keeping up with the Joneses" spending that characterized the 1950s and 1960s. Instead, she says, people's status symbols thirty years ago tended to be right in their own neighborhoods. And although some overspent, it often wasn't destructive because neighbors tended to have somewhat similar incomes. Today, in contrast, Schor's research shows that "the need to spend whatever it takes to keep current within a chosen reference group—which may include members of widely disparate resources—drives much purchasing behavior." By the end of the 1990s, American consumption accounted for some two-thirds of the country's GDP, or some $6 trillion—an essential lubricant for the entire world economy, most of which was growing more slowly than the United States despite the global "comeback" that began in late 1998.

Just how dependent the entire globe had become on the whims of the American consumer shows up clearly in data on the role of U.S. imports in the growth of world output. In 1995, U.S. imports amounted to about 4 percent of the industrial world's total gross domestic product. In 1999, that percentage had grown to about 7.5. In commenting on the strength of the American economy in the late 1990s, James W. Paulsen, chief investment officer of Wells Capital Management, observed that people have been baffled about "why auto sales are off the chart and why housing sales are so strong." His data on the American consumer's ability to buy cheap imports provide an important part of the answer.

But it wasn't only the flood of imports that served to pump up consumer spending in the United States. The American consumer also went on a debt binge. As we have seen, the personal savings rate in the United States actually turned negative in the second half of 1998 and early 1999, even though employee contributions to 401(k) plans are counted as savings. There had been a tendency to pooh-pooh this decline, since official government data on savings does not include capital gains scored in a soaring stock market as income. It is perfectly true that stock ownership by the better-heeled American family was increasing. But the median family—the one that divides the top half from the bottom half—had only $2,000 worth of stock.

Despite the Clinton "prosperity," a growing number of Americans existed with no adequate financial cushion. In 1995, the median value of household financial assets was a mere $9,950. By 1997, well into the stock market boom, nearly 40 percent of all baby boomers had less than $10,000 saved for retirement. Indeed, 60 percent of families had so little in the way of financial reserve that they could only sustain their lifestyles for about a month if they lost their jobs. The next richest 20 percent could only hold out for three and a half months. Yet these families were not immune from taking risks in the stock market.

Still, it should not be imagined that a lack of financial resources was a problem confined to the less well-to-do. What was perhaps most striking was the extent to which upscaling had undermined savings among the nation's better-off households. In 1995, one-third of families whose heads were college educated did no saving. The vast majority of Americans said they could save more but reported themselves unwilling to cut back on what one study calls "the new essentials." Indeed, throughout the 1990s households took on debt at record levels, and the largest increases were not among low-income households but among those earning $50,000 to $100,000 a year. (Sixty-three percent of these households were in credit-card debt.)

The dangers of underplaying the degree to which the consumer was overspent go well beyond the mere statistics. During the 1990s, there had been a profound change in the way the media covered statistics regarding consumers and workers. To reporters who covered labor figures and consumer numbers during the 1970s and 1980s, it was obvious how things had changed. For the most part, these numbers were now being interpreted by journalists intent on showing how they affected the stock market. In the past, they may have been reported by a consumer or a labor reporter, but now they were usually critiqued by a Wall Street reporter.

For example, in former years, if statistics were released indicating that labor costs had gone up five-tenths of a percent, a labor reporter would have regarded this number as benign, since the reporter would have put it into an overall labor perspective showing that wages had in fact only inched forward over the last twenty years. But since wage costs are something that Wall Street analysts and reporters regard as highly inflammatory and negative for the stock market, these tiny increases in the 1990s were reported by the TV financial cable press as being "bad for the market" and as costs that would somehow have to be repressed so that the market could keep climbing. To make matters worse, this interpretation was then morphed onto the network nightly news as what was happening in the economy. In newly efficient "news hubs"—such as those at NBC, which "shared" information among NBC, MSNBC, and CNBC— these trends automatically came to be interpreted for millions of Americans in terms of their effect on the stock market.

As media companies merged and reemerged during the 1990s, it became more and more common for the material of one "hub" reporter to be recycled on his or her local television station, the Internet, and the local newspaper, since they were all increasingly part of the same media conglomerate. And this local "hub" reporting would then be recycled to national "hubs," so that, in the end, there were fewer and fewer reporters covering union news, consumer swings, or changing job conditions from unique perspectives. "Hub" reporters who filed too many stories that were "out of line" with conventional thinking not only had problems but often didn't have time to argue with bosses, as they ran up and down ramps, reading the same story on television, typing it onto the Internet, and filing for their newspaper.

If the consumer stopped using credit cards or workers struck for higher wages, it was increasingly viewed as offensive and negative behavior by the media. Although many people wrote about the effects of entertainment seeping into the hard newsroom, nobody seemed to care about the stock market perspective that now permeated all newsrooms and increasingly distorted what was really going on in the American economy. John Kenneth Galbraith's famed observation that "the stock market became central to the culture," was, of course, written about the 1920s. But it is clearly even more applicable to the Bush-Clinton-Bush economy. It is a distortion of vision for which the average American would eventually pay dearly.

There is widespread awareness that the 1980s and 1990s witnessed a revolution in household technology. But it is not often understood that parallel conditions existed in the 1920s. Some economic historians have in fact argued that the invention of the small fractional-horsepower electric motor used in appliances was almost as important in propelling the American economy in the 1920s as the computer and the Internet were in the 1990s. One reason was that these appliances played an important role in freeing American women to enter the labor force.

Factories used brand-new high-tech management skills to bring to market a huge proliferation of new consumer products at low prices. And American business became hooked, as never before, on making bundles on the American consumer. If they could be persuaded to buy and buy lavishly, the whole stream of six-cylinder cars, cigarettes, rouge compacts, electric iceboxes, cloche hats, and straight, long-waisted knee-length dresses set off by luxurious silk stockings would go on selling forever. Advertisers planned elaborate national campaigns, consulted with psychologists, and employed poetic copywriters to cajole or intimidate the consumer, if need be.

Installment buying became common, and by the latter part of the decade, economists figured that 15 percent of all retail sales were on an installment basis. When stocks were skyrocketing in 1928 and 1929, it is probable that hundreds of thousands of people were buying goods with money that represented, essentially, a gamble on the business profits of the 1930s. First the rich, then the middle class, and finally, workingmen in the 1920s had the opportunity to buy the many new consumer products that began appearing on store shelves in the 1920s. And for the first time, the United States began to accept the revolutionary idea that middle class and even poor Americans were in a position to finance their consumption.

Yet many families could not afford the products they saw in new department stores or in magazines. In spite of the country's overall prosperity, tens of millions of Americans were living frugally or in poverty. Even when they had steady work, many blue-collar workers could barely afford to shelter and feed their families. When unemployment, seasonal layoffs, or sickness struck, their families were plunged into desperate circumstances.

An earlier era of social reform had set up remedial lending societies, whose mission had long been to lend to the poor, but they were essentially viewed as a form of charity. Yet in the 1920s, though it was the subject of heated debate, the idea of lending to ordinary people began to be accepted. By the end of the 1920s, outstanding installment debt had risen to $7.6 billion, and two out of three cars sold were bought on credit. This is undoubtedly a far larger number than most people now realize.

Although little of the writing about the 1920s stressed the role of consumer debt, there is substantial evidence that an "overspent" consumer was also a characteristic of that period. Workers in the 1920s, like workers through most of the 1990s experienced a decline in real wages. This may seem surprising to generations of Americans who learned in school that Henry Ford began paying workers his famous $5 a day, a number way above the average wage in the economy, back in 1920. What they fail to recognize is that those workers were still earning the same amount in 1929.

Ford's highly publicized salaries were the most dramatic of a broad range of paternalistic plans offered in the 1920s by large companies. Among the benefits offered were company pensions, stock-purchase plans, subsidized housing or mortgages, insurance, and sports programs. Some textile employers in small Southern towns even built churches and hired ministers for their employers. These forms of "welfare capitalism" were voluntary on the part of employees, aimed at stopping the huge national turnover of workers who often quit their jobs because of long hours, which caused deep fatigue and illness.

Company unions often sponsored these programs, and they were often used to keep bona fide unions out. The 1920s was one of the weakest periods for unions in the twentieth century. Members of what were considered to be the most radical unions—several in New York City—had been jailed and deported in the early 1920s in a reaction to the Red revolution in the Soviet Union. After 1923, the sharp drop in union decline ended, but the decade saw little real activism. The union movement made little headway in organizing "new era" industries such as autos and petrochemicals. Only those unions unaffected by technological change, such as the building trades and the Teamsters, saw any real growth.

Free Market Ideology

And yet the world was so full of so many things to do—so many people were so happy and so successful. . . . What one thing to take up and master—something that would get him somewhere . . .

—Theodore Dreiser, *An American Tragedy*

There is no doubt that Theodore Dreiser's Clyde Griffiths felt the power of the newly emerging free market in the 1920s, and doggedly set out to "get somewhere" no matter what that meant. Griffiths would have been comfortable in the 1990s. By then, the worship of the free market was so strong that the old-fashioned word "capitalism" began to be viewed with suspicion. Indeed, perhaps because of its political roots, there was a growing tendency in the 1990s to banish the word "capitalism" from ordinary vocabulary and news stories. And that is simply because the term "free market" tended to draw attention away from an economic power structure that embodied arrangements, institutions, and indeed government decisions that favored owners of capital over those who earn their living from work. CNBC and CNNfn, for example, almost never discuss "capitalism" as the force that is helping out viewers. It is always the "free market"—open to everyone rolling out of bed and tapping on their laptop as they watch cable television and exercise. As the use of the word "capitalism" declined, people were lured into forgetting that they live not only in a world of market arrangements but also in one dominated by a particular system of power relationships.

There is, of course, no question that capitalism had time and again demonstrated that it is a powerful force, fully capable of producing great periods of prosperity. And just as in the Netherlands of the seventeenth century, when the real creativity of creating new products began to run out and the investment houses dominated the economy instead, capitalism at its best moved on to another habitat of creators and tinkerers, and the Dutch market began to be overpriced, bloated, and ripe for a blowout. It was this historical rhythm that had again been ignored at the end of the twentieth century. The investment houses and their media-savvy analysts were pitching American families to stay involved in the worship of a market that had already profited mightily from three decades of research and government sponsorship, producing the computer revolution in California. But by the late 1990s, that market had become dreadfully overpriced. This was in effect the dark side of the market mania, which, after gloriously feeding off the inventions of "new economies," generate manias, panics, recessions, and depressions. But this time it involved many more people, and many more Wall Street analysts telling them to buy on the dips.

The true nature of economic systems is usually revealed in times of economic turbulence. The proof of the victory of free market ideology in the late 1990s was the way that international economic institutions—particularly the U.S.–dominated International Monetary Fund (IMF)—sought to contain the Asian economic crisis of 1998. The entire effort was to impose programs that left capital free to move across borders. Instead of allowing the troubled countries of Asia to impose capital and exchange controls, policy was aimed at keeping international investors as happy as possible by forcing up interest rates. The effect was to cause most of the core countries of East Asia to stagger under heavy debt loads they could not meet without great pain. In late 1998, many of the countries of Asia did partially emerge from the shadow of the condition Paul Krugman used for the title of one of his books, *Depression Economics*. But the recovery fizzled in most of them in the postmillennial decade. For its part, Japan—the leading economy of Asia—lay prone throughout the period.

The Asian crisis began to show up in July 1997, when Thailand was forced to devalue the baht. Several weeks later, the devaluation of Malaysian, Indonesian, and South Korean currencies hit workers and businessmen hard, eventually throwing hundreds of thousands out of work across Asia and into severe poverty, as retirement savings fell in value and salaries vanished. By the end of 1998's first quarter, the Pacific Rim was sinking fast: Indonesia's economy shrank by 8.5 percent, Thailand's by 6 percent, Hong Kong's by 2 percent, and Malaysia's by 1.8 percent. And by the end of the summer of 1998, it was clear that Japan was in a depression and Russia in bankruptcy. And closer to home, America's North American Free Trade Agreement (NAFTA) partners—Mexico and Canada—were suffering under the twin blows of sharply depreciating currencies and sagging stock markets.

When Asia seemed to be recovering in 1999, it was taken as a tribute to the wonders of a dose of free market medicine. The conservative American free market model was held up as the example of what other countries must do if they were to revive their economies and receive international aid. Underlining this phenomenal clout was the behavior of the International Monetary Fund during the Asian meltdown of late 1997 and early 1998, and the Russian crisis of late August. As a condition of granting loans, that supposedly international body forced troubled countries to raise their interest rates, even though the United States was responding especially to the Russian crisis by cutting rates. The IMF also urged Asia to get rid of crony capitalism, even though, as U.S. Senate hearings on campaign practices in the 1996 elections abundantly showed, the period was one of high crony capitalism in the United States itself. And subsequent investigations revealed that the floor of the capitalist temple, the New York Stock Exchange, was riddled by front running and other forms of manipulation. Yet the United States reveled in a sense of moral superiority.

But was it the IMF program that was really responsible for damping down the crisis? Paul Samuelson once likened the performance of policy officials to that of a xylophone player in a striptease show. "They are fascinated by the intricacies of their performance. But the real action was going on somewhere else on the stage." Indeed any analysis of the reason the Asian crisis did not persist and spread points not to the wisdom of Alan Greenspan or Robert Rubin and their cohorts, but rather to a prosaic piece of plastic in the wallets and handbags of the average American consumer: the credit card. The main factor that imposed limits on the damage done by the Asian crisis was, of course, a surge of exports to the United States, financed as we have seen mainly by mounting levels of consumer debt. An economist at Credit Suisse First Boston hailed the average American as "the consumer of last resort," the savior of the world economy. It was American hubris of the highest order! Indeed, it went far beyond anything that was seen in the 1920s.

The 1990s: Have Policymakers Learned Anything from the 1920s?

[B]etween John Maynard Keynes and Milton Friedman, we thought we knew enough to keep that from happening again.

—Paul Krugman, *The Return of Depression Economics*

Krugman was commenting here on the precipitous declines in the economies of Asia's tigers, the near bankruptcy of Russia, and the rapid spread of Asia's problems to Latin America in the second half of 1998. These problems did not, of course, bring the world economy down. As we have seen, the consumer binge in the United States propped up global demand sufficiently so that Asia began a painful turnaround and world stock markets soared. But it is fair to wonder what would have happened had the American consumer not been so obliging. Or what could happen if the maldistribution of income and the rise in consumer debt slows consumer spending in the next decade.

To answer these questions, looking at the 1920s as a template is especially helpful. Globalization is, of course, much further advanced now than it was in the 1920s, but in a fundamental sense, the economy of the 1920s was certainly global enough to cause plenty of trouble. Perhaps the most widely acclaimed expert on the causes of the Great Depression, MIT economic historian Peter Temin, notes: "The major industrial countries were highly interdependent . . . the origins of the Depression lay in the interaction of exchange rates and international capital movements. Its continuation lay in the transmission of currency crises and banking panics as well as in the diminution of commodity demands." In that period, of course, much of the problem was the consequence of World War I, the defeat of Germany, and the imposition of reparation payments. But as Temin underlines, a key cause of the evolving depression in Europe was the neglected fact that Germany had by the end of the 1920s become a huge debtor nation, much as the United States had by the end of the 1990s.

Many of the same profound dislocations that Temin describes began to be seen in the late 1990s, close to a decade after the end of the Cold War. And just as in the decade after World War I, the general economic climate in most of those years since the Berlin Wall came down has been one of exceptional buoyancy and boom. Yet the failures of the international trading system in the 1990s are evocative of similar problems that emerged in the late 1920s. The spread of the free market to Latin America, Eastern Europe, and especially Asia led to sharp increases in world trade and in international capital movements. Of course, they operated in a different matrix from the 1920s: At that time the problem was a creaky gold standard. In the 1990s, the problem was a flexible exchange rate system, designed to replace the gold standard. It produces giant, de facto devaluations. International monetary institutions set up to monitor sudden and swift financial problems—especially the IMF—are equipped with inadequate resources and operate on obsolete economic theories.

The international crisis of 1998—though somewhat contained by the IMF and the United States—nevertheless raises serious questions about the sustainability of economic growth. Although the crisis remained hidden for much of the decade, it revealed an overwhelming problem never really faced before on such a large scale: the integration of the work and wages of a developed world population into a worldwide economy that came to rely heavily on a huge supply of emerging world workers whose effective wages shrank as a result of currency devaluations in their own countries.

The assumption that the world has learned how to prevent another international financial cataclysm has been in place since the 1950s. Yet in the late 1990s, the entire response of the world economy, particularly as measured by the flow of monies across international boundaries, was alarmingly similar to the conditions existing in 1929 and in the early part of the 1930s. The difference is that in the 1920s, it was Germany that was the recipient of large capital inflows, whereas in the 1990s, it was the United States. It is truly remarkable, for example, that the trade-weighted dollar appreciated by some 20 percent during the Clinton years, even though the United States ran a cumulative trade deficit of about $1 trillion over the same period.

The American capital magnet operated with amazing power during periods of market turbulence. This is shown, for example, by the huge movement of capital—$700 billion—that flowed into the United States at the end of the first quarter of 1998, when the Asian crisis was at full tilt. This figure amounts to 7 percent of America's GDP and is larger than the entire GDPs of such countries as South Korea, Thailand, Indonesia, and Hong Kong.

This was not supposed to happen. The conventional view was that the institutions set up after World War II, especially the International Monetary Fund, would have both the moral authority and the money to prevent such wild imbalances from appearing in the world economy. Unfortunately, these assumptions proved wrong. Private markets grew so quickly that they swamped the ability of the IMF to exert heavy influence on capital flows. Political pressures in the United States prevented a quick increase in the IMF's resources, as Congress balked at providing IMF funding. The entire inability of the IMF, backed by supplications from U.S. Treasury officials, notably Treasury Secretary Robert Rubin and Deputy Secretary Lawrence Summers, proved that the assumption that international organizations could prevent a crisis was dead wrong.

The tendency of capital to flow to the strongest market in a crisis was hardly unknown. Movement of capital to the Bank of England was a major feature of the financial crises of the nineteenth century, as Walter Bagehot showed in a 1917 essay on the money market. And more important to the argument of this book, a similar flight of resources to the United States was a primary feature of the international financial crisis that started with the crash of 1929.

The most severe financial stringency in that period appeared in Europe with the failure of the Credit Anstalt, an Austrian bank. In the wake of that failure, the most important monetary asset of the time, gold, migrated to the United States so that by the beginning of 1932, the United States was in possession of some 90 percent of the world's official gold stock. The movement of gold into the United States had precisely the same origins as the $700 billion capital movement in the first quarter of 1998. International finance wanted its resources in the safest market. And in the world of 1929, where the gold standard prevailed, capital inflows into the United States, in the end, resulted in huge gold inflows. It is also worth noting that the inflow of gold into the United States did not help. The reason, of course, was that commodity prices were falling around the world, making it impossible for business and consumers to pay back their loans and robbing banks of the incentive to make new loans. In fact, as is well known, despite the plethora of gold reserves in the United States in 1929, the banking system set out on the road to collapse.

No such calamity appeared in the late 1990s. Yet it is unrealistic to assume that a sudden capital movement into the United States or into another country deemed safer for the moment will not occur in the decade ahead. The 1990s are not the opposite of the 1920s; they are its mirror image.

Chapter 6

The Postmillennial "Hangover": Why the 2000s Will Feel Like the Brave New World's Version of the 1930s

[It was] that quaint period, the thirties, when the huge middle class of America was matriculating in a school for the blind. Their eyes had failed them, or they had failed their eyes, and so they were having their fingers pressed forcibly down on the fiery braille alphabet of a dissolving economy.

—Tennessee Williams, *The Glass Menagerie*

As the post–September 11, 2001, stock market lurched up and down, investors were being plagued by the same kind of schizophrenic advice that the country as a whole had been receiving from the Bush administration. Citizens were being told to live normal lives but be on the lookout for smallpox, anthrax, nuclear bombs, and the al-Qaeda network's cells all over the world. But they were also being told to be bright, cheerful, and stubbornly upbeat about the American stock market. It would all work out well in the end. This, of course, meant somehow internalizing all the downbeat information: the virtual certainty of a recession; consumer debt that was ridiculously high not only in the United States but around the world; a higher unemployment rate; a global economy that was rapidly losing steam; and last but not least, an international war in which no one could predict its course, length, or eventual outcome.

Yes, the American family was being told to deny all of this unsettling information and go about business as usual. For those who would slavishly follow Wall Street, this meant spooning most of their savings into American equities. Never mind that Congress was mainly doling out money to corporations that had been financially threatened by the terrorism. Never mind that those worker-investors who had fallen between the cracks and were often walking around with no unemployment insurance were "toughing it out" on their own. As the new decade moved into 2002, the question overhanging the American public was increasingly clear: Should it continue on in the role of investor, obediently moving in and out of the market and bottom feeding off "cheap" stocks as thousands more were laid off week by week?

We believe that speculation on the exact shape of economic recovery is the wrong way to look at the prospects for the markets, just as speculation on the exact course of the war on terrorism is the wrong way to confront the new dangers facing the United States. The focus instead should be on the longer-term forces that will determine America's economic performance in the postmillennial decade. And, as we have seen in our comparisons of the 1990s with the 1920s, forces have been set in motion that virtually foreordain a sustained slowdown in the rate of economic growth both in the United States and in the other advanced industrial countries.

Because that growth slowdown will undermine the stock market performance that is central to the success of 401(k) plans, it is a severe threat to the American family, and it will persist even if the war on terrorism has a reasonably satisfactory outcome. In historical terms, this is so because the forces making for slower growth were visible well before September 11. Five debilitating forces, in place before that harrowing date, were already at work:

- The sustained boom in the information technology industries that characterized the 1990s will give way to a prolonged slowdown in the postmillennial decade. That does not mean that there will be no recovery from the essentially cyclical tech slump of 2000 and 2001. But that recovery will be weak because there will be great difficulty in digesting the excess capacity that was created in the second half of the 1990s.

Equally significant, there will be a radical change in the economic impact of new investment in information technology. In the 1990s, the information technology industries created many new jobs, both in companies that were producing high-tech products and services and in the companies that were their customers and needed new people who understood the new technology. In sharp contrast, high tech will be a job destroyer in the postmillennial decade because the new products that come to market will be geared to making high tech more efficient by replacing workers with equipment and computer programs that replace high-tech labor itself.

- The United States will be bedeviled by the fallout from the mountain of debt piled up by the private sector in the 1990s. In that decade, the burden of that debt was mitigated by falling interest rates, which enabled both consumers and corporations to refinance their obligations at lower and lower interest rates. Rates fell repeatedly in 2001 and 2002; in those two years the Federal Reserve cut rates eleven times, with the Federal Funds rate falling to 1.75 percent, a figure not too far from zero. The implication for the postmillennial decade is that neither consumers nor corporations will be able to save much on their interest payments. On the contrary, interest rates are likely to increase because the government will have to borrow more in order to offset a deficit caused both by slow growth and decline in tax receipts and the cost of fighting the war on terrorism.

- Great stock market booms like that of the 1990s lead to lax accounting practices and downright fraud, both among corporations and in the securities industry itself. The lesson of the 1930s is that economic slowdown and weak markets create an atmosphere of suspicion that eventually results in revaluation of the misdeeds that characterized the boom years. Some of those misdeeds came to light in 2000 and 2001. More will be discovered during the remaining years of the postmillennial decade. The effect will be to undermine confidence in the economy and the stock market.

- Globalization is likely to continue to depress the wages of old-line workers in the postmillennial decade while putting new pressures on the white-collar occupations, even in high tech. In the 1990s, well-paid American workers in old-line manufacturing suffered, but the effects were offset by an explosion in information technology and in new services created by the computer and the Internet. No such luxury is in prospect for the next decade. Instead, information technology will shrink white-collar employment just as surely as it shrank manufacturing employment in earlier decades. Only cutting-edge technology will survive intact. Routine information-processing tasks will be outsourced at higher and higher rates to the cheapest possible work sites.

• Perhaps the most dangerous of all will be the mindset of the United States. This is the psychological trap that could paralyze the country. In the 1990s, Americans had suspended their disbelief and had begun to think that the nation had found the key to perpetual prosperity. That is a surefire prelude to trouble, because it hinders the switch to the new set of economic policies that will be required by the drastic slowdown in growth that is sure to come. The danger of allegiance to the free market grows as an economy slows, as does the risk of relying on monetary policy amid low interest rates to put an end to recession and slow growth.

Why High Tech Will Hurt, Not Help

The vision of an ever-expanding technological frontier future is firmly fixed in the American mind. At its root, perpetual prosperity for the family is based on the wonders of the information and communications revolutions. The great information boom of the closing years of the twentieth century was indeed one of the great technological revolutions of the modern world. The evidence lies in the enormous wave of investment in new technology, new production facilities, and new communications. Adjusted for inflation, investment grew at an average annual rate of 9.2 percent between 1994 and 1999. Historically, that investment surge far exceeded the growth rates of investment during the longer periods of the railroad boom in the second half of the nineteenth century and the auto boom of the 1920s. In the 1990s, Bill Gates, as it were, outboomed Henry Ford and J. P. Morgan.

It was not only the rapid growth of investment that made the 1990s unique. It was also the almost total fixation on the new technology and the neglect of the rest of the economy: Investment in the new information and communications sectors represented a higher proportion of total investment than had railroads and autos in the past. It was almost as though there was only one string to America's economic bow. There was more focus on the computer and the Internet, on satellites and cell phones, on routers and servers than there ever was on steam engines and rails or on autos, tires, and service stations. The boom of the 1990s was startlingly concentrated in one sector of the economy. In a cover story in *BusinessWeek,* Michael J. Mandel showed that "new economy investment" accounted for 75 percent of total investment in the 1990s. That was higher than the proportion invested in railroads in the new economy of the late 1890s and the proportion invested in autos in the new economy of the 1920s. Under Clinton-Gore, the country's old-line manufacturing base continued to disappear, just as it had during the Reagan years in the 1980s.

Innovation kept coming and coming in the new economy. Forecasts of a technological slowdown, and they were fairly common during the 1990s, proved incorrect. Did investment in the personal computer seem to be slowing down? Software took its place. Did software seem to be showing some signs of slowing growth? The investment in the Internet took its place. Innovation followed innovation in swift sequence, and it seemed that nothing could bring it to an end.

But the leap from a new technology to a trouble-free prosperity is not something that history would lead us to expect. Indeed, the historical record shows that the introductions of new technologies is anything but trouble free. There were many convulsions in the world economy in the seventeenth and eighteenth centuries, and the nineteenth century saw many panics, particularly that of 1873 and 1893, associated with steel, textile machinery, and the railroads. Similarly, the boom of the 1920s was followed by severe trouble both in the U.S. economy and the global economy as a whole.

Fundamental to this book is the idea that the downswing in major tech cycles can't be stopped or fully offset by economic policy. In writing this book, Bill Wolman's memory often went back to the days when he was part of an army of 400 vice presidents at Citibank. In those days, his boss always used to say that if anyone could solve a nation's economic problems by waving a magic wand, he would wave it. In the environment of the early years of the new decade, faith in the existence of a magic wand is widespread, particularly among economists.

Deep down, they all feel that the right monetary policy and the right tax policy can always keep the economy moving forward, not as rapidly in some periods as in others, but forward, nevertheless. Yet evidence shows there is no such magic wand that can be waved to evoke a strong response from investment in technology. On the contrary, history suggests that technology investment follows a path of its own that is only marginally affected by monetary and fiscal policy. Indeed, it seems possible that technology itself can create swings in a "new economy" so severe that they are beyond the ability of government policy to counteract effectively. And that is particularly true if "privatization" of health care, pension systems, and other services has become so deeply embedded in the economy, as it was in the 1990s, that government in its diminished role as public caretaker can do little to counteract these swings. The day after the giant futuristic energy-trading corporation Enron declared bankruptcy, economist Paul Krugman wrote in the *New York Times*, "It's highly likely that millions of American workers will have near-Enron experiences, learning to their dismay that big chunks of their retirement savings have evaporated."

One major effect of cycles in innovation is to create a dual economy in the countries in which they occur. In his story in *BusinessWeek,* Mandel documented the emergence in the 1990s of a startling prosperity gap. Through a careful classification of industries, Mandel identified a new economy sector that encompassed only 20 percent of the U.S. economy. It seemed larger because of the disproportionate attention it received from the Clinton administration and in business news coverage during the 1990s.

This "new economy" was found in industries whose output is information. The remainder of the workforce was stuck in industries producing tangible goods and noninformation, personal services like haircuts or even education and health care. The difference in performance between the 20 percent "new economy" and the 80 percent "old economy" was vast. Between 1994 and 1999, the real wages of new economy workers rose by 11 percent, while real wages in the rest of the economy rose by only 2 percent. The differences in the profits performance of the two economies were even more amazing. Between 1994 and 1998, old economy companies representing 80 percent of the economy accounted for only 25 percent of the profits of the companies included in the S&P 500, even though they had roughly 70 percent of all the revenues. That, of course, meant that the new information-based companies accounted for 75 percent of all the profit gains, even though they had only 30 percent of the revenues.

Americans who worked in the old economy industries saw their pay gains fall below wage increases in the new economy sector, creating deep fissures that had not existed before. Teachers, for example, were finding that they had to get more education just to stay in place. In the health-care industry, real wages actually fell as health-care reform squeezed profits and prices. The shortages of nurses that drove up salaries in the 1980s and early 1990s had largely disappeared, and salaries had pretty much peaked by the late 1990s. For many Americans then, the 1990s continued to be tough, despite the widespread increase in consumer confidence and seeming boom conditions in many parts of the old economy. The construction industry, the historic home of high wages and strong unions, for example, continued to lag throughout the 1990s, with average workers earning 10 percent less in inflation-adjusted wages in 1998 than they had earned ten years earlier.

What accounts for this great gap? A large part of the explanation appears to lie in an exceptional concentration of productivity gains in a narrow sector of the economy. In a research study that shook up the economics profession in 1999, a past president of the American Economics Association, Robert Gordon, argued that virtually all the productivity gains of the 1990s were concentrated in the computer industry itself. His figures show that the productivity of this industry increased at a rapid rate, while productivity in the rest of the economy increased by only 1 percent per year, a figure not too different from the one that characterized the stagnant 1970s. Gordon's findings more or less corroborate Moore's law, which states that the amount of computer power that can be bought for a real dollar doubles every eighteen months. This means that the price of computer power fell dramatically, as did the price of many services offered on the Internet. Productivity gains in the new economy, then, accounted for almost all of the acceleration of productivity growth in the late 1990s. So, despite its huge investment in computers during the 1990s, the rest of the American economy did not witness acceleration in its productivity growth. For better or worse, all of the United States found itself swimming in the wake of the computer revolution.

This kind of schizophrenic "dual economy" is by its very nature much more vulnerable than one in which growth is balanced in diverse sectors of the economy. Economic numbers demonstrate that the same "dual economy" existed in the 1920s. We have already seen that a broad range of new products—household appliances, new materials such as rayon, cosmetics, and cellophane—were every bit as popular as were organic foods, recreational vehicles, and exercise equipment in the 1990s.

Consider the intimate link between the auto industry and the boom and crash of the stock market in the 1920s and 1930s. In the 1920s, the single biggest force for growth was the tripling of auto production and a similar expansion of capacity in its satellite industries such as steel, rubber, and highway construction. The Standard & Poor's Index for automobile stocks more than quintupled between 1925 and the spring of 1929. During the same period, the market as a whole increased "only" by 144 percent.

But when auto sales reached their peak in April 1929, it was the signal that boom times had ended—not just for autos but for the rest of the economy as well. In the next four years, carmakers' stocks dropped as far and as fast as they had risen. A few big players such as General Motors survived and even continued to be profitable, but many other manufacturers such as Auburn, Franklin, and Pierce Arrow disappeared, along with most of the money of the people who had invested in them. But the concentration of industry that resulted from this consolidation wave hardly saved the American economy in the 1930s. Indeed, it may have made things worse.

The same kind of concentration wave characterized the information process industries in the wake of the crash in the Nasdaq. Virtually every new wave of technology has been unstable in the past, with sharp declines in investment following sharp increases.

And that is not the end of the looming problem. Often, a fall in investment is followed by stagnation that persists for a long period of time. Moreover, the classic example of "the bigger they are, the harder they fall" is pertinent. The most severe declines and the longest slumps tend to follow the most powerful technological upswings. Thus, the effects of the depression that started in 1873 lasted close to a decade.

Similarly, the great boom of the 1920s was followed by the prolonged slump of the 1930s. It appears to take time for an economy to digest technological advance, and the process of digestion can be depressing and disruptive.

The clues to this process are to be found in "creative destruction," the famous paradigm invented by economist Joseph A. Schumpeter. Worshipers of Schumpeter, and there are many on Wall Street and in right-wing think tanks, are prone to view the creation and destruction as simultaneous processes, and they are partly correct. But it is also true, as history has repeatedly shown, that destruction can follow the creation and carry with it prolonged periods of economic stagnation. That was visible in textile technology as far back as the early nineteenth century, the period made famous by the gloomy parson, the Reverend Thomas Robert Malthus. Stagnation also characterized the second half of the 1870s, following the railroad expansion of the preceding decade.

More recently, the 1930s provide a cogent and chilling example of how the emergence of a dangerously unbalanced economic duality—new and old economies—can contribute to a prolonged period of stagnation. Economist Michael A. Bernstein's examination of why the Great Depression lasted far longer than any other cyclic downturn in American history may have lessons for the postmillennial decade. Bernstein looks at the unique coincidence of a typical downturn in the business cycle with a fundamental change from an old to a new economy, similar to the transition that was occurring in the 1990s. Bernstein argues that contrary to then prevailing opinion, the 1929 crash occurred at a time when investment dynamism had already shifted from autos to such new consumer-driven industrial and commercial sectors as food processing, mass retailing, household appliances, medical care, and recreation. But the cumulative size of these new sectors, in terms of investment activity and employment, was simply too small in the 1930s to lead an overall economic recovery. Even as firms in these sectors quickly recovered their sales, investors, and profitability, they could not overcome the drag imposed on the economy by those old sectors, such as primary metals, textiles, and lumber, that still accounted for large shares of national output and employment. Had the panic of 1929 occurred at a later point in this secular transition, when the new sectors had added some heft to their lean, energetic frames, the trauma of a decade-long depression might well have been averted. If Bernstein is right, a dual economy plagued the 1930s.

There is evidence to suggest that the Clinton-Gore administration could have done much more to nurture America's old-line industries, which continued to disappear at a rapid rate during the 1990s, just as they had in the 1980s. The assumption seemed to be that the "new economy" was so powerful that anyone who got himself educated could become incredibly successful. Silicon Valley today, though, is filled with unemployed tech workers and "for sale" signs. If there had been a more balanced approach between the "old economy" and the new, the chances are that the United States would have been much less dependent on high tech after the Nasdaq fell in March 2000. There is a good chance that the New Democrats helped set the country up for slower growth and higher unemployment because of their neglect of the old economy.

This does not mean that the new economy does not have at least one substantial area of real growth ahead. It is obvious that the real new technological frontier lies in the biotechnology areas. There is no doubt that in the end, biotech will have far more profound consequences for the American economy than anything thought of by Bill Gates. But it is also highly likely that major increases of biotech investment will not occur swiftly enough to replace the kind of investment dynamism that drove information technology in the 1990s. Biotech was still a small industry. It is still probably a decade away from becoming a major source of new jobs.

Meanwhile, virtually every aspect of production, distribution, accounting, and management control could easily move onto the Internet with devastating effects on white-collar employment. Although many Internet companies went out of business in 2000 and 2001, business over the Net will increase over the decade. Moving data over the Net to countries with low white-collar wages—even for accountants, actuaries, architects, and those in other professions—is a huge money-saver and will become an extremely powerful force in production and distribution. Indeed, it does seem that the movement of most services that do not have to be rendered face-to-face—like haircutting—into the hands of consumers will almost inevitably move toward the Net. The elimination of bricks and mortar will inevitably result in huge cost savings for business.

That is not to say that other jobs will not appear in an economy whose distribution system will be totally transformed. United Parcel Service's famous "men in brown" have already become members of a huge army delivering Net-bought products. Its main competitor, Federal Express, was seen as the harbinger of great things to come in the movie *Bowfinger*, as a FedEx truck headed toward the small home of Steve Martin's middle-aged moviemaker, who was on the verge of bankruptcy.

Huge amounts of money were obviously made in the 1990s, providing the hardware and software that were necessary to the information revolution. But the fortunes made by those who provided building blocks for the Net are no guarantee that fortunes will be made by most of those seeking to sell or provide services on the Net. It may also be tough to make money on the new broadband pipeline that will come into every American home over the next decade, a pipeline that will simultaneously bring telephone, television, and the Internet, and make all kinds of databases widely available.

One way to think of the broadband Net is as a utility that provides essential services to the consumer. These services—water and electricity being critical examples—can be of enormous value to their users. But these are not sectors of the economy where high profits have been sustained for long periods of time. The electric utility industry is earnest and uninteresting. The water supply is important and threatened, but it's not a place where private capital flourishes. There is, indeed, a school of thought represented by Wingham Rowen, a British writer and TV producer, who argues that the fate of the broadband Internet is to become a public utility, either owned by government or closely regulated by government. That is certainly what happened to the private companies that were the first providers of a piped-in water supply to the cities of both Britain and the United States. It is also what could happen to the broadband computer network as it develops. Profits, in short, are not guaranteed. The airlines meet an essential need. But the industry as a whole is hardly profitable.

We are not Luddites. We do not believe in breaking machines. We do not question the benefits of technology. But our analysis has led us to the conclusion that the great tech investment boom of the late 1990s is almost certain to be followed by a sustained slowdown in the rate of growth of capital investment that will shrink the economy's rate of economic growth. The late 1990s witnessed a huge growth in investment in information-technology industries, financed not only by corporate revenues but also through the proceeds from stock sales by companies that were in effect just getting started. The excesses of the 1990s and the neglect and loss of "old economy" manufacturing industries will make the economic situation of the United States extremely precarious in the postmillennial decade, a decade we believe parallels the 1930s. The United States is in no condition to cope with the dark side of a technology cycle.

Debt: Not Just a Headache, a Migraine

From the late 1980s through the 1990s, the United States literally got away with a form of economic hocus-pocus. Because of its power and the unquestioned creativity of its economy, it became the Mecca for the world's capital. The result was to create global trouble—a vast imbalance that showed up most clearly in the American balance of trade. Between 1985 and 1999, the United States ran a total balance of trade deficit in goods and services of slightly over $1.5 trillion. That deficit, which would not have been remotely possible for any other country, financed a huge surge in consumer spending by American families. The effect, of course, was not only to place families, but the entire country, in debt. Meanwhile, the American public was focused on forecasts suggesting that the U.S. government finally had a balanced budget.

The alarming trade deficit was for most Americans a distant economic statistic with little meaning. Yet the American consumer could get away with spending so much only because the rest of the world was ready to hold American debt. The threat was that the deficit could grow so large that foreign countries would become reluctant to hold dollar assets. The effect would be a falling dollar and a reduced willingness of foreigners to invest in the United States, hurting economic growth.

As we saw in Chapter 5, the rise in consumer debt in the 1990s was far sharper than in the 1920s, although the role of debt in that dazzling decade was greater than most analysts have been willing to admit. That, in itself, would suggest that the American economy will have difficulty in coping even if the slowdown in tech spending proves to be only moderate. But the debt hangover from the 1990s will be even more severe than in the 1930s. It's not just the level of debt that counts. It is also the kind of debt buildup that occurred as the twentieth century came to a close.

Despite its size, the debt buildup of the 1920s was a domestic matter. That, of course, meant that whatever difficulty American debtors may have been in, the money that led them into hock was owed to other Americans. In a sense then, the money was moving from the pockets of workers in overalls to the richer pockets of executives, or as they came to be called in the 1990s, "suits." In sharp contrast, the 1990s witnessed a huge buildup in monies owed to foreigners. With a large trade deficit between 1990 and 1999, the amount of money that Americans owed foreigners increased far faster than the money owed by foreigners to Americans. Given the aura of prosperity that prevailed, it is hard to realize that by 1999, the size of the American trade deficit ran at 4.4 percent of the nation's GDP, far more than for any other country and far more than the United States had ever seen in its entire history. In the 1920s, by contrast, the United States actually ran a trade surplus.

The worship of the corporation in the 1990s also deflects attention from another source of careening debt. Throughout the 1990s, Wall Street breathlessly cheered the corporate community for buying back its stock. When a company announced a stock buyback, its stock usually rose, giving option-drunk managers more and more incentive to take on debt in order to buy back stock. Between 1990 and 1999, the new debt taken on by corporations rose steadily each year, ballooning from $173 billion to $886 billion. The irony was that despite the high reported profits of the late 1990s, the American corporate sector ended the decade deep in hock.

Only one sector tightened its belt in the 1990s, and that of course, was government. Deficits shrank sharply in the decade, partly because of rapid growth in tax receipts, resulting mainly from the impact on income of the boom in tech investment. The federal deficit also fell because of sharp cutbacks in the growth of programs designed to aid the poor.

There was, of course, a question of the extent to which the government surpluses were produced with smoke and mirrors. Many of the cuts made in the 1990s were of this sort, particularly those resulting from the spending caps imposed in 1993 in the compromise between the Bush White House and the Democratic Congress and reinforced in 1997 in a compromise between the Clinton White House and a Republican Congress. Yet any serious analysis of budget projections for the opening decade of the twenty-first century made even before the bin Laden attack on the World Trade Center raised doubts about whether the cuts in ordinary government spending—all the way from environmental protection to the State Department—could be sustained.

The September 11 attack on the World Trade Center will obviously accelerate the swing from surplus to deficit in the federal budget. Although the eventual costs of the military buildup and homeland defense are not yet clear, they are certain to undermine the federal deficit, as will the impact of the $100 billion stimulus bill signed by President George W. Bush in 2001.

But even before the attack, the total rise in debt in the 1990s put the United States in hock on a massive scale. A study for the Levy Economics Institute showed that the ratio of the total increase in debt to the total increase in GDP was exceptionally large in the 1990s. Nor was that the end of the problem. Despite the low figures for government debt, the Levy study indicates that the sum of monies owed to foreigners and the monies owed by corporations led to a ratio of total debt to total GDP beyond anything that the United States, or any other advanced industrial country, had ever seen.

This is obviously debt of a migraine level. It is conceivable, of course, that the huge flow of capital from abroad will continue to wash into the United States. But today's international financiers do not need to have the acumen of the legendary gnomes of Zurich to realize that there is something unsustainable about the growth rates of debt that fueled American growth in the 1990s. It did not seem that way in the opening years of the new millennium. It is nevertheless likely that as the American economy slides down the declining curve of high-tech investment, money will begin to flow out of the country, seeking a haven in what will then perhaps be the faster-growing economies of Europe and the Pacific Rim.

In the end, what is amazing is not that the trade deficit, given the U.S.'s profligate ways, grew at a headlong pace in the 1990s but that it did not grow faster than it did and that it was financed as easily as it was. For most of the post–World War II era, Western Europe and Japan slowly gained ground on the United States by adopting U.S. technology and adding some innovations of their own. In 1970, U.S. per capita income was 31 percent higher than that of the other industrial nations. By 1991, the difference had narrowed to only 10 percent. But with the arrival of the Internet age, the gap began to widen again, reaching 22 percent in

1999. "It was," as Luc Soete, an economist at Maastricht University told *BusinessWeek*, "historically unique. For the first time in the post-war period you have a growing divergence, the pulling away of the leading technology country."

Unlikely as the continued rise in the U.S. currency in 2000 and 2001 may make it seem, it remains probable that the dollar will begin a prolonged decline that could last far into the postmillennial decade. And with import prices therefore rising, it is likely that the magic that held the American inflation rate down in the first two years of that decade will again move under the magician's hat. As a consequence, the sustained slowdown in U.S. growth and a decline in the dollar will combine with rising government deficits, which we believe are likely to raise interest rates in the United States relative to those in the other advanced industrial countries.

This will be a result of the nation's visible debt crisis. But an invisible debt crisis also emerged in the late 1990s. A question that is central to the state of the market—and the probability that it will rise or decline—is what percentage of overall stock investment is being financed by a home equity loan or credit card, in other words, financed with other people's money. That, of course, comes down to the critical issue of how much debt underlies the valuation of stocks at any given moment of time.

When asked this question, stockbrokers tend to give a reassuring answer that normally provides a high comfort level to the average investor. There is no chance that a dangerous level of debt underlies the market, they say, simply because debt in the market is regulated by the most sacrosanct name in the financial community, that of the Federal Reserve, which has, as one of its regulatory functions, power over the extent to which Wall Street is allowed to finance the purchase of stock on margin. Margin is, of course, a simple concept. If say, General Electric stock is selling for $100 a share and the margin requirement is 10 percent, you must have $10 in your account; if it is 20 percent, you have to put up $20, and so on. Through the decade of the 1990s, that margin requirement was not at those low levels but rather at 50 percent, a seemingly comfortable figure. The difference between the price of a stock and the amount of money that must be put up to buy it is typically borrowed from the broker and is often called a broker loan.

Broker loans are also called "call money." The reason is that the loan has no fixed payment date. Instead, the broker can demand repayment at any time. Typically, margin loans are "called" when the amount of cash put up is inadequate to represent the required proportion of cash needed to support the stock. Say that a customer has borrowed $50 to buy a $100 share of GE. Then, if the price of the stock falls to, say, $90, a "margin call" will go out. The reason, of course, is that if the stock has to be sold at $90, the customer will realize less than 50 percent of the value of the stock and would only have $40 to repay the $50 loan. Therefore, when the dreaded margin call occurs, the customer may have to sell the stock and take the $10 loss. The broker will get $50 dollars, but the customer will have only $40 left in the account. Now just imagine that the required margin is 10 percent; then a 10 percent fall in the price of GE would wipe out the value of the account, and the customer will be left financially empty-handed in the brokerage account. Hence, the dread of margin calls.

The 50 percent figure that prevailed for over a decade is alleged to be comfortable because it is widely believed to be high enough to prevent the market from undergoing the same margin-related convulsion that is alleged to have occurred as part of the Great Crash of 1929, when the Federal Reserve required a margin of merely 10 percent.

But no such reassurance is merited by the facts. To begin with, research on the true level of margin requirements in 1929 reveal that 10 percent margin accounts were about as scarce as really rich people. Brokers may not try too hard to protect their customers, but they are ordinarily assiduous in taking measures that they believe are self-protective. Research on the state of margin debt in 1929 indicates that virtually all brokerage houses required not a margin of 10 percent but rather of 50 percent, or the same level that prevails today. And if that is true, there is no more protection against the withering effect of margin calls now than there was before the Great Crash of 1929.

But that is far from the end of the relevant comparisons. Back in the 1920s, there were no real credit cards; instead, a few "valued customers" were granted small metal identification plates called "charge plates." Americans, especially those in the frugal Midwest, for instance, in Toledo, Ohio, did have home mortgages, but research shows that families lived extremely frugally to pay these mortgages off, so that they could proudly own their own homes. It took the liquid 1990s for homeowners to casually borrow on home equity loans in order to infuse instant cash into their brokerage accounts.

The ready availability of these forms of borrowing power to the middle class strongly suggests that the level of debt supporting the market in the current decade is probably far higher than in the 1920s. The government collects no data about the proportion of credit card debt and home equity borrowing used to support stock market investment.

But, though the exact facts are hard to come by, there is every reason to believe that debt plays a more important role in this decade's stock market than it did in the 1920s, and the reason should be obvious. Today's market is, more than ever, a family market, and credit is far more plentiful for the average family than it was in the 1920s. In talking about this point to bankers and brokers, we have heard many stories about families using home equity loans to buy stocks, of buying stocks on credit cards, and even of people who have borrowed on their 401(k) plans to leverage their position in the stock market. When the real story of the market of the 1990s is fully told, it is almost certain to reveal that much of the rise has been fueled by an expansion in consumer borrowing. The implication is that margin is more of a problem for the current decade than it ever was in the 1920s. Edward Hyman Jr., president of International Strategy and Investment, has consistently argued using persuasive data that there has been a high correlation between the level of the Nasdaq and the rate of growth of consumer spending ever since the beginning of the 1990s. That, of course, is highly consistent with the notion that margin is being provided by credit cards and, especially, home equity loans.

Corruption: The Aftermath

[E]mbezzlement. . . . Alone among the various forms of larceny it has a time parameter. Weeks, months or years may elapse between the commission of the crime and its discovery. . . . At any given time there exists an inventory of undiscovered embezzlement . . . it should perhaps be called the bezzle. . . . In good times, people are relaxed, trusting, and money is plentiful. . . . In depression, all this is reversed.

—John Kenneth Galbraith, *The Great Crash*

The chain of events that followed the Enron affair will lead to a fundamental change in the political and investment atmosphere. To anyone who earned a living as a financial journalist during the 1990s, no contrast was more striking than the reaction to stories about corruption and immorality in government and in business. In the 1990s, stories about government corruption were read, relished, and endlessly rehashed on television. At least in the case of cabinet-level officers, suspicion of corruption led to the appointment of an endless series of special counsels to investigate: the secretary of the interior, Bruce Babbitt; the secretary of agriculture, Mike Espy; the secretary of labor, Alexis Herman; and, of course, the president himself. And when the attorney general refused to appoint a special council to investigate campaign finance during the 1996 presidential campaign—particularly payments received by the Democratic Party from China—the press hurricane hit with fury.

No such reaction followed credible revelations of misdeeds in the private sector. In its August 9, 1999, issue, *BusinessWeek* magazine published a story that raised the possibility that the president of the New York Stock Exchange looked the other way despite his personal knowledge of trading irregularities on the floor, the result of assiduous reporting by Gary Weiss, the *BusinessWeek* finance reporter who has won journalism prizes for uncovering the activities of the mob on Wall Street. Fine, the public seemed to be saying, it is OK to land on the mob, but please, Richard Grasso, president of the New York Stock Exchange is making me rich, so lay off!

Part of the relative indifference was simply that the public had no stomach for the investigation of an institution that it deemed vital to its prosperity. The explanation of the indifference to evidence of misdeeds in the corporate sector lies, of course, in the time dimension of what Galbraith calls the "bezzle" cycle. As long as the economy is strong and the stock market is going up, corporations have an easy time concealing their problems and the public has little appetite for hearing about them. But when the economy slows and the market declines, the entire atmosphere changes. Galbraith's "bezzle" cycle is therefore an almost perfect explanation of both the revelation of Enron's problems and the public's outraged reaction. It also obviously explains why the politicians in Washington leaped into action with a host of congressional hearings and Justice Department investigations. In the 1990s, as in earlier bull markets, money was plentiful, business was good, and Galbraith's "bezzle" was easy to hide. There were, of course, exceptions when things went really wrong. Questionable practices were examined at Long-Term Capital Management when it lost bundles in the futures markets in 1998. And the Bank of New York was the object of a certain opprobrium in 1999 when its intimate link to laundering money found its way from the International Monetary Fund to Russian mobsters and political figures. But that, after all, has to do with Russia, and besides, the Bank of New York was ratted out by Republic National Bank of New York, which had had plenty of dealings with Russia on its own.

In a sense, Wall Street's connection to the mob officially became a part of the popular culture in 1999, but even then it was done with an affection, a humor, rather than as a high-profile investigative riff. The Home Box Office television series, *The Sopranos,* nibbled around the edges of Wall Street's involvement with the Mafia. Weiss, who had reported heavily about the mob and Wall Street in the last years of the 1990s, wrote about his "take" and the view of some of his "inside" contacts on the Sopranos and the Street. The series, Weiss wrote, "certainly exudes authenticity . . . Wall Street . . . [is a place] where wise guys have been staking a claim. Tony Soprano's cousin Christopher has gotten a brokerage license by having someone else take the test for him, as happened quite a bit in real life. He is running a brokerage house where two thugs beat up a broker for not selling the house stocks. "One alleged wise guy," added Weiss, "insists that the scene was taken right out of the court record from his stock-manipulation case." But, Weiss, a big Soprano fan himself, warned, "the real Mob would be a totally different HBO series from *The Sopranos.* It would be grimier. It would be nastier. And there would be nothing the least bit adorable about a real-life Tony, who is portrayed in the series as a sympathetic family man whom viewers can relate to, even though he has, well, a peculiar job." One trader who knows mobsters well told Weiss: "They're a bit like a cross between my old Italian uncle and Charles Manson." It was this affectionate, cleaned-up view of sometime mob involvement in Wall Street (which in fact only represented a small sliver of *The Sopranos'* overall plotline) that amused but did not seriously interfere or confront in any way the deep exuberance and high stakes surrounding the market.

As the United States entered the new millennium, Galbraith's "bezzle" cycle continued in its mysterious ways. It will be years before we will be able to tell how deep the corruption in the corporate sector actually ran during the great boom. Although if history is any guide at all, the odds are it will prove to have run very deep. After all, in the wake of the Great Crash, Richard Whitney, president of the New York Stock Exchange, and Albert H. Wiggin, variously president, chairman of the board, and chairman of the governing board of Chase Bank, were shown to be unscrupulous operators and speculators and were discredited. Charles E. Mitchell, known as "Sunny Jim" (head of National City Bank, which later merged into First National City Bank, renamed Citibank and more recently combined with Travelers Insurance into Citigroup), actually ended up on trial but was acquitted by a New York jury. Three of the largest financial fish of the 1920s obviously landed on the beach. There is no suggestion here that these same institutions or their successors are similarly culpable in the 1990s. Big financial fish will again be netted. But the "bezzle" cycle will have to run its course before the full extent of Washington complicity in corporate corruption comes to light.

The complexity of financial dealings and the sophistication of creative accounting make it likely that revelations of corporate misdeeds will continue for some years. In the past, corruption in Washington usually came to light far earlier than on Wall Street. The press did not have to wait through the 1920s to unveil the Teapot Dome Scandal. That happened in 1922. Similarly, it did not have to wait for a declining stock market to unearth the political corruption of the 1990s. Veteran Washington columnist Elizabeth Drew's searing analysis of contemporary inside-the-Beltway politics forecast a dark political "hangover" from the 1990s. "The cumulative impact of the downward spiral of our politics . . . was enough to cause widespread despair on the part of the public. We saw the inability, or unwillingness, of the politicians to deal with our broken, corrupt campaign finance system—our most serious problem—and the brutal, and ultimately successful, attempts to stymie those who tried."

Carl Bernstein remarked in a television interview in early fall 1999 that American politics—mired in corruption and money—was in trouble "in a way that it had never been before." He was obviously in a position to know; along with Bob Woodward, he was part of the *Washington Post* team that unmasked the Watergate scandal resulting in the resignation of President Richard M. Nixon.

The Great Global Unraveling

William Greider titled his brilliant 1997 book on the impact of globalization *One World, Ready or Not*. Wall Street, flushed with the great gains scored in the bull market that had started fifteen years earlier, had placed a huge bet on the belief that the world was ready for American-style free market capitalism. And it was a bet that received solid backing from the great American corporations that began to change their perspective. Companies like General Electric, Microsoft, and Intel based their corporate planning on the assumption that economic growth would be far faster in the emerging world than in the United States.

This belief was widely communicated to the American public. Ad after ad was placed on television showing the egg-bald smooth-talking Mark Mobius of the Franklin Templeton Funds speaking from exotic locations and bragging that he could find excellent companies with great prospects no matter where he looked in the emerging world. But the truth was that the performance of markets in the emerging world was often mediocre at best. Chile, in particular, was widely perceived as the country that had learned the free market lesson the most thoroughly. Even in Chile, however, the stock market gains were moderate in the second half of the 1990s, though that country was held up as the exemplary case where even the Social Security system had been privatized. And while we were in Chile in those days, we saw firsthand that mutual funds were being sold on street corners next to marvelous Chilean grapes, perhaps a testament to Wall Street's belief that privatized Social Security would truly broaden the market.

The illusion of a smoothly emerging world transition to a free market was thoroughly shattered by the international financial crisis of 1998. Those markets had not fully recovered by 2001. Bill Greider was vilified and ridiculed by the *Economist* for allegedly not understanding economics when his book first came out. As it turned out, however, Greider was right and Wall Street was wrong. Greider was hung out to dry for having neither the economic numbers nor the economic sophistication to prove his case. But his travels around the globe gave him an all too clear-eyed view of what was soon to emerge.

When the Asian crisis of 1998 struck, Alan Greenspan moved quickly to paper it over. He cut interest rates three times in rapid succession. His triple interest play, coupled with more than $120 billion in loans from the IMF, along with the United States and other industrialized countries, did arrest the precipitous decline around the Pacific Rim and led to a halting recovery in the afflicted countries.

But market meltdowns almost always tell a longer-term story: the Great Crash was followed by the Great Depression, just as the tumble of the Nikkei in Japan in early 1989 ushered in a troubled decade. We readily grant that there was a recovery in the emerging world in late 1998 that continued until U.S. consumer spending began to slow in 2001. But it is nevertheless our belief that the crisis of summer 1998 was not just a onetime thing but rather revealed weaknesses in both the U.S. economy and the world financial system that will last not for just a few months, or even a few years, but rather for perhaps a decade.

The reason is straightforward: There will be a continuing increase in the number of jobs moved abroad, and imports will continue to rise because they will be cheap. As a consequence, the deflationary pressures emanating from the developing world are likely to remain intense—far more severe than either governments, investors, or businesses expect. The result will be continued disappointment for companies seeking to expand, putting strong downward pressure on investment in new plant equipment, the driving force in any economy.

At the same time, Asian currencies that have continued to depreciate well into the postmillennial decade will reduce the purchasing power of producers on the Pacific Rim. That will put a lid on American exports to Asia. The impact is likely to be severe. American exports to Asia tend to be high-end goods, dependent on rapid income growth for sales success. And with depreciation limiting the real incomes of Asians, American exports are likely to suffer just at the same time the United States is awash in cheap imports.

The bin Laden attack could change relations between the developed world and the industrialized world profoundly for a sustained period of time and in ways that will create difficulties. We've seen changes of this sort before. During World War I, a number of developing countries—such as Peru, with its coastal sugar factories; Malaysia, and its rubber plantations; and India's cotton producers—supplied commodities to help out war production in the developed world. When the war ended, they just kept on producing. By the end of the 1920s and into the 1930s, there was oversupply of many primary products, resulting in severe deflation in the developing world.

Although relatively powerless, opinion leaders in the developing world came to the conclusion that their countries had been used by the advanced countries. When the depression came in the 1930s, the prices of primary products, on which the developing world was so dependent, collapsed much more dramatically than those of manufactured goods, which they bought from the West. "'Students rioted in Cairo, Rangoon and Djakarta, not because they felt that some political millenium was in striking distance,'" writes Eric Hobsbawm, "but because depression had suddenly knocked away the supports which had made colonialism so acceptable to the generation of their parents. . . . A mass basis for political mobilization came into existence." At the same time, the slump destabilized both the national and international politics of the dependent world.

A similar mass basis for political mobilization has been created by the bin Laden movement. The oligarchic governments of the so-called moderate Islamic states have proffered support to America's war on terrorism. But they are also telling Washington that it will have to pay a price for those concessions. That price could easily include a lowering of such barriers to imports as the quotas on textiles from Indonesia and steel from South Korea. At the same time, the United States may be more willing to reduce its pressures for such changes as the lowering of taxes on imported cars of the kind that have been imposed on South Korea and Thailand.

If the new basis for mass political mobilization provided by the war on terrorism persists, it could build on the rise in economic nationalism that began to show itself in the late 1990s. In the emerging world in those years, pressures to impose capital and exchange controls could be seen everywhere. In Europe, continued high unemployment led to major political rifts, especially in France and Germany over the appropriate role of government as compared to the free market. And even in the United States, there were major rumblings among those left behind in the old economy—as witnessed at the World Trade Organization meeting in Seattle, where thousands of demonstrators protested environmental and labor issues related to globalization. And it wasn't just radical demonstrators who were concerned about the WTO. There were increasing signs that the Democratic Party, led by Tom Daschle and Richard Gephardt, was prepared to fight hard for fair labor rights and a go-slow globalization policy. In the post-Clinton years, more Democratic politicians were beginning to lose their zeal for 1990s style globalization.

With its institutional hand on the deep pulse of the working families around the world, the Roman Catholic Church convened a Rome conference of bishops in the fall of 1999, concentrating on the state of the global economy. The focus was on changing political conditions at the end of the 1990s. In a sermon at All Saint's Church in Rome on Sunday, October 10, 1999, the Anglican bishop of Europe, who was invited as an observer to the conference, noted that "there was great optimism at the beginning of the decade after the Berlin Wall came down. The world was filled with hope. Now, close to ten years later, there is much more cynicism and unfortunately a new ultra-nationalism, as a result of unemployment and other economic problems, rising up in a number of countries throughout Europe. We must be realistic—not overly optimistic, not overly cynical, about what all this means, and how to deal with it." This is clearly an observation that takes on even more force in the wake of the American-led war on terrorism.

Despite the willingness of many diverse governments to join the antiterror coalition, the outlook for global economic cooperation leads to conclusions that are less than reassuring. There is no doubt that the resurgence of growth in the United States and its impact in generating a huge growth in imports is what really saved the day after the Asian currency crisis of 1998. But as the American economy's growth rate sags, the threats of rising economic nationalism mount and there are no guarantees that the world trading and financial system will continue to flourish. As the downside of the tech cycle cramps the ability of the American consumer to "shop till you drop," there may be little left to prevent the global financial and trading systems from groaning and creaking.

The Psychological Trap

Even after the tech boom came to an end in the opening years of the postmillennial decade, the United States remained convinced that its leadership position in world economic growth would remain unchallenged. That belief had been seen before, both in the United States in the past and in other countries. And each time it has erupted, it has proved fatal, and not just because it produced a stock market crash. It is a form of triumphalism. It produces a widespread feeling that the economic mixture that worked to create prosperity in a particular country in a particular phase of global economic development will continue to work wonders even when conditions change. That is the great psychological trap for the United States in the next decade.

"History teaches that nations and regions can rise and fall in the flick of a decade. In this fading century, Europe, America and Asia have run the cycle many times, tripping up on their own hubris, then regrouping to come back." These quicksilver races featuring dramatic ups and downs in economic leadership within a couple of decades are in sharp contrast to the centuries-long hold former economic powers—such as the Dutch and the British—held in earlier centuries when capitalism came into its own. But they are the new reality of a closely integrated world economy.

In recent history—the half century following World War II—countries have traded places as economic growth stars at an increasingly fast pace. Initially, the United States made an easy transition to the post–World War II economy and became the world economic leader as Europe worked through the monumental losses incurred by the war. Europe struggled with low productivity, an adverse balance of payments, and generally slow growth. This period lasted from 1945 to the beginning of the Kennedy administration in 1960.

But with the onset of the early 1960s, that period seemed to come to an end, and Germany—with its machine tools, fiscal discipline, the Volkswagen and the Mercedes—seemed to lie at the center of world trade while the United States moved into a slower growth period and Asia remained stagnant. Then came the very late 1960s and early 1970s, when Japan began to emerge as the star of the economic firmament with its home electronics and the Toyota. By the 1980s, it appeared that Japan and its East Asian satellites would probably replace the United States as economic leaders of the free world. But by the 1990s, of course, Japan had become stuck in a long-term economic slump and a stagnant stock market, which lasted throughout the decade, while the United States reemerged as technologically brilliant and all but erased the idea of a twenty-first Pacific century.

These alternations in growth and economic leadership tend to be forgotten in the euphoric moments of economic triumphalism. But just the history of the years since the Cold War already tell us that leadership once gained is hard to hold onto, and once lost can easily take a decade or more to recover. And understanding the reasons that triumphant nations tend to slip back is vital. Put simply, but correctly, they boil down to this: Through some combination of luck and skill, a nation attains leadership. Competition then arises that tends to undermine that leadership and economic success.

As the postmillennial decade moves on, the economic race will take on a new dimension: The developing world will be a more effective competitor with the industrialized countries. Through most of modern history, what is now the emerging world was held back by anti–free market forces such as colonialism, or antimarket ideologies like communism or left-wing socialism. But as the last quarter of the twentieth century drew to a close, these forces began to dissolve. And while it is certainly true that Asia and Latin America suffered severe setbacks, there is no serious reason to doubt that these areas will revive and indeed become formidable competitors to the United States. It is perfectly possible, indeed plausible, that continental Asia and especially its big countries, China and India, will become fully competitive with the old industrial world and have their periods in the sun of leadership. And the old industrial engines in Asia, such as Taiwan, will constantly reinvent themselves. By early 1999, Taiwan was already beginning to pull ahead in the massive global semiconductor business, and bets were on that Taiwan would soon become the major contract producer of newly designed chips for companies all over the world.

There is a real danger that in the postmillennial decade, the American middle classes will act as if they had matriculated "in a school for the blind," to use Tennessee Williams's vivid characterization of the 1930s. What that middle class has above all failed to see is the danger inherent in a world where stocks become an item of mass consumption. That creates a country of fantasy in which the numbers central to the calculations of the average family make no sense whatever. The family market will not produce economic security, fund education, and lead to an elegant life for the average American. Proving that is not a question of rocket science. It takes only simple arithmetic and a compound interest table.

PART THREE

THE ELUSIVE SEARCH FOR FAMILY SECURITY

THE HISTORY OF PENSION PLANS in the United States is deeply disturbing. Its main lesson is that the American pension system has been designed throughout its history to serve the interests of corporations and other employers rather than those of the American family. And that is true not only of private pension plans but also of the Social Security system, which is, of course, the province of government. The implication is that the American family will not only have to save to insure its financial future but will also have to be on the right side of the political fights that are likely to determine the future of family well-being.

That Social Security is vulnerable to an assault by the corporation might seem surprising. But in sharp contrast to the other great industrialized countries, the United States resisted a government plan to provide what can only be described as modest benefits long after the other industrial countries, led by Germany, introduced public pension systems as far back as the 1880s. It took the severe depression of the 1930s to overcome resistance to the foundation of the Social Security system in 1935. And it was only after a cynical deal in 1972 between President Richard M. Nixon and the powerful chairman of the House Ways and Means Committee, Wilbur C. Mills, that the system achieved the corporate support needed to extend Social Security to the majority of workers and, importantly, to provide cost-of-living allowances (COLAs), so as to protect retirees from the ravages of inflation. And of great current importance, the administration of George W. Bush is pushing hard for at least a partial privatization of the system, which would make benefits subject to the vagaries of a stock market that is unlikely to be strong in the postmillennial decade.

The private pension system has, throughout its history, been subjected to erosion every time the corporate sector has decided that fewer employees should get benefits and that the benefits should be smaller. Each time the American economy has been afflicted by recession or slow growth, the corporate sector has been able to get government to come down on its side, rather than that of the workers. Over the last two decades, the most disturbing trend has been the drive to substitute weak 401(k) plans for old-style defined benefit pension plans. There has also been a tendency for pensions to be cut back or even vanish at the first signs of economic trouble. The most recent examples, of course, were the cutbacks in corporate contributions to 401(k)s that occurred in 2001 and 2002 in the wake of the economic slowdown during the previous two years. The American family continues to be the victim of a history showing that their pensions are anything but secure. The implication, as the Enron case has most recently shown, is an almost desperate need for legislation to prevent the corporation from victimizing its employees on the flimsiest excuses.

Chapter 7

Power Play:
The Attack on Social Security

The scene is the opening years of the postmillennial decade. In the midst of Republican tax cuts, faith-based initiatives, and plans to privatize Social Security, the figure of Andrew Undershaft, one of George Bernard Shaw's most famous characters, exploded onto the New York stage during the summer of 2001 in a remarkable production of Shaw's 1905 play, *Major Barbara*. In a rave review, *New York Times* theater critic Bruce Weber wrote that Undershaft, "a brilliant, tunnel-visioned despot—he's a weapons manufacturer—[is played as] a sleek rumbly voiced executive more than comfortable in the unambiguous conviction that his selfishness is good not only for him but for the nation and even for the souls of its citizens." He slyly tells the young aspiring politician who wants to marry his daughter, "When I want anything to keep my dividends up, you will discover that my want is a national need. When other people want something to keep my dividends down, you will call out the police and military. And in return you shall have the support and applause of my newspapers, and the delight of imagining that you are a great statesman." Transpose Undershaft, as Shaw created him close to 100 years ago, to the United States, and he is, as it turns out, a living, breathing corporate apologist of the early twenty-first century!

Undershaft's advice to the aspiring politician provides a penetrating insight into corporate hardball. The history of employee benefits in the United States is testament to a system of rewards geared much to the interests of the corporation, not to the interests of the workers. When it suits their purpose, corporations do show more generosity in providing employee benefits. But when they believe that benefit levels are hurting profits, corporations have been relentless in scaling back. The implication for the average American family is clear: Employers cannot be trusted to maintain the benefits promised in employee handbooks. If conditions change, benefits will surely be peeled back in the future, just as they have in the past. This became abundantly clear in the slowdown that began six months after the new century opened. It was health-care benefits that were the first victim. The number of retirement systems that promised generous health-care benefits to retirees shrank, copayments for current employees rose sharply, and prescription drug benefits became scarcer, with their costs to employees rising sharply. Around the nation there was a growing realization that 401(k) programs were far more fragile than employees had been led to believe. And it wasn't just Enron employees who became acutely aware that, as earlier in history, companies would cut back pensions when it suited their purposes. But more than that, everyone recognized that pension plans based on stock were highly vulnerable to bitter disappointment. In a vivid example, it was revealed that Lucent's matching contribution to the money their employees put in was made in Lucent's own stock, which had plummeted from its peak. And to top things off, the terms of Lucent's 401(k) prevented employees from even selling the stock until they were fifty-five years old. Major Barbara would have been shocked! But Undershaft would have understood.

And what is remarkable, as we shall see later in this chapter, is that corporate interests have played a major role, not just in private pensions but in the design of the Social Security system itself. The original Social Security system never paid out nearly enough to the average retiree to keep a person even close to staying above the poverty line because business wanted it that way. The industries in which workers were covered was kept small in number because business wanted it that way. Amazingly, the Social Security system was expanded to a full national retirement system by the Nixon administration in 1972 because corporations at the time wanted it that way. And the current assault on the system and the drive to privatize, at least part of it, is an explicit and dangerous attack on what some experts on Social Security call the

"Social Security wealth," built up by many Americans after the 1972 re-forms. Although there is little evidence to support their case, business believes that the Social Security system is reducing the amount of capital available to the corporation and increasing its costs.

The weight of history, then, gives strong reason to believe that the promise of retirement prosperity and good health care is one that the employee simply cannot trust. And what was true of private employee benefit plans in the past is the best possible guide to what will happen in the future. And, yes, the 401(k) stands in a long tradition of employee benefits that tend to be taken away or reduced if the going gets tough. History shows that the 401(k) is likely to be anything resembling a panacea. It's a good bet, in fact, that the drive to reform 401(k)s in the wake of the Enron debacle will fall far short of an ideal.

That had already become apparent at the end of the great boom of the 1990s. Chances were that those middle-aged Americans who had con-scientiously saved the top amount in their 401(k)s from the early 1980s on, until early 2000, and had incomes somewhere above $75,000 a year had put away a comfortable amount of savings during those boom years, to withstand the postmillennial decline in the market. Others were not so fortunate. The 30 percent of Americans who made $7 or less an hour usually didn't have access to 401(k)s or old-fashioned pensions, either, for that matter. Those in between these two groups—called the "Missing Middle" by social-policy expert Theda Skocpol—had suffered a severe erosion of benefits, leaving them highly dependent on the hope of a stock market revival to give them enough money to live on during their retirement years.

Many Americans who had access to 401(k)s often didn't or couldn't make monthly contributions, and those who were able to got much smaller matching contributions from their employers than their well-paid bosses. Others were suffering the consequences of the inadequate informa-tion offered by employers about their pension plans and had little idea of what the end result would be when they were too old to work anymore.

This scenario had come about as a result of a century-long tug-of-war between corporate interests, labor unions, and progovernment reformers, who were, for the most part, on the losing side of the twentieth century's pension battle. The history of social policy in the United States is totally different from that in its European and Canadian counterparts. It has resulted in a complex patchwork quilt of programs that work for many during boom times like the 1990s but were a true disaster in the 1930s, and most probably will be disastrous in the postmillennial decade as well.

Indeed, it doesn't seem to take long for benefits to erode once the economy runs into trouble. Between the last quarter of 2000 and the middle of 2001, profits declined sharply. The weakness of the highly touted 401(k) system immediately became apparent. Even though the slowdown did not begin until the last quarter of 2000, a tumbling stock market brought down the value of the average plan by about 10 percent, and many plans were abandoned as companies went under. To make matters worse, the tech slump revealed that some famous companies quickly cut back. The record reveals surprising examples of employees suddenly deprived of company contributions—not just Enron, but even Ford.

Effective 401(k) reform faces an uncertain future. We are living in an era when vast sums are spent by the corporation to support think tanks and hire propagandists who ridicule Social Security and other public programs while throwing flowers at the feet of the gods of the market. It is hard to combat the picture of the wise corporation headed by the great CEO in an era that ridicules politics and extols the free market. But the fragility is nevertheless real and has been a recurring theme of U.S. economic history. That is what the average American investor must understand. And that is why we are taking a tour of that history in this chapter.

If he lived today, Undershaft would most likely be the most effective proselytizer for abolishing Social Security and replacing it with individual retirement accounts that President George W. Bush could ever imagine. Undershaft, a British munitions maker, may spout the party line of the Bush administration. But he recognizes the Bush-Cheney-O'Neill cant for what it is. Undershaft, as Weber rightly points out, "sees things like charity, faith and what we now call 'family values' as dogma— hypocrisies to defend the status quo as morally good." Some on the Republican right are true conservatives who strongly believe that what their party defines as "family values" constitutes a moral dictate. And we salute them. But to the Bush inner circle, they are secondary, useful in defending the sanctity that really matters to them—a "free market" that supposedly preserves corporate profits.

Shaw understood the kind of capitalism that generates the power to address social needs at a cost that the corporation can afford. That power is, of course, monopoly. Undershaft is in a position to make a plausible case for his corporation. He is an arms monopolist in the opening years of the weapons race that results in World War I. Undershaft is, indeed, a businessman with an infinite amount of capital sufficient to take care of all of Major Barbara's social projects. And her social activist colleagues are bowled over by the model village that Undershaft has created around his manufacturing plant. "Heavens, what a place," says one. "Did you see the nursing home!" "Did you see the libraries and schools?" says another. "Have you gone into the insurance fund, the pension fund, the building society, the various applications of co-operation?"

Fast forward a hundred years, and you would imagine that free market capitalism had, in fact, produced Undershaft's paradise in the United States. To hear Wall Street tell it, Americans who know how to take advantage of their opportunities can, in fact, arm themselves with appropriate insurance funds, pension funds, subsidized mortgages, and even health insurance to provide the basis for a secure life, to an extent Shaw apparently hadn't even thought of.

In fact, almost the exact opposite is true. We do not question the virtues of a free market if they are properly understood. A truly free market does not preserve monopoly—it undermines it, leaving the economy free to innovate and new companies free to challenge the status quo. But companies constantly under attack by competitors are by their very nature vulnerable to economic vicissitudes, especially in downturns. And this means that a serious program to provide protection to the majority of Americans must be social rather than corporate.

The Self-Help Delusion

It's been almost a century since *Major Barbara* was first produced. For a hundred years, politicians, corporations, and unions have dangled attractively worded benefit and retirement plans in front of the American public. But only two public programs, Social Security and Medicare, have proved to be a reliable source of income and health insurance for the vast majority of Americans.

That both Social Security and Medicare are under serious attack should not be in any doubt. Wall Street, particularly in the booming late

1990s, had a way of ridiculing Europe and Japan as having become "hidebound" and inflexible economies bent on preserving their social insurance policies at the cost of rapid economic growth. It mattered little that these same countries grew far faster than the United States in the 1960s, 1970s, and 1980s, even though their government social insurance systems had been in place for far longer.

America's social insurance system was late in coming. Just three years after Shaw wrote *Major Barbara,* Great Britain passed nationwide pension legislation to provide retirement funds for elderly Brits. And even the Brits were late. Two decades earlier, Chancellor Otto von Bismarck, the original "compassionate" conservative, decided to defang the powerful labor movement of Germany in the late 1880s, and by co-opting it to serve the cause of German nationalism, gave Germany a pension system. The rest of Europe gradually fell into line. Even Canada put in a national pension plan in the 1920s.

It took the cataclysm of the Great Depression to shake the United States out of its hostility to public social programs. From the end of the Civil War to the 1930s, Social Darwinism dominated American policy. The prevailing ideology, as correctly pointed out by Richard Cloward and Frances Fox Piven in their classic *Regulating the Poor,* was: "The doctrine of self-help through work which distinguished nineteenth-century capitalism flourished in its purest and fiercest form in the United States. . . . The promise of America was not affluence, but independence; not ease, but a chance to work for oneself, to be self-supporting, and to win esteem through hard and honest labor." The very notion of a relief system "seemed blasphemous" to many in the country.

None of this, of course, is to say that the doctrine of self-help prevented the appearance of vigorous social and political reform movements between the end of the Civil War and the Great Depression. Indeed, the rise of a union movement, the emergence of the suffragettes, Robert La Follette's Progressive Party and a host of social reformers, including Justice Louis Brandeis, rejected Social Darwinism. The famed lawyer who became a Supreme Court justice wrote a book, *Other People's Money,* urging reforms to prevent the way in which Wall Street was deceiving the public in his day. But though they were active, the reformers could point to few concrete successes at the federal level.

One nineteenth-century program did escape the tyranny of self-help, but with ironic effects. The plight of Civil War veterans led to the first public pension system in the United States. Congress passed a substantial pension plan for veterans after the war. As it turned out, virtually all of the benefits went to those who were Northern and white. Over the years, the Civil War pension plan was often amended and "improved." But what the changes really improved were patronage, political corruption, and "pork-barrel" spending. The result was that the pension program ended up costing double the Civil War itself.

Ann Shola Orloff, one of the nation's leading experts on American social policy history, has written that in the early twentieth century in Britain, for example, "the problems of the aged served as a unifying focus for the political activities of reformers and some labor leaders, helping to cement a cross-class alliance in favor of new social-spending programs." In contrast, in the United States, the problems associated with the aged—poverty, but also mismanaged Civil War pensions—served to drive apart groups that might otherwise have cooperated politically to push for a modern system of social protection.

The corruption in the Civil War pension system had a perverse effect. It heightened suspicion of any broad-based pension legislation similar to those being passed in Europe after the turn of the century. "Thus," adds Orloff, "the trajectory of events in the United States was quite different from that in Europe, and the successful establishment of workers' compensation in many states was not followed by similar successes in instituting old-age pensions or social insurance." But this was, in some ways, a minor cause of American reluctance to institute social insurance.

Though there is no evidence that social insurance systematically destroys the incentive to work, the idea that it does continues to be a dominant factor in American politics and social policy. It was unquestionably a major factor in the cynical welfare reform program signed onto by the Clinton administration in 1996. The director of one welfare-to-work program we spoke to in the South Bronx was privately appalled by what was happening to those who had gone through his training program. "In 2002," he says, "many former welfare recipients we thought were successful have since lost their jobs, their benefits often no longer exist, and we have very few new jobs coming into the center that we can even tell them to apply for. They are in really scary shape financially." Thus, although the doctrine of self-help sometimes does merit genuine respect, it is always worth keeping in mind that Social Darwinism—the idea that social policy should be guided by the survival of the fittest—is a questionable ideology that serves the interests of the rich and powerful more surely than the interests of the average family.

The belief in self-help that still permeates even the poorest Americans does not guarantee that their work will be rewarded. In her best-seller, *Nickel and Dimed,* Barbara Ehrenreich recounts the experiences she had after temporarily leaving her comfortable middle-class life during the economic boom of the late 1990s. To gather data for her book, following in the footsteps of George Orwell, she labored alongside the one-third of American workers with an income of less than $8 an hour—waitresses, nursing-home attendants, and housekeepers. Ehrenreich, who comes from a blue-collar background, writes that she "grew up hearing over and over, to the point of tedium, that 'hard work' was the secret of success. No one ever said that you could work hard—harder even than you thought possible—and still find yourself sinking ever deeper into poverty and debt . . . the Democrats are not eager to find flaws in the period of 'unprecedented prosperity' they take credit for; the Republicans have lost interest in the poor now that 'welfare-as-we-know-it' has ended."

Evidence of the kind that appears in Ehrenreich's book, showing that the plight of the American poor is not caused by their unwillingness to work and work hard, has never undermined the American doctrine that self-help can conquer all. Indeed, the majority of American social insurance programs that evolved over the twentieth century—Lyndon B. Johnson's Anti-Poverty Program, Aid for Dependent Children (AFDC), and others—became hugely unpopular and have been drastically reduced or done away with over the years because they have not attracted middle-class support.

Indeed, the idea that only the middle class has the work ethic to merit government insurance and health programs largely explains how the American Social Security system works. In Europe, the social insurance systems tend to be comprehensive, including both the middle classes and the poor. Welfare checks are usually written by the same government department or agency that provides retirement checks to the middle classes. That makes the American system of Social Security unique. Alone among the social programs in the industrial world, the Social Security system, expanded to include Medicare benefits in 1965, has been targeted from the beginning on America's middle class and has always been described as an insurance program, not as a welfare program. Indeed, because the Social Security tax is a tax on wages, most Americans on Social Security find the idea that they are receiving a handout deeply offensive. And they are right.

Because most Americans perceive Social Security as earned through a life of hard work, it has expanded over the years, despite frequent business opposition. As a result, the United States has not developed a comprehensive "welfare state" in the European sense. Instead, the federal safety net has developed into a bifurcated two-tier system. The upper tier is Social Security; the lower tier includes programs associated exclusively with the poor that have been far less popular than Social Security and much more vulnerable to being cut back or done away with, like many programs in President Lyndon B. Johnson's Great Society effort. That has left Social Security as the only great long-term bulwark between the possibility of poverty in old age and a decent existence. And those who have compared how the United States provides for its middle-class older population argue that today's Social Security system serves the middle classes at least as effectively as government programs in Britain and Canada. That may come as somewhat of a surprise to many on the left, but it is nevertheless true.

The Roosevelt Phase: The Birth of Social Security

For those living in the conservative, probusiness 1920s, it would have been impossible to predict that Americans would ever support anything resembling the Social Security system. As the United States emerged from World War I, there were signs of life on the political left and in the union movement. Many on the left thought that the 1919 Red revolution in Russia would be the beginning of a whole new activist era. But the reverse occurred. A "Red scare" was used to suppress the more radical leftists, many in the unions. And there were arrests and deportations.

The assault on radical reform worked. Labor launched a series of bloody confrontations just after the war ended. But they were plowed under by a conservative establishment that fed politically on the anti–Woodrow Wilson sentiment of the postwar years. "Southern textile workers rose in strikes which were almost revolutionary in their fury, but were repressed at times with equal brutality," writes Frederick J.

Hoffman in *The Twenties*. The coal industry, faced with the competition of oil and electricity, sought to move its base from Pennsylvania to the nonunion fields of the South. "Bitter strife ensued in both North and South, but the operators won," Hoffman writes. And before Franklin Delano Roosevelt was elected president in November 1932, "John L. Lewis and his United Mine Workers (UMW) were so thoroughly beaten there was a possibility that the union would vanish."

In the 1920s, a defanged union movement became an organization that Harding and Coolidge could love. The only workable response to the anti-union sentiment was devised by the head of the American Federation of Labor, Samuel Gompers, the most famous cigar-roller since Carmen. He opted for a go-slow, integrative approach that was anything but threatening. After he became head of the AFL, his cautious approach began to pay off in limited gains made during the tight labor markets of the prosperous 1920s. By the end of the 1920s, some unions offered retirement benefits (covering about 20 percent of all members), which were obviously influenced by the political tenor of the times. They looked more like mutual aid and self-help societies than robust union pension plans. Found in the railroad, construction, and printing trades, their cautious approach was the only thing that could work in the anti-union judicial environment of the time. God forbid that Gompers would have supported anything resembling federal Social Security. As we've already noted, he was, as H. L. Mencken once said, "Tame as a tabby cat."

Without the depression and the massive unemployment and deep poverty that characterized the period, the Social Security Act could never have been passed. The progressive wings of both the Republican and Democratic Parties were vastly overpowered by the probusiness, antilabor agendas of conservative Republicans of that time. Yet there were some models at the state level. New York governor Franklin D. Roosevelt, along with several other reform-minded governors in the 1920s, had supported pension legislation for their states. And it was Roosevelt's staff, many of whom went along with him to Washington in 1932, that really worked to pass the Social Security Act of 1935.

Even though the original Social Security system was hardly universal in scope, it did cover the foreign-born, lower-paid, ethnic working class. Despite the flaws in the union movement's early attempt at creating pension systems, it deserves credit for its legislative support of expanding the scope of Social Security. But that support could not overcome conservative resistance to an American plan as comprehensive as the European plans that had long before been put in place. Roosevelt sensed correctly that if he wanted to get Social Security legislation passed, he could not include a health insurance component in the package because of vigorous opposition by the American Medical Association. As it turned out, 1935 was the high point of Congress's willingness to go along with FDR's domestic reforms. In the years following, a strengthened coalition of congressional conservatives gained strength.

Roosevelt's aides decided early on to make old-age insurance "fiscally sound" and contributory so that it would not be considered an "assistance" plan for the needy. That is one reason that by the time it was passed, the original Social Security legislation was remarkably meager. It covered only certain classes of workers in preferred occupations. Low-wage industries such as agriculture and domestic service were exempted. The reason was opposition from Southern congressmen and senators, who were not only fearful of damage to their rural economies but also well aware that the majority of all blacks were employed either on the farm or as maids and other domestic servants. And at a time of dramatic unemployment and much poverty, the insurance benefits for those older workers who were included in legislation did not begin until 1942. Meanwhile, 50 percent of Americans over sixty-five depended on others for their support in the mid-1930s, at a time when the proportion of the aged in the population had doubled since 1900.

Despite conservative opposition to Social Security, it provided immediate assistance to business, partly by giving executives a clear conscience when they cut off pension benefits for lower-paid workers. Their reasoning was that these workers would do fine because they were covered by Social Security benefits. Companies felt freer than ever to skew their pension plans toward higher-paid workers so that the percentage of income replaced by a pension plan would increase with earnings.

One enduring legacy of Roosevelt's Social Security was the preservation of the notion that beneficiaries were collecting benefits because they were imbued with the work ethic. Benefits were earned only through contributions based on employment. And from the beginning, the stress was on the idea that Social Security would be financed by its own tax system, not by general revenues. The stress on keeping the system fiscally sound without recourse to other revenues was also there at the outset and has lasted to the present day. That was what Albert Gore's continued reference to the "lockbox" in the 2000 election was really about.

After seeing to it that Social Security was deeply restricted, the financial industry's response was to fill in the gaps that it had in large part created. It was in many ways a forerunner to the way it capitalized on the emergence of the 401(k) close to fifty years later. In the late 1930s, insurance companies created all kinds of new annuities to peddle to high-income workers, who, at that time, tended to view Social Security not as a program for themselves but one designed for the poor, despite Roosevelt's care that it was not, indeed, an assistance program. It seemed that the new Social Security system had unleashed a demand for all kinds of insurance, and the industry boomed. And this feeling that Social Security is a baseline antipoverty program persists to this very day and may partly explain support for privatizing the system.

The Lyndon Johnson Years

The years following World War II saw massive growth in government programs in Britain and Canada. But in the United States, the great triumph of policy was the GI Bill. Social Security did make one important change. After his surprising win in the 1948 election, President Harry S. Truman had enough of a majority in Congress to extend Social Security coverage to major segments of agriculture and domestic service that had escaped Roosevelt. There were also some increases in benefit levels, but the "result was that during the period between the end of the war and the mid-1960s, there was a continual erosion of the economic status of the American elderly," notes John Myles. "Benefits did not keep pace with the general rise in the standard of living or replace the labor market income being lost through a rising retirement rate. The combination of low benefits and a rising number of retirees was progressively pauperizing the American elderly."

Yet an unlikely stage was being set for a radical improvement in the lives of older Americans. A series of events—the assassination of President John F. Kennedy in 1963, race riots in a number of large Northern cities where unemployment rates ran as high as 36 percent, the emergence of the civil rights movement, led by Martin Luther King Jr., and the assassination of Dr. King himself set the stage for the first great expansion in federal programs since the New Deal. When writing this book, Anne Colamosca remembered her experiences as an undergraduate at Temple University, where she was attending summer school during the race riots of 1964 in North Philadelphia. Fires, pillaging of local stores, and a sense that anarchy could take over the city at any time frightened the wits out of the white middle-class and blue-collar citizens. As far as they were concerned, these demonstrations had come out of nowhere, and they felt threatened. They also thought that the blacks had come to Philadelphia to get welfare payments and had every reason to be grateful. But they didn't want to know that the black unemployment rate was at an astronomical 36 percent, although the city itself was still doing well economically!

It is usually said that the catalysts for President Johnson's social programs were the assassination of President Kennedy and the Democratic sweep in the 1964 presidential election that left Barry Goldwater and the Republican right in tatters. But the origin of the Great Society, and its Social Security component, Medicare, has deeper roots. There is a strong argument to be made that Johnson's programs were adopted because of a belief that they would stave off more serious political disruption in many of the nation's largest cities. That the first really reformist Congress in thirty years passed the nation's most far-reaching national health-care program was in essence a side benefit.

Events of the first half of the 1960s not only led to Medicare but also to the capacity of business to prevent Social Security reform. From its inception under the New Deal until the mid-1960s, the dominant strategy of business and conservative critics was not to dismantle Social Security but merely to "hold the line, wherever that line might be at the moment. Until 1965, this was a successful strategy; after 1965, it failed and failed massively."

Yet even with business in retreat, "one of the most striking aspects of the implementations of Johnson's Medicare and Medicaid is that it greatly benefited those who had been mostly opposed to the enactment of the two programs—physicians and the AMA," writes Helene Slessarev, in an essay about this social transition period. Both Medicare and Medicaid were set up as systems to be administered through private health-care delivery. As a result, doctors' fees increased after Medicare was implemented.

The Surprise of the Richard Nixon Years
(No, Not Watergate!)

John Myles has argued persuasively that the major step taken in the development of America's modern welfare state for the elderly occurred not under Franklin Roosevelt's administration, but under Richard Nixon's. The reforms of the late 1960s and early 1970s are responsible for the fact that Social Security now does its job more effectively. Social Security developed a political constituency that made it immune, at least temporarily, to political attack. When the Nixon reforms were complete, as Robert Ball, head of the Social Security Administration remarked, the United States had a "new social security program."

In an effort to deal with inflation, the Johnson administration had increased Social Security benefits 13 percent in 1967 and raised the level of covered earnings from $4,800 to $7,800. But Nixon went further, faster. Increases in benefits in 1969 and again in 1972 raised real, inflation-adjusted benefits by 23 percent in just three years. Even more important, in its long-term implications, it was the 1972 legislation that guaranteed further cost-of-living allowances into the future. The decision to add a COLA to Social Security had major implications, not only for retirement benefits but for many other government and private programs, such as union contracts, that provide inflation protection.

Because cost-of-living allowances have become a feature of the American economy, it is critical to understand that the decision to grant them in Social Security was intended to benefit business rather than the average family and therefore conforms to the fundamental thesis of this book that except in crisis, family benefits are changed whenever the power structure decides to do it. Prior to the outburst of inflation that followed President Johnson's decision to escalate the war in Vietnam at the same time as he was fighting his war on poverty at home—the famous "guns and butter" policy—business was satisfied with the post–World War II "social contract" that linked wage gains to productivity increases. That was certainly true in the early 1960s. Business liked the system because productivity gains had actually exceeded wage gains between 1961 and 1965. After inflation began in 1966, it was profits that were hurt. Between 1966 and 1972, real wages rose a sizzling 18 percent; productivity, by only 13 percent.

The result was a change in the balance of power that the corporations hardly intended. Labor's share of national income rose, and profits were squeezed. That was an outcome that corporations were unwilling to take, especially from a Republican administration. The result was a cynical abandonment of the free market by President Nixon. In August 1971, the Nixon administration imposed wage controls, to halt the erosion of corporate profits. But the popularity of Social Security and its strong constituency essentially defeated Nixon's intentions. As we have already seen, cost-of-living allowances were added to Social Security, and Americans won the largest real increases in their "retirement wages" in the history of the Social Security program.

Nixon's decision to grant cost-of-living increases changed the character of Social Security in a fundamental way. What had started off as a meager program had become a source of wealth for the average American—"Social Security wealth," as Myles calls it. And when the program changed, all Americans on the system became richer because their retirement income had increased. But the government did not have to pay out the largest share of its commitment immediately, because only those who were already retired got bigger Social Security checks right away. The reason is that benefit increases resulting from COLAs were never paid for in higher Social Security taxes. Wages may go up when inflation accelerates, leading to bigger tax collections for the Social Security fund. But there is no guarantee that the taxes on the higher wages will be adequate to fund the additional cost of the system. Still, the COLAs solved a business problem in the inflation and Watergate-haunted years, 1972 and 1973. Retirement pay comes due sometime in the future. But in the short term, a decision to raise it can defer current wage pressures. And the Nixon Social Security reforms meant that workers were granted deferred retirement benefits, while employers avoided the cost of significant increases in current real wage bills.

The Great Social Security Debate: Where Does Social Security Stand Now?

More than sixty-five years after the Social Security Act of 1935, the system has finally advanced to the point where it provides the major source of retirement income for the vast majority of older Americans. One remaining weakness springs from discrimination against women who have spent many years working for wages that were far lower than those paid to men, working in comparable jobs. These women can end up with lower Social Security benefits than women who may never have worked. That's because women who claim Social Security as dependents often receive benefits based on their husband's high income. The other weakness springs from the U.S.'s unequal wages. Because this skews income distribution prior to retirement, it produces a very high level of relative poverty among the elderly after retirement, especially among women.

The married middle classes get the best deal from Social Security. This explains why Social Security, unlike other sectors of the American welfare state, has proven so resistant to conservative political attack. Its natural political base is not the poor but rather the broad middle class. That is not to say that the average American family pretends that it can retire and pay all of its bills from Social Security income. But at least for the middle class, the system is a vital building block in a decent retirement. The real issue is not whether Social Security should be privatized; it is, rather, whether it should be expanded to provide better protection in the slow-growing economy of the postmillennial decade.

A Social Security Crisis?

An astounding change occurred in establishment attitudes toward Social Security after the passage of the Nixon program. Up to that point, the relationship between American business and the Social Security program had always been ambivalent. As we saw earlier, there were periods in which corporate America saw the expansion of the system as in their interest, and other periods in which it roundly opposed Social Security improvements. But by 1972, the modernization of America's welfare state for the retired population was a fait accompli. And business did not like what it saw.

The result was the discovery of the Social Security "crisis." There is a tendency to believe that worries over the bankruptcy of Social Security first became serious in the 1990s. But the idea that American society was about to collapse under the weight of an aging population and rising Social Security entitlements was ironically a part of the Nixon legacy that would never go away. Ronald Reagan came to power in 1980, announcing that it would be necessary to slash Social Security in order to save it. And by the time the Republicans had shoehorned George W. Bush into power, the assault on Social Security had become intense. In early 2001, President George W. Bush appointed a commission to study the future of the system. Every single member that he appointed had already gone on record in favor of at least partial privatization of the system. The only thing that seemed to be preventing a quick capture of Social Security by Wall Street was the inconvenient fact that the stock market had begun its slump before Bush was even elected. As a consequence, the American public may in the end have at least one reason to be thankful for the sickening dive in the Nasdaq in 2000 and 2001. It may have at least delayed the fateful day when the 401(k) hoax totally captured the field.

But the relentless attack on Social Security is certain to continue. We have seen that the Vietnam inflation induced the corporate power structure to sanction a strengthening of the system. Deflation will almost certainly have the opposite effect. So, in the deflationary period that we foresee, business is almost certain to launch a major assault on the system that goes far beyond the mere idea of privatizing some 2 percent of employee contributions, which seems to be what Bush had in mind when he created his commission.

Thomas Byrne Edsall dates the origins of the mobilization of corporate America's fascination with the notion of a Social Security crisis to November 1972. That was the period when Nixon's Social Security reforms were in the air. The Business Roundtable, whose main purpose was to restrict the influence and bargaining power of organized labor, came into power as a policy forum and lobbying agency for America's largest corporations. Edsall describes the resulting change: Rather than using up their political capital by competing with one another for a larger share of the government pie, corporations now joined together in the struggle to advance interests they shared—defeating consumer protection and labor law reforms, enacting favorable tax legislation, and rolling back America's recently modernized welfare state for the elderly.

Business put a lot of effort into developing the resources needed to promote the idea that Social Security was facing a crisis. America's educated elite was targeted as one of the main enemies of traditional business interests. To turn this situation around, business began to put large sums into the creation of think tanks and policy institutes to nurture scholarship and research, among them the American Enterprise Institute and the National Bureau of Economic Research, in addition to the Employee Benefit Research Institute. The hunt was on to discredit Social Security.

Much of this research was of reasonably high quality, showing that an increase in Social Security tax rates was needed to fund Nixon's Social Security reforms. But some dubious studies resulted from the zeal to support conclusions favorable to the Roundtable's point of view. One notorious example was a National Bureau of Economic Research study that was conducted by Martin Feldstein. It purported to show that Social Security had reduced the U.S. savings rate so severely that the nation's capital stock had fallen by one-third. In its December 11, 1978 issue, *BusinessWeek* ran a story citing research showing that Feldstein's main numbers were implausible. When confronted with that criticism, Feldstein blamed the error on two graduate students who were working for him and had committed a programming error. When that error was corrected, his data suggested that Social Security did not decrease the savings rate. Although Feldstein's study did not survive scrutiny, Feldstein himself and his comfortable conservative views not only survived but flourished. He is now president of the National Bureau of Economic Research.

The attack on Social Security, backed as it was with big money spent by opponents of the system, has been sustained and powerful. One reason, as John Myles points out, "is the pattern of intellectual production: from learned journal to political essay to the business press, and finally, to the mass media." It was a pattern repeated many times. The claims varied. Myles has cataloged the attacks: Social Security was going broke, Social Security was a bad buy, Social Security was too generous. As Myles puts it, by 1981, when the Reagan administration came to power, "the 'crisis' of Social Security had successfully penetrated American culture, both high and low." In the end, however, the American public rejected the argument and even Martin Feldstein admitted that as long as the voters were prepared to support it, Social Security could not go broke.

Yet as the boomers move closer and closer to retirement, the attacks on Social Security become more and more shrill and still threaten the system, as George W. Bush's appointments to the 2001 commission show. There is no doubt that the dramatic drop in the number of workers that is supporting each member of the retired population poses severe problems for the nation's retirement system, particularly since health-care costs are rising far faster than the consumer price index as a whole. The authors readily agree that reforms will be needed. But we radically reject the notion, for which there is not one shred of credible evidence, that privatizing all or part of the Social Security system will make things better. This is what the right-wing think tanks would have us believe, along with an alarming number of politicians, including Democrats as well as Republicans.

Ending or privatizing Social Security would obviously put the burden totally on the private pension system, but the history of private pensions in the United States is fraught with disappointments: bankruptcies, broken promises, and changes in the system that hurt employees when business believes that it has to cut back on expenses. It is to the checkered and often harrowing history of the private pension system that we now turn. There is no better way to raise needed doubts about 401(k)s and other private pension schemes. Broken promises have abounded in the past, and they are almost certain to become more lurid in the future.

•◆•

Chapter 8

Pension Power: Who Has It, How They Got It, and How It's Used Against the Family

Every story has a moral if you can only find it.

—Lewis Carroll, *Alice in Wonderland*

As in an Alfred Hitchcock movie, real-life truth has a way of coming out in unexpected ways. The prosperity of the 1990s had obscured the "easy come, easy go" nature of 401(k) plans. But as the plumes of smoke billowing from the World Trade Center were finally damped down in early November and the economy was officially declared to be in recession, American families began to realize that their pensions had suddenly fallen into the category of other corporate "perks."

Most American families had forgotten or had never realized that 401(k)s were created in order to free corporations from funding and guaranteeing that they would pay pensions to their retirees. But after the terrorist debacle, corporations began announcing that they had found a new way to cut costs. Companies, among them Daimler-Chrysler's U.S. unit, Chrysler, the Wyndham International hotel chain, and Bethlehem Steel, all suspended their 401(k) matches to save money as the economic downturn deepened in late 2001. Equally troubling was that the early birds, like Chrysler, were setting an example of what other corporations might do if the recession continued or if the long-term growth rate of the

U.S. economy declined. It wasn't only that the early 401(k) cutters were well within their legal rights in slicing or eliminating their 401(k) "matches"; they were also under no real pressure, with unemployment rising, to offer new employees 401(k) plans without making them wait a long time to enroll.

It is vital to realize that the quick corporate attack on 401(k)s in the difficult autumn of 2001 springs from the deeply embedded flawed logic of the American pension system and therefore can easily happen again. Cutting back on benefits is perfectly consistent with the entire history of private pension plans in the United States. Walter Reuther, the famed head of the United Auto Workers Union who made his mark in the decade following World War II, would have understood it very well. Reuther understood that the fatal flaw of the American private pension system was that it was not administered solely or even primarily in the interest of the workers on whose behalf contributions were being made.

Instead, the main decisions about pension plans—their "governance," as the ugly technical language would have it—have always been made by the corporations that carry them and by the unions that bargained on their behalf. Although Reuther was obviously a union official himself, he was opposed to any pension system that did not insulate the worker from manipulation by these outside interests. As a consequence, he favored a pension system administered by the federal government and totally free from manipulation by either business or unions. This was because Reuther had long found company programs distasteful. He thought their coverage was incomplete, their financing indeterminate. To him, they smacked of old-fashioned paternalism.

These flaws have persisted to this very day. The reason, of course, is that attempts to reform the system run into a wall of corporate lobbyists. And to make matters worse, employees are delivered into the hands of their company's human resources department, where for many years they have run into an environment dominated by people trained to view pensions as what Notre Dame's Ghilarducci calls "personnel devices."

In the 1980s, most large American corporations changed the name of their personnel department to "human resources" department. Most companies probably thought that this new name was worker-friendly, even "warm and fuzzy." But looking at people as resources is in fact dehumanizing. It implies that companies want their employees to think of themselves as physical objects: zinc ingots, vats of sulfuric acid, or if they were lucky, computer chips. Just think of the problems that humans present to managers. "Human" implies emotion and individualized behavior, often erratic and unpredictable. If only human resources could be treated like slabs of zinc, surely the company could control costs and quality more easily. What could be better than making human resources more and more susceptible to the dictates of the market? Surely contract work is more controllable than the work of real employees. It could be hired with no long-term commitment and terminated with no guilty conscience. And in fact, throughout the 1990s, the proportion of workers covered by health insurance and pensions declined, the pay of more and more workers was linked to short-term profitability, and contract workers soared in number.

When new employees come in the door, they get little warning about what has happened to pension plans in the past, and what could easily occur in the future. The company invites them to an orientation session, designed to impress them with the firm's benefit plans. These sessions take the "high road," full of the profession of good corporate intentions.

A description of flaws in the pension system or a suggestion on how the average family must defend itself are not part of the story that the typical corporation tells its current employees or those people it wants to hire. That is because there never was a time in American history when the interests of the average employee were clearly and unambiguously the central concern of those who administered or legislated the nation's private pension system. And it is harrowing that economic conditions are changing in a way that could make the next decade the worst ever for private pensions since the 1930s. If anything, the forces arrayed against the interests of the average worker are more powerful than ever. Pension power does not lie in the hands of individual employees but rather in the hands of powerful interests—the corporation and its hired guns in Washington, the accounting profession, and pension consultants generally—interests that are always tempted to use this power against workers. There are many ways in which the American pension system is used: to turn pensions into a disappearing act; to discriminate against women; to provide funds for corporate purposes, like financing mergers, that are not intended to provide family security and, indeed, often undermine it; to provide excuses for union busting that have no legitimate foundation in union abuse of pension monies; to turn full-time employees into contract workers; and to further the interests of those who would advance so-called free market causes, at the expense of the worker.

The Incredible Shrinking Pension

In 1875, the American Express company introduced the first industrial pension plan in the United States, according to Ghilarducci. What has happened since is one for Ripley's Believe It or Not. In a fundamental sense, the American pension system has changed little since then. Even minor improvements have been hard won. Mostly, it's been a grueling, tough fight with a lot of setbacks along the way. There have been many attempts to raise retirement income and to increase the chances that employees will actually get the benefits that they have been promised. But to this very day it remains true that the level of benefits paid out is low, as compared to the size of the pension investment funds. Companies still manipulate their pension funds with creative accounting that serves to boost their earnings per share. They still arbitrarily change their pension plans when it suits their purposes. Employees are still victims of the way pension fund rules are written. Yes, especially the 401(k). The Enron affair is only the most vivid example of the continuing pension hoax. Many other companies required their employees to take the company contribution in the form of stock, which could not be sold for a considerable period of time. The Enron debacle led to an increased scrutiny of 401(k) plans by Congress and the media. Indeed, the American pension system often looks as if it takes two steps forward, followed by three steps back. That is the dangerous implication of the history of private pension plans.

Enron's shenanigans are evidence that, incredible as it may seem, the pensions of Americans have actually deteriorated in the prosperous 1990s. That's true even though the amount of money in the hands of traditional pension fund managers—approximately $6 trillion in 1998—had soared. Figures compiled by Ghilarducci tell the story: Between 1980 and 1998, the value of private pension funds, in real terms, grew by 413 percent. Over the same period the average pension benefit, adjusted for inflation, declined by one-third. To top it off, there was an actual 2 percentage-point shrinkage in the share of retirement income provided by private pension plans.

Over the same period, coverage has stagnated. The proportion of the workforce covered by private pensions has hovered around 50 percent since the 1970s. Coverage rates are higher than average for middle-aged workers (61.5 percent) and those in large firms (67.3 percent). Unionized and high-income workers have the highest rate of coverage, 78.7 percent and 79.6 percent, respectively.

Ghilarducci asks, "Why are pension funds so large and benefits so small?" With the 413 percent gain in the inflation-adjusted value of pension funds, it's obvious that the answer does not lie in any failure of pension fund assets to keep up with the market.

Instead, Teresa Ghilarducci finds the explanation of the disparity between large funds and small benefits in the way in which pension investment and benefit decisions are made. Corporate pension sponsors who manage 90 percent of defined benefit money are torn between using investment gains to improve pension generosity and financing other vital and pressing corporate needs. She underlines that there are strong incentives for agents (money managers) to act in ways that may harm those whom they represent—the pension beneficiaries.

And defined contribution plans, like the 401(k), which became prominent in the early 1980s, haven't made things any better. The real bonanza was for the bosses and their investment bankers on Wall Street. The 401(k) is dirt-cheap. It costs the employer 50 percent less than a traditional pension. And to make it even better, the 401(k) relieves the company of any "sticky" long-term obligations to retired workers. Both of these advantages make corporate annual reports look a whole lot better. There are no down-the-road liabilities. As economists would put it, the 401(k) shifts all the risks—extending into an uncertain future—onto the departing worker.

At the end of the 1990s, only 9 percent of income to the elderly came from private pensions; six times that amount, or 54 percent, came from Social Security. This was the outcome of over a century of evolution of the private pension system. It makes a joke of the right-wing assertion that Social Security is a bad buy, and that, at least by implication, the average worker can do better by relying on the private pension system. This right-wing assertion is truly ridiculous. The truth of the matter is that it is the private pension system that is the bad buy. Tax breaks showered on private pension funds take a large bite out of federal revenues:

Over $50 billion a year, or an incredible one-third of the average annual budget deficit in the 1990s, was lost each year because pension savings are tax deferred. Yet less than half of the nation's private sector labor force is covered by employer pensions. What is sometimes true in theory just hasn't worked out that way in over 100 years of practice. This is a chilling thought going into a period when the stock market, we believe, faces a long period of stagnation. And it makes one ponder over what percentage of Americans will still have access to comfortable private pensions in ten, twenty, or thirty years. Our belief is that as the pace of globalization quickens as a result of the worldwide coalition against terrorism, the American workforce will receive even fewer pension benefits, as corporations will easily find other well-educated workforces abroad to do skilled white-collar work.

What explains the miserable history of the private pension system? Social Security benefits have not exactly been generous, but they have at least grown over the past twenty years. When adjusted for inflation, Social Security has done better than private pensions for one simple reason: The actual pensioner has no role whatever in decisions over the rules for private pension plans. People may think that they control their 401(k)s, and to the extent that they can change their asset allocations, they do. But the public has exercised little control whatever over the rules that govern 401(k)s, or the fees that are charged for managing them, or the size or form of company contributions. In Social Security, by contrast, nothing can be done without an explicit decision by Congress. And at least Washington politicians must go to the voters. That's what gives the average American some power over the system.

But when it comes to private pensions, the United States is unique among the industrialized countries in granting companies the sole control over pension plans as long as they meet government rules. The exceptions are pension plans covered by a collective bargaining agreement between a company and a union. These plans are administered by joint trustees, but in practice the role of the union is strictly circumscribed by the Taft-Hartley Law of 1947.

The effect has been to allow the corporation to use its pension fund as a financial resource through which it can acquire other companies or jack up its earnings to satisfy Wall Street. Indeed, the money has, in practice, been used for almost anything. Ghilarducci argues that the rules issued by the Employment Retirement Income Security Act (ERISA) in 1974 were written "to minimize moral hazard from underfunding and faulty and incomplete information." Since ERISA was passed, pension funds have grown dramatically and "there [has been] an increasing disonance between the concept of pension trust as irrevocable payments to workers and pension funds as an unexplored corporate resource."

Despite the passage of ERISA in 1974, the use of corporate pension funds to serve company interests continued to flourish. "During the 1980s recession in the steel industry, Continental Can Company used a sophisticated computer program to identify [those workers] just about to vest in their pensions and fired them," writes Ghilarducci. Later, the U.S. federal court found that "the company had constructed an elaborate system that kept track of employee eligibility for generous early pensions." Continental Can even had "a secret accounting system that it did not deny developing." The company's defense was "bold," Notre Dame's pension expert explains. Although it was later convicted of violating age discrimination law, Continental Can claimed the existence of its system "was legal and [it] was innocent of wrong-doing because . . . pension costs were not important factors in the company's administrative costs." Enron's top executives could well have been mentored by these people!

How Corporate Pension Power Is Used Against the Family

The private pension system has a long and complex history. What stands out, however, is that the corporation always has enough power to attenuate reform and continue to use pension monies to serve corporate financial interests at the expense of the American family. The best way to show this is to look at several critical periods in the long development of the system still in place at the beginning of the twenty-first century.

The fact that America's national social pension plan—the Social Security Act of 1935—came decades after national plans were in place in much of Europe and Canada is key to understanding why the American pension system is so different today from plans in other developed countries. Germany in 1889, Great Britain in 1908, and Canada in 1927 all adopted federal programs that would provide pension assistance to their citizens. Because of a combination of social factors in the United States, after World War I most pension activism revolved around company and union pensions for a tiny part of the American population, rather than taking the form of a countrywide push by reformers for a national government program. From that point on, social insurance in the United States swerved off the road leading to universal social insurance. And even after the passage of Social Security, the United States pension system continued to develop on a three-prong track—Social Security, union, and company pension plans—none of which, by themselves, have proven to be completely financially sustaining for those who retire. One reason is that in some sense, these three systems have competed with one another over the years for attention and funding.

Although many American companies opposed the passage of the Social Security Act, its passage did not lead to the demise of company pensions during the 1930s. On the contrary, the corporation felt that it had to do something to maintain executive perks. Companies argued that because Social Security benefits were so progressive and skewed toward low-income workers, they felt obliged to supplement pensions for their high-income earners. Ghilarducci argues that a number of new company pension plans were actually adopted during the 1930s. As many companies saw it, the Social Security Act eliminated the need to provide pensions for their nonmanagement employees.

Along with passage of the Social Security Act of 1935, other progress was made in the 1930s, despite the depression. Almost all pension plans were backed by the accumulation of reserves, interest was guaranteed on contributions, and benefits to surviving family members became more widespread.

Yet the fragility of the private pension system persisted through World War II. At war's end, complaints over unmet retirement income needs were partly responsible for the rapid union, employer, and government development of private pensions after World War II. Abuses prompted the Internal Revenue Service to promulgate antidiscrimination rules and regulations in the 1950s, but the possibility that employers would misrepresent pension promises and abuse pension funds was overlooked.

It took a long time for Washington to even begin to attempt to correct these abuses. It was 1974 before Congress passed the famed ERISA, the Employment Retirement Income Security Act of 1974. And it was only in 1984 that Congress passed the Retirement Equity Act (REACT), which required firms to cover workers immediately upon hiring. The REACT requirement that spouses must provide approval in writing before participants can elect to forgo survivor pensions so as to enjoy a larger pension was one of the few victories for women's pension rights.

How the Private Pension System Discriminates Against Women

As a simple matter of longevity, the inadequacies of the pension system have been far harder on women than men. What might be called pension discrimination against women affects Social Security and private plans alike. Of the 34 million Americans who were over sixty-five in 1998, 20 million were women, and only 14 million were men. And the difference rises with age. The older the demographic cut, the bigger the proportion of women. Indeed, many elderly women in the United States have already come close to running out of pension money or live with the frightening prospect of falling into deep poverty.

A few years ago, the pension problem was highlighted among a group of women at the Riverside Church in Manhattan who were discussing a number of social issues. Suddenly, the conversation turned personal, and someone asked, "How many women here believe they could in fact become 'bag ladies' and actually run out of money later in life?" Almost everyone in the group of twenty-five spontaneously raised her hand. As the conversation continued, stories of divorce, loss of jobs, mental illness in the family, and prolonged physical illnesses were all included as reasons for financial concern. Women in the group included an artist, a physical therapist, a corporate executive, several full-time mothers, and two women who were themselves caretakers for older people. It seemed clear that many of the women had thought about the possibility privately but had never voiced it to other people.

In many respects, the women's movement deserves credit for moving the inadequacies of pension protection for women at least close to the front burner. The movement forced policymakers and analysts to begin to face the gender consequences of inequality in all pension areas. The pension system has always been male oriented. Women who have been in the labor force and rely on benefits based on their earnings are usually worse off than married women who have the option of basing their benefits on their husband's income. The reason is simply that women have not received equal income for equal work.

The good news is that the position of women whose pensions are based on their own earnings show signs of improving. There has been a shrinkage in the margin between what men get paid and what women get paid both in the economy as a whole and in specific jobs. Between 1980 and 1999, women's pay rose from 62 cents for each dollar that men get paid to 75 cents.

But in other respects, women continue to seriously lag. In 1984, Ghilarducci wrote that women only received 22 percent of all pension income and men 78 percent, even though women live far longer than men. The situation of women in the Social Security system is somewhat better, but still totally unacceptable. Women received 34 percent of the income paid out by Social Security. And little has changed.

A reduction in gender inequality still has a long way to go. Women are disadvantaged because they are extensively employed in industries that are often uncovered by private pensions. Women tend to work for small employers who have weak or no pension plans. Often, the plans that exist in these companies tend to limit coverage for younger workers while at the same time requiring relatively long employment before the worker becomes eligible. Women, more often than men, are forced to take part-time work, as they try to balance work and family obligations. This means that even when women and men are in the same industry, men are more likely to be vested and get pension coverage.

Ironically, although women's wages have been inching up and making the gender gap less ominous, private pension plans like the 401(k) are, in effect, putting pressure on the entire workforce to move in the direction that women workers were unfortunately in for all of the twentieth century and into the twenty-first century—that of part-time, contract workers, a "feminization" of the politics of pensions, if you will, under the guise of self-help and entrepreneurship. It was only in the 1980s and 1990s that the whole concept of a comfortable "rollover" from a worker's 401(k) into a private IRA became part of the psychological terrain of the times. It, of course, had existed since the early 1980s, but only when the Street required constant layoffs—no matter how high profits were, or appeared to be—did the idea of "rollovers" really take hold. Financial consultants on cable television saw "rollovers" as just another great way to make money. Separating from the company was no longer a heartrending emotional and financial experience, they said, when a "rollover" offered such juicy prospects. And the whole separation changed during the mid-1990s to just another career step, with another whole set of doors opening up. The image of the lonely contingency worker with no benefits at all from the company never became part of the "new economy" scenario in which workers rolled effortlessly along from one job to another with their "rollover" pension.

The Reputation of the Unions for Uniquely Bad Pension Fund Management Is Unjustified

Over the years, Washington has enjoyed nothing more than the spectacle of a congressional investigation of corruption in the management of union pension funds. It immediately calls forth visions of tough guy Jimmy Hoffa's Teamsters union, of his conviction for jury tampering. But the truth of the matter is that some of the best pension funds in the country are administered by the labor movement. It's also true that the union movement has been the most consistent and effective force in creating pensions and has fought some of the determined battles to establish pension rights.

Unions have a good record of winning pensions for their membership. By 1979, over 83 percent of union members were covered, compared with only 39 percent of nonunion workers. The coverage rate gap between union and nonunion workers has remained steady since then. This is so even though, since the beginning of the 1980s, globalization has made it harder for unions to protect their members against a general erosion of benefits. Unions have made these gains even though their hands have been tied by the famous—or more rightly, infamous—Taft-Hartley Amendment of 1947 to the National Labor Relations Act. Taft-Hartley barred the sole control of pension plans by unions. Instead, control was vested in a board made up of representatives of employers as well as of the unions.

Unions have always gotten more flak than companies for the way they administer pension plans, even though there is no serious evidence that their misdeeds are more flagrant than those of the bosses. Call it the "Hoffa effect." In 1957 and again in 1959, Senator John L. McClellan of

Arkansas held highly publicized hearings on the International Brotherhood of Teamsters' pension plan. The star witness was Jimmy Hoffa. His nemesis was Robert Kennedy, then chief counsel of the McClellan committee. The subject was the use of the pension funds accumulated since Hoffa negotiated the union's first pension plan in 1955. Nevertheless, Kennedy failed to gain indictments until Hoffa's conviction for jury tampering in 1964. The long struggle between the Justice Department and Hoffa made the public, and unions themselves, wary.

The Teamsters continued under fire into the 1970s. Ray Marshall, Labor Secretary under Jimmy Carter, continued investigating the Teamsters' pension fund and in 1977, put pressure on Frank Fitzsimmons, then Teamsters president, to resign. At issue were a number of scandals, one that led to Richard G. Kleindienst, an attorney general under President Nixon. Teamster notoriety has, of course, carried over to the new millennium, as the battle between Jimmy Hoffa's son and Ron Carey showed in 2000.

Despite this history, there is no serious evidence that the flagrant abuses of pension funds were any more prevalent in the union movement than in the corporation, or on Wall Street, for that matter.

When a "True Believer" in the Free Market Occupies the White House, the Pension System Tends to Wane

Ronald Reagan became president in 1980, ushering in the first period since the 1930s when private pension coverage fell and the finances of remaining plans became more insecure. No such new government plans could be seen anywhere in Washington during the Reagan years. On the contrary, the Reagan decade witnessed almost annual changes in funding standards. Terminations were made easier, as were the rules that prevented corporations from grabbing pension funds and using them for other purposes. The result was "blatant usurpation of pension funds for sometimes dubious corporate use[s]." The results were frequent changes in management and far shorter time horizons for business decisions of the kind that make management feel it necessary to maintain strong pension systems.

Corporations won greater incentives for, and freedom to, use pension funds for their own financial purposes. The effect was not much different from the "abandonment of plans during depressions and the sheltering of profits in pension funds during the past hundred years."

So blatant were corporate pension grabs during the Reagan years that even a normally prostrate Congress was nudged into levying taxes on the amount of money that companies shifted from their pension plans into other uses like financing takeovers.

Nevertheless, when George Herbert Walker Bush took over in 1989, he tried to outdo Reagan by sponsoring legislation that made it easier than ever for companies to borrow from their employees' pension funds. It seems likely, in fact, that the villains of the junk bond era of the late 1980s, Ivan Boesky and Michael Milken, were aided by the "white-shoe" Bush administration. The famed hearings on insider trading conducted by then Wisconsin senator William Proxmire, in the wake of the indictments of Boesky and Milken, showed that it was highly likely that worker pension fund money made up a "large proportion of institutional investors' funds" used by the corporate raiders. That's because over 30 percent of new capital coming into the stock market in those days came from pension plans. Thus, it is quite likely that much of the insider trading of that nefarious period was fueled by workers' money, without their consent or even their knowledge. It is no excuse to say that the trustees who represented the workers on the boards of the pension funds made the loans in hopes of reaping profits for workers.

The Clinton administration "went along" with the notion that the stock market, and the 401(k), had ushered most of the nation into "lotus land." The administration never came to grips with the reality of the situation that, in fact, inflation-adjusted, private pensions were slipping in value for the average American. The Clinton administration flirted with the idea of partially privatizing Social Security but in the end did not do much direct harm, although it did reinforce the great 401(k) hoax by constantly hyping the charms of the new economy.

There is every sign, however, that George W. Bush is hell-bent on playing his father's game. Within six months of becoming president, he appointed a new Social Security Commission. Each and every member had already declared in favor of privatizing at least part of the Social Security system. For the moment, at least, the private pension system appears as though it has a good chance of encroaching on Social Security. It appears that Bush still worships at the feet of the 401(k) icon.

In conclusion, despite the huge growth in pension funds, there is little evidence that the true owners of pension monies have much impact on the way their money is used, despite many predictions to the contrary. Particularly in the 1970s, many analysts argued that because worker ownership of corporations was growing since pension funds owned more and more stock, workers could use their ownership position in ways that would better serve worker interests.

The belief, especially among liberals, was that labor would control investment and production decisions by stewarding the "largest lump of money in the world." The hope was that worker pension power would bring a new form of overall worker power, a type of workers' capitalism. As it turned out, however, corporations retained control of pension fund management and often used it to further their own goals, rather than those of their employees. That is the problem that dogs the American pension system to this very day. Indeed, it raises fundamental doubts about whether the 401(k) reforms that were demanded in the wake of the Enron debacle will really change anything. The lesson of pension history in the United States is that as long as Americans derive their pension rights as employees rather than as citizens, their pension monies will be vulnerable to misuse.

Something has clearly gone wrong, and it has ominous implications for 401(k) plans. Corporations and Wall Street are in charge of the show. Predictions of worker capitalism have turned out to be just another fantasy. And as a consequence, the average American family continues to be faced with the need to look after itself by beating Wall Street at its own game.

PART FOUR

BEATING WALL STREET AT ITS OWN GAME

THE FUNDAMENTAL THESIS of this book is that a long-term reaction to the stock market exuberance of the 1990s will set the tone for the current decade. We have seen that the great stock market booms that ended in 1901, 1929, and 1966 were followed by prolonged periods of market stagnation or decline that lasted for at least twenty years, and we have given our reasons for believing that the early part of the current century will be no different.

That is why we have entitled this part of the book "Stillwater Investing." Investors will have to cope with an environment in which they will have to gear their strategy to a stillwater market: It will take a very long time indeed for broad market averages to significantly exceed the highs achieved in the first half of the millennial year 2000.

There is an approach to investing that can succeed in this new environment. A successful transition to the new era must begin, however, with stern determination to drown out the noise that emanates from Wall Street's house gurus and their disciples. Our guide details the major ways in which Wall Street assaults the mind of investors with a steady flow of opinion and reports designed to encapsulate arguments for why "now" is almost always a good time to buy stocks and a bad time to sell them. The attempt to seduce the investor into buying stocks shows up across the board, from the Orwellian language that Wall Street uses to financial reports designed to make corporate earnings look a lot better than they really are.

Freed of Wall Street's thrall, investors are ready to implement the positive program. It stresses the lessons of history. It depends on strategies that draw on the records of earlier periods of market stagnation to determine the appropriate prices at which to buy and sell stocks. It gives heavy weight to the argument that periods of overall stock market stagnation favor investments in high dividend stocks. It gives bonds, particularly U.S. Treasury bonds, whose yield is indexed to inflation, an important role. This approach will clearly identify periods in which stock market investing can be highly successful even in a still-water environment.

Chapter 9

Stillwater Investing: Drowning Out the Noise

It will not come as a surprise to those who have read this book that we became extremely skeptical about the stock market in early 1998. And the record of our investments will show that we pulled out of stocks early in the spring of that year, just before the Standard & Poor's 500 began to sputter. Our investment records will also show that we moved into bonds at that time. And a comparison of the returns to ten-year treasuries with the total return to investing in the S&P 500 Index shows that these bonds outperformed stocks in the ensuing four years. That is not to say that we have never made investment mistakes, because we certainly have. But in our defense, we have never made the mistake of taking what Wall Street says at its face value.

To us, the key to investment survival is drowning out the noise that comes from the Street on the cable financial channels, in the personal investment magazines, and, above all, from the brokerage houses themselves. In the circle of people that we know well, listening to Wall Street has often proved fatal. One couple who knew Abby Joseph Cohen and were dazzled by her media glitter sat by and watched the value of their investments fall by 20 percent in the year before the World Trade Center bombing. A close friend and neighbor, a hardworking fifty-eight-year-old physical therapist, saw the value of her portfolio fall by 25 percent in the twelve months following the March 2000 peak in the Nasdaq.

Instead of developing a healthy skepticism about Wall Street as a whole, she blamed the collapse in her portfolio on bad advice from the particular broker she was using. And her response was to change brokers. She had bought the popular line in 2001 that her portfolio needed "rebalancing," to use the word that was so prominent in Wall Street's advertising in the summer of 2001. Unfortunately, her redesigned portfolio fell steeply before the terrorist bombing on September 11, 2001. Another close friend was suckered by her broker into suddenly taking a high-tech flier in late 1999 that ended with the loss of about $75,000, a big chunk of her hard-earned savings. That is not to say that we feel smug. We don't. But it remains true that virtually every personal story about stock market woes that we have heard resulted from the same mistake: taking what brokers say seriously.

In contrast, the people we know who have steered clear of trouble in the millennial stock market decline were broad-gauged and knew that Wall Street's message is always designed to sell stocks. Indeed, the two people among our friends who did the best during the tech debacle are conditioned to ignore what brokers are saying. One, a man who had left the practice of corporate law to do human rights work, was extremely skeptical of the close bond between the Clinton administration and Wall Street and its twin act in cheering the market. In 1998, he took all of his money out of equities. The other, an ex-cop from upstate New York who later went to the University of Chicago business school and turned into an iconoclastic money manager, was extremely skeptical of the idea that the twenty-first-century corporation had devised ways of managing that put the "old-fashioned" business cycle to rest. His chief mantra is: "Only invest in an idea that is so strong that even the most incompetent manager in the world can't mess it up, because an incompetent manager is what you are almost certain to get." He is gloomy about the outlook for the next decade because "the new economy doesn't amount to much, and the old manufacturing economy in the United States has been allowed to all but disappear during the 1980s and 1990s." He gets his jollies mainly from selling short and has made so much in the market that the only money that he manages these days is his own.

It is important to realize that the "noise" that must be blocked out comes from sources that are harder to ignore than the cant that emanates from the Street itself. Subtle and pernicious deception also emanates from the great universities and research organizations. That is what makes a guide to "noise suppression" an essential element of investment success in what shapes up to be a difficult economic and financial decade for the United States.

That what Wall Street says must be treated with caution and skepticism was in vivid evidence on the morning of September 17, 2001, the day the markets reopened after the World Trade Center terrorism. The raw emotions as a result of the thousands of deaths—many of them Wall Street veterans—was real. Make no mistake about it. There was real heroism and real grief about those losses. There was a real coming together of those who worked in Lower Manhattan, and a patriotic feeling that everyone should pull together and keep the market afloat for all the world to see.

One problem was that the market was already in deep trouble, long before the awful events occurred. So, in effect, American families were being asked to keep their money in a marketplace that was already unsafe and deeply insecure before the terrorists came anywhere near the World Trade Center buildings. And while the top 20 percent of families had done extremely well in their 401(k) and other similar pension plans, a much higher percentage had barely made a dent in the amount of money they would need to accumulate in the not too distant future in order to keep a roof over their heads and pay their medical bills. This was the awful irony of the September 11 debacle. Families were being asked to put their lifelong savings in harm's way because bin Laden had attacked New York City. It seemed to have nothing to do with the reality that the market itself had been fading fast for well over a year, raising the most destabilizing prospect for the United States: the specter of millions of American families with little pension money.

A second problem was the persistence of what is a common practice in virtually every industry in the entire industrial world: trade puffery. It is a common practice for every industry to develop a vocabulary that works to "keep the truth from the children." That was evident on the morning of September 17. All the public stress was on the fact that Wall Street's systems were running well, on the beneficial effects of coordinated interest rate cuts by the Federal Reserve and the European Central Bank, and on the reassuring statistics showing that the U.S.

markets had fallen far less than those of Europe and Asia. But the private talk among the pros was focused on an entirely different and gloomier point. There was a sense that the terror had radically changed the market outlook.

The real feeling on the floor of the exchange was that the great stock market boom of the 1990s was fed by the peace dividend that flowed into the American economy after the end of the Cold War. That dividend, the pros seemed to be saying, helped the economy to recover quickly after the Gulf War and kept it moving during a decade when defense spending fell from 8 percent of GDP to 4 percent. The war on terror will obviously change those numbers, though it was obviously unclear on that dramatic day by how much it would do so. But there was widespread conviction on the floor that the end of the peace dividend would make it far harder for the market to go up.

Yet the pros are not free of delusions of their own. On the day that the market reopened, even some of the genuinely smart guys on Wall Street fell victim to American triumphalism. Edward Hyman Jr., president of International Strategy and Investment, drew comfort from numbers showing that the American market had declined by less on that day than the amount European markets had declined over the four days that followed the World Trade Center attack. On this basis, he concluded that the United States had sturdier markets than Europe.

That, of course, was possible. But an alternative explanation of the superior performance of Wall Street is more plausible. Up to September 11, the United States had proved relatively immune to attack from international terrorists. After that attack, there was recognition that the United States had entered a new war in which it had no experience. The same thing cannot be said of a continent that had seen Irish Republican Army bombings in London, Algerian attacks on France, and Basque assaults in Spain. The relative calm on Wall Street on the day the market reopened may not have reflected any superiority of the United States but rather a lack of experience with terrorism. It may indeed have been that Europe understood far better than the United States the somber, long-term implications of terrorist assault. American triumphalism has been a feature of Wall Street rhetoric throughout the 1990s. Yet on September 17, 2001, serious questions emerged on whether that triumphalism will prove to be justified by a new set of facts.

The Street's Orwellian Semantics

If thought corrupts language, language can also corrupt thought.

—George Orwell, "Politics and the English Language"

We believe that it is useful to compare the language of the Street with that of Big Brother in George Orwell's *1984*. This is so even though we have no reason to believe that Wall Street is morally or politically obtuse as compared to the rest of the United States. Rather, we have used this dark Orwellian parallel to drive home the unquestioned fact that the language of Wall Street is deeply deceptive and misleading. War may not be peace on Wall Street, as it was in Orwell's *1984*, but the semantics of the Street often make it seem that events are exactly the opposite of the words used to describe them. To us, the most Orwellian words on Wall Street are "correction," "volatility," "consolidation," and "capitulation." All are euphemisms, dangerous and deceptive ways of drawing attention away from what is really happening.

Wall Street's redefinition of the ordinary meaning of words makes it difficult to drown out the "noise." Wall Street almost always uses the word "correction" as a euphemism for decline. Correcting behavior always connotes something of a triumph for virtue in the recognition of past mistakes. It is worth reflecting, however, that ordinarily what is being corrected are the prices of stocks that have been driven up by those who have followed Wall Street's advice. Andrew Smithers, a brilliant British analyst, has never hesitated to come forth with honest forecasts that are obviously sometimes bearish. As we have noted, he once told us that he could make a lot more money being bullish than being right. And often in his career, being right simply meant forecasting a market decline in a way that could never be mistaken for some form of equivocation. In his book *The Great Crash,* John Kenneth Galbraith pointed out that 1930 and 1931 were characterized by one correction after another.

Wall Street, of course, has another euphemism for periods in which correction follows correction. When the market's attempts at rallies result in a series of stumbles, the euphemism becomes "consolidation." The euphemism appears to describe fairly long periods in which the market does nothing except "consolidating" a series of losses. "Consolidate" is obviously a solid word, appearing to connote the formation of a "base"—another euphemism—from which the market can again rise. The difference between "correction" and "consolidation" appears to be simply how many bad forecasts have been made in the past. Apparently, the market "corrects" after one over-optimistic forecast and "consolidates" after a series of over-optimistic forecasts.

"Corrections" and "consolidations" occur, mind you, even though, in Wall Street's tortured use of language, the decline did not occur in the first place. Instead of saying the market is declining, Wall Street often merely says that it has become "volatile." In years of following the market, we have seldom heard the Street mention the word "volatility" in periods when the market is rising. In the early months of 2001, the market staged a recovery from its decline in the preceding year. That recovery ended in April 2001, and the market, especially the Nasdaq, began to sink again. Market comment kept confusing the decline with something it called "volatility." Yet there are indexes that give a precise measure of the intraday and day-to-day volatility of the markets. The index that is most frequently used is the VIX. It is an ice-cold fact that that index was extremely low between April and September 2001. The truth is that the market was not volatile at all. It merely declined in a manner that was extremely steady by historical standards.

It obviously has plenty of competition, but our favorite euphemism is the word "capitulation." When the market defies other euphemisms and continues to decline, Wall Street calls on a military analogy as a sign that things are really getting serious. In a steeply sinking market, the Street begins to look for a situation in which anyone who has been thinking of selling actually does the foul deed. There is virtually no use of the word "capitulation" in the military lexicon that seems to connote that the unit, army, or country that has capitulated is, instead, laying the base for a comeback. The result of capitulation is, of course, a trip to a prisoner-of-war camp or to a peace that imposes severe penalties on the country that loses.

But not so on Wall Street. Here, capitulation means that all those who wish to sell have done it. The suggestion is that the supply of stocks at the prevailing price has shrunk to nothingness, leaving those who believe that the market will rise in total control of the situation. The implication is that the market will rise again. But as with "consolidation," it's perfectly possible that sellers still remain on the sidelines and will eventually drive the market down even further.

The semantics of Wall Street mean that the average investor faces many barriers in drowning out the "noise." The trick is to recognize the euphemisms and realize that they really belong in an Orwellian world, not the real world in which the average investor is trying to cope with a legion of problems—job loss, college expenses, and vanishing retirement funds.

Wall Street's Nickel Knowledge

University placement departments will tell you that by any objective standard, Wall Street attracts the best and the brightest of the graduates who want a career in business. Yet the advice that the Street gives to the average investor costs the average investor far more than it is worth. The record, in fact, shows that it is incredibly difficult for money managers to beat the market averages. The disturbing implication, of course, is that it is extremely important for the average investor to drown out the investment advice coming from even the most prestigious investment houses in the world.

After the debacle that afflicted the Nasdaq in the opening years of the decade, there was a tendency to blame conflicts of interest for bad advice. Two of the great stars created during the tech bubble, Mary Meeker of Morgan Stanley, and Henry Blodget, formerly of Merrill Lynch, were accused of trimming their recommendations so as to satisfy the investment-banking arms of their companies. The reasoning was that it was extremely costly for the research department of an investment house to issue a "sell" recommendation at the time that its investment banking department was floating a new issue of stock for the same company. And, in fact, during the heyday of the tech boom, investment bankers promised their potential clients that if given the investment-banking business, the firm would support the client company's stock.

Holes in the "Chinese Wall" that traditionally separated the investment-banking and research departments of the great brokerage houses unquestionably led to much overly bullish investment advice. The ethical breaches of the late 1990s were less flagrant and less odious than the insider-trading scandals of the 1980s, made famous by the character of Gordon Gekko in the movie *Wall Street*. But they nevertheless represent a stain on Wall Street's reputation that will be hard to live down.

Yet no investor should be under the illusion that bad investment advice results from questionable acts by dishonest people. Bad advice does not exist merely in the dark corners of the Street. Rather, it is endemic to the system and emanates from the most honest investment managers on a regular basis.

Bad investment advice is not confined to the conflicted analysts who work on the "sell" side of the business and are under pressure from their firms' investment bankers. It is also chronic among analysts and money managers who work on the "buy" side of the business. Analysts and money managers who work for mutual funds, pension funds, and the like earn their livings purely from making money for their clients. They have no incentive to recommend or buy a stock to satisfy investment bankers.

Yet there are reams of evidence that even the most honest and objective of the pros consistently underperform the stock market. The average money manager does not beat the market but rather produces results that are inferior to those produced by the basic stock market indicators. In the last five years of the 1990s, the average equity mutual fund earned 19 percent a year—a rate at which $10,000 grows into nearly $24,000, but relative to the Standard & Poor's 500 stock index, that performance was characterized by *BusinessWeek* as "woeful." An index investor would have $35,000—a 28.5-percent compound average return. In all, just 7 percent of all equity funds beat the S&P in the last five years of the 1990s.

This underperformance is sometimes concealed from the public because virtually every kind of market does produce money managers who, for a time, seem to be stars. For many years, Fidelity Magellan, which was first under the management of Peter Lynch and then under Jeffrey Vinik, outperformed the majority of mutual funds and the market itself. Yet Magellan fell on its face in the mid-1990s because it did not climb aboard the tech bandwagon. In the late 1990s, the Janus Fund was a huge star because its money was concentrated in tech, but it underperformed woefully in the tech decline of 2000. The lesson for the average investor is to realize that there is no consistent performance in the mutual fund business, or in other money-managememt businesses, for that matter. The odds are strong that last year's money management hero will be next year's loser.

The reasons that bright, well-trained analysts and money managers can't beat the market averages are rather like Winston Churchill's description of the Soviet Union: "an enigma wrapped in a mystery, wrapped in a puzzle." For that reason, the question has intrigued some of the top minds in the academic world.

The hunt for an explanation of this systemic failure on Wall Street had its first major success at the University of Chicago. That institution houses the Cowles Foundation, which is the nation's historic center of econometric research, the branch of economics that uses sophisticated statistical techniques to analyze economic problems. Early in its history, the Cowles Foundation compiled a careful record of stock market performance that went back all the way to 1803. We have already met that record in the work of Professor Jeremy Siegel. But as a simple accident of birth, he came to use that record late.

The original and most famous analysis of the Cowles numbers was conducted by Fisher Black and Eugene Fama in the late 1940s. In studying stock market movements over a long period of time, they concluded, in words that had become famous, that the stock market is "a random walk." By this, they meant that movements in stock prices, be they second-to-second or year-to-year, looked very much as if they had been produced by chance. To a statistician, this meant that, for example, you would do better in forecasting the price of say, General Electric, by pulling numbered Ping-Pong balls out of a cage than if you studied the past movements in the price of GE stock, or anything else, for that matter.

Their work gradually became famous. Such remarks as "you can do better" in selecting stocks by throwing darts at the stock market tables in the *Wall Street Journal* than you could through careful analysis are often heard. The vision was solidified in the academic mind by those who pointed out that a monkey with a dartboard could outperform the brightest and best-trained analyst.

Random walks have always been controversial within the academic community itself. The random walk theory baffled such analysts as Professor Anthony Loo of MIT, who said that it defied his belief that a smart person who worked extremely hard could not earn his pay through studying stock market patterns.

Although the random walk theory remains controversial in the academic community, the average investor would be smart to take it seriously. Burton G. Malkiel, a former member of the President's Council of Economic Advisers, argues that in a lifetime of experience, he has never been able to find anyone who can consistently beat the market.

The academic world has worked hard to find out why Wall Street looks very much like a random walk. Its reasoning points to a theory called "perfect information." The idea is that all publicly available information is incorporated in the price of a stock at a given moment of time. And if that's true, it means that stock prices can only be moved by events that are unexpected and that are unknown to any specific analyst before they are known to everyone else. It is important to notice that the random walk theory does not preclude the possibility that those who possess inside information that is not generally available can make gobs of money. That's the way Gordon Gekko made his. But what Gordon Gekko did was, and is, illegal.

The possibility exists that Wall Street analysts, in their interviews of company executives or by carefully scrutinizing company books, can come up with pieces of information that are not widely known to the public. That is certainly the impression that companies who employ these analysts like to give to their clients. But the possibility that the average investor can benefit from bits of early information is severely limited by the new financial disclosure rules that were imposed on Wall Street by the Securities and Exchange Commission (SEC) in early 2001. These rules forced companies to disclose their results to everyone at the same time. In 2001, these rules also led to the pattern of early warnings of earnings disappointments that so disturbed the markets in the months before earnings were actually reported. So, even if the random walk theory is not exactly true, the possibility of beating the market by listening to what brokers say virtually vanished from Wall Street in the opening months of that year. Some have argued that the new financial disclosure rules are hurting the investor by increasing uncertainty. However, we regard them as highly desirable, simply because they reduce the chances that the average investor can fall victim to those with inside information. That surely improves the position of the small investor. Because investors of that type do not generate huge commissions for brokerage houses, there is almost no chance that they would be the ones to get the information quickly enough to benefit. Instead, they are far more likely to be suckers, selling to rich investors at too low a price or buying from them at too high a price.

Random walk analysis makes it seem as though the task of making money in the stock market is impossible. But this is, as we will see in the positive rules discussed in the next chapter, anything but true. In fact, the very data that Fisher Black and Eugene Fama used to develop the theory of the random walk does open up huge possibilities of success for the family investor. The trick is to understand the implications of market history. They tell the investor when price-earnings ratios are so high as to virtually demand that the investor sell stocks and when they are so low so as to make stock investment an excellent bet.

Drown the Water Hog: Creative Accounting

In early spring of 2000, Anne Colamosca was asked to do a piece for the *Columbia Journalism Review,* the major publication of the Columbia University School of Journalism, about the ethics of journalists taking stock options as a part of their pay compensation. The concern of the *Review*'s editors was that any journalists who accepted options became directly dependent for their livelihood on the profits of the publication they worked for.

In the end, Anne's piece, "The Options Option," concluded that accepting options as compensation did not compromise the ethics of the journalists to whom they were awarded. That, indeed, was the same conclusion that was reached by the *New York Times,* which in December 1999 sent 143 editorial employees e-mails informing them that they would be receiving stock options in the company. This represented a radical departure for an organization that, like most traditional media companies, had in the past confined its list of newsroom optioneers mostly to people at the top of the editorial pyramid. "If you look at the incredible profits that media companies have made over the last several years, it's clear to me that most journalists are still vastly underpaid," said Marshall Loeb, former top editor at *Fortune, Money,* and the *Columbia Journalism Review.* And Gene Roberts, a former *New York Times* managing editor who now teaches at the University of Maryland School of Journalism observed, "A handful of editors have gotten stock options for years. I never noticed that having stock options changed the way these editors covered the news."

Roberts is right in arguing that options do not change the way that journalists do their job. But it does not get around the real problem that options pose for the average investor: Their grant promotes a kind of "creative accounting" that results in giving a false and overly bullish picture of the true revenues and profits of the companies that grant them.

Central to the argument of this book is an analysis of the size of the pool of profits that underlies the value of stocks. The water hog plants itself in the middle of the African river and mechanically eats up everything that comes within the range of its massive bite. But its appetite is never really sated. When the corporate economy is looked at from that point of view, it becomes clear that any move by high corporate executives to expand the share of the profits pool that accrues to them hurts the average investor and undermines the argument that the stock market is an effective vehicle for insuring the financial future of the American family.

In all that was written and celebrated about stock options during the great boom of the 1990s, the most important fact was obscured from the average investor. When the corporation grants stock options and the options are sold at a profit by employees, the company gets a huge tax break. When employees exercise the option, they discover that they must pay the regular income tax on the money they receive from the sale of the stock. And what most investors do not realize is that the tax withheld from the proceeds of the sale can be counted as a credit against the tax that the corporation pays. That means, of course, that the higher the market goes and the more options that are exercised, the lower the corporation's tax bill becomes. The other side of the coin, of course, is that the more options that get exercised, the greater the number of shares that the corporations have outstanding. And that, of course, means that the value of the shares in the hands of ordinary investors is diluted. In a simple example, a corporation has 1 million shares outstanding before options are granted. After, say, options on 100,000 shares are exercised, it has 1,100,000 shares outstanding. That means, of course, that the profits of the company must be stretched over more shares, and that in turn reduces earnings per share for the average investor who is holding the company stock. Options were therefore a good deal for a company's employee during the great boom, but they undermined the value of the shares in the hands of the ordinary investor. Hard as it is to believe, companies granted their employees options and in so doing ripped off their shareholders.

Those with first dibs on the way income is generated by a corporation are hardly the members of the average American family; on the contrary, decisions that affect the distribution of the corporation's income are vested by law in boards of directors and in practice in the executives of the corporations themselves. A real clue to what went on during the great prosperity of the 1990s was provided by a rather famous *BusinessWeek* story that demonstrated that overwhelmingly, corporations were giving their top executives huge increases in pay and stock options that far exceeded in size the wages and other benefits that were accruing to average workers. In 1998, thanks to a pay structure that "linked most executive compensation to the stock market through huge option grants, the head honcho at a large public company made an average $10.6 million," a "36 percent hike over 1997—and an astounding 442 percent increase over the average paycheck of $2 million pocketed in 1990." That 36 percent raise "compares to 2.7 percent for the average blue-collar worker; one-tenth of a percentage point above 1997's salary take. White-collar workers got 3.9 percent." To put it mildly, at this most basic level, the share of the profits pool going to the average family was diminished by the huge financial hauls taken in by top corporate executives. In a story for *Forbes* magazine, written before she moved over to the *New York Times,* Gretchen Morgensen analyzed the overstatement in earnings of 100 companies that resulted from issuing options in large numbers. She concluded that in 1995, the reported earnings of these companies were 30 percent higher than they would have been if the options had not been granted in that year. Her conclusion was based on a study by Smithers & Co.

Some companies play the options game in a relatively straightforward way. Once they determine the strike price at which the option can be exercised, they maintain that price at its original level for as long as the option lasts. Other companies, however, load the options deck. Should the market price of the stock decline, these companies tend to issue new options whose strike price is lower than that of the options originally issued. In cases like this, of course, executives who are compensated with options do not bear the same risk inherent in a falling market as does the general investing public. This options game bears a characteristic that is a principal focus of this book. When the game turns averse to the establishment, the rules of the game change. That is because those with first dibs on the stock market are not you, even if you are a typical worker, or even if you are a middle manager, a rich doctor, a successful lawyer, or even a creative small businessperson. Decisions on how much stock to issue and how to divide it up are inherent in the corporate establishment.

The options game is the most flagrant example of how the stock market is stacked against the average investor, but it is not the most insidious. That honor goes to the subtle campaign that has been waged by the corporation to induce workers to accept lower wage increases in exchange for bonus pay that depends on how well the company is doing. When business is strong, this is obviously an appealing argument. But should business conditions deteriorate, the effect is to tilt the economy in a way that allows the profits pool to grow at the expense of the rate of wage increase. This is obviously a great game from the corporation's point of view. Remember that wages account for some 65 percent of corporate revenues and pre-tax profits for only about 10 percent So any game that can induce workers to accept a 1 percent decline in the corporate wage bill balloons profits. Suppose, for example, the case of a corporation with $100 million in revenues that pays some $65 million in employee compensation. Now, further suppose that it manages to talk its employees into accepting only $64 million in wages. That is a mere 1.5 percent reduction in wages. But because profits are only about $10 million, that same million-dollar reduction in wages results in a 10 percent increase in profits. The great allure of a low wage policy and of an attempt to induce employees to accept bonus compensation instead of regular wages becomes apparent. And remember, because of the way stock options and other forms of incentive compensation are stacked in the favor of top executives, it is undoubtedly a long-term losing game for the individual employee.

It is perfectly true that the average worker did not seem to be disadvantaged during the great boom. Sure, between 1981 and the end of the century, wages grew at only three-fourths the rate at which profits grew. But at the same time, employment rose and unemployment fell. And because inflation was low, the purchasing power of wages seemed to increase.

But this appeared to be offset by what seemed to be a wonderful development. More and more employees began to get bonuses, most often in the form of stock options. Supervisory and professional employees got the lion's share of the options. According to Hewitt Associates, 10.8 percent of the compensation of managers and professionals was profits-based in 2001, up from 3.8 percent in 1991. Although ordinary employees also received bonuses, the fact is that the bonuses of the bosses rose far faster than those of average employees, even when it was at the expense of the size of the profit pool available to the ordinary stockholders in the corporation.

It should be realized, of course, that variable compensation tied to profits is one of those places where the rule of "not-so-easy come, easy go" applies. It took a period of extraordinary profitability and tight labor markets to induce companies to let their employees take a peek at profits through their paychecks. But when profitability began to fall in 2000, this compensation showed signs of vanishing. This is a classic example of our fundamental rule that when they begin to pinch the established interests, benefits to ordinary families will be taken away.

Disturbing as the trend toward making the employee more and more dependent on the size of the profit pool may be, it is not the most chilling aspect of the assault on the security of the average family. That honor goes to "creative accounting"—the trend toward financial machinations that have generated a phony impression of how fast profits are growing. In some sense, at least, the evidence for phony profits is arcane. But it does become accessible in the "biographies" of the great American corporations in the past two decades. One accessible story is what happened at IBM in the years after it purchased Lotus in 1995.

First, the role of "special charges." Big Blue purchased Lotus for $3.2 billion in cash. Normally, when one company acquires the assets of another company, it must depreciate the purchase price over a long period of time. That results in a need to subtract the cost of the purchase in even amounts over, say, ten years. But when IBM bought Lotus, it adopted a form of creative accounting that allowed it to compress the cost into the first few years after the purchase was made. The effect, of course, was for IBM to be able to infuse the record of its profits growth with a false glow of prosperity. In effect, IBM acted so as to reduce its profits in the early years, while increasing them later on. That, of course, meant that it hiked the rate at which its profits were growing.

Here is how it worked. IBM's goal was to quickly charge off the cost of the Lotus purchase in order to boost the long-term rate of profits growth that it reported to Wall Street. The company hired professional appraisers, who assigned $1.84 billion of the purchase price to an asset classification called "software technology under development." That turned $1.84 billion into what was, in effect, a one-time current expense that did not have to be depreciated. IBM could thus immediately wipe off the balance sheet a large part of the cost of buying Lotus. In addition, another $290 million was charged off over the next two years. The net effect was to vaporize 67 percent of the purchase price of Lotus, reducing the need to depreciate two-thirds of the cost of Lotus and subtract the depreciation from earnings for a sustained period. The effect, of course, was to increase reported earnings way above what they had actually been. There was nothing illegal about this. It was a maneuver that had become commonplace in the American corporate world and was sanctioned both by the SEC and the accounting profession's famed Financial Accounting Standards Board, or FASBE.

This would never have been done before the great stock market boom of the 1990s. The immediate expensing of a large part of the purchase price of Lotus reduced the book value of IBM. In earlier times, that would have made it appear as a dangerous financial venture, and one not to be undertaken lightly. But that changed in the 1990s, when Wall Street and investors began to notice that mergers that seemed to involve strange new accounting techniques helped rather than hurt the price of the acquiring company's stock. It, of course, would have warmed the heart of the accountant who is a central character in the Broadway smash musical, *The Producers*. He, after all, was the inventor of the term "creative accounting."

That was not the end, but only the beginning, of creative accounting at IBM. In addition to using special charges to make depreciation vanish, IBM aggressively repurchased hundreds of thousands of its own shares many times, expending sums well in excess of its reported quarterly earnings. These stock buybacks, according to calculations by Charles Parlato, reduced the number of shares outstanding by approximately 20 percent between 1990 and 1998. Parlato's calculations indicate that these maneuvers allowed IBM to report 1998 earnings per share at 20 percent above what they should have been. Between January 1990 and the fall quarter of 1999, the investment return to IBM shareholders increased by some 500 percent. This indeed is a wonderful performance, but the effect was to decrease the book value of IBM by 45 percent. At the same time, its dividend yield decreased by 64 percent.

The impact of these maneuvers on IBM's reported earnings was staggering. According to Parlato's calculation, IBM's earnings per share in

1998 would have been approximately $1.69, or 48 percent below the reported $3.29. The price-earnings ratio at the end of 1998 would have been approximately 55, rather than 28. And most dramatically, IBM's earnings per share would have fallen from $2.63 in 1990 to $1.69 in 1998, a 36 percent decline. These numbers, as Parlato says "speak for themselves."

They also speak for most of America's giant corporations. Parlato's calculations, for example, are that International Paper boosted its 1998 earnings per share by approximately 233 percent using maneuvers similar to those of IBM; U.S. Steel boosted earnings by 204 percent; GM, by 104 percent; Kodak, by 46 percent; Corning, by 38 percent; Allied Signal, by 36 percent; and AT&T, by 34 percent.

These are companies that have used both creative accounting and buybacks to enhance earnings per share. But Parlato also has made some calculations for companies that have focused mainly on stock buybacks to boost earnings per share. These include The Limited, which boosted earnings by 45 percent; Schering-Plough, by 19 percent; Briggs & Stratton, by 17 percent; and Becton, Dickson by 15 percent.

The mergers/write-offs/buybacks game that has been prevalent in the later years of the great Clinton bull market will have devastating consequences. It has, of course, had the effect of pushing reported earnings growth above the realistic levels that would have prevailed under sound accounting practices. But it has also given price-earnings ratios the appearance of being lower than they actually are.

It is also critical to realize that the new valuations game was played not only among new economy companies but also by old economy companies. Even though these companies have not been particularly technologically creative, their accounting maneuvers have boosted the growth of earnings per share far beyond where traditional accounting methods would place them. The important consequence is to undermine the idea that unrealistic valuations are confined to high-tech companies so that average investors can protect themselves by rotating into old economy companies. This has, in fact, been conventional investment advice, peddled endlessly by so-called value managers on the financial airwaves for the past ten years. But just as this advice has been useless and counterproductive during the bull market, so it will also prove grossly misleading over the next decade.

Value investing has become a joke because it has been undermined by "creative accounting." The fact that the only way many companies were creative during the boom was by manipulating their books makes things incredibly more dangerous in any bear market that persists over the next decade.

Investors may have saved money if they quickly rotated from tech stocks into old economy stocks in the wake of the Nasdaq crash that started in March 2000. But that rotation is no guarantee of safety. The financial machinations in the old economy are certain to take a toll on old economy stock prices over the next decade. Booms do not only create wealth, they create problems.

Don't Be Gulled by Analysts

In and of itself, the overstatement of the rate of earnings growth through the use of creative accounting would have left the average investor with a horrendous problem in assessing the prospects for this difficult new decade. Unfortunately, however, it is only half of the problem that emerged during the boom of the 1990s. Equally troubling was the emergence of a problem that can be described as "the new metrics." The idea here was that companies had taken on a value that simply could not be measured by the standard old-fashioned price-earnings ratios that had been used for decades.

This problem emerged in its most ridiculous form in statements analysts were making about the stocks of new economy tech companies that were consistently losing, not making, money. For these companies, it became fashionable for analysts to use valuations based on the rate of growth of revenues, rather than of earnings. It was almost as if the old saying "The hell with the profits, look at the turnover" had come to life. Webvan.com, a San Francisco company that delivered groceries to your door, plunged from 25 in December 1999 to virtually zero in December 2001. It turned out, of course, that their costs drove them to the wall in an industry where supermarket chains like the West Coast Safeway were operating on margins that have always been paper thin, often 1 to 2 percent of sales. These new metrics proliferated during the boom and left many who believed that they were reflecting reality far poorer at the end of the boom than at the beginning.

When companies actually were making money and experiencing rapid profits growth, the metrics really became bizarre. As the market reached its frenzy in the second half of the 1990s, a set of books appeared promising virtually infinite wealth to anyone who invested in stocks. The idea was that a new economy justified price-earnings ratios that were stratospheric by historical standards.

Dow 36,000, by James K. Glassman and Kevin A. Hassett went even further. The essential argument of their book is that stocks are a safer investment than bonds. The reason, they said, is that whereas the returns on a bond are fixed, the dividends on a stock, paltry as they were at the end of the 1990s, would continue to grow. What if a company pays no dividends à la Microsoft? Not to worry, say Glassman and Hassett. What Bill Gates has in mind—yes, that's the argument—is building up the value of his company so he can sell it some day. That would indeed be news to Bill Gates, who seems obsessed with keeping his company and nourishing its growth rate, while avoiding dividend payments to stockholders like the plague. Indeed, dividends were pooh-poohed as antique relics of another age throughout the 1990s both by Wall Street and, often, the financial press. The disdain for dividends resulted from a faith that a company that reinvested its profits would fare far better than one that looked after the maiden aunt in the 1950s.

The Glassman-Hassett book took Wall Street by storm because it seemed to be a respectable, old-fashioned kind of argument that nevertheless justified ridiculous stock prices. Glassman, in fact, became the Henry Kissinger of the investment world, collecting as much as $30,000 for his speeches. Even Alan Greenspan told Congress that the Dow 36,000 argument could not "be dismissed out of hand."

Obviously, Glassman and Hassett believed that the rise in stock prices in the great bull market of the 1980s and 1990s did not go far enough. Their book came out in late 1999, just in time for its sales to benefit from the millennial moonbeams. At that time, the p/e on the Dow Jones was 30. Glassman and Hassett said it should have been three to four times the prevailing p/e at that time, between 90 and 120. That, mind you, was not a statement about how p/e's would grow. It was a statement of what p/e's rationally ought to have been in 1999, according to them. So, all you have to do is split the difference between three and four and you get their Dow 36,000 figure (three times the 12,000 level that the Dow had approximately achieved at the end of 1999). It is worth stressing that Dow 36,000 was not a forecast. It was a statement of what the market was worth in the second half of 1999. The authors frequently use the term "perfectly rational price" (PRP) in their book. The Dow's PRP, they assert, was 36,000 in 1999.

But is a stock really a safer investment than a bond? There are, to put it mildly, very strong reasons for doubt. The Glassman-Hassett argument is based on the notion that many companies show a consistent record of paying dividends and that the amount of dividends paid has steadily increased through time. Their book is full of ritual worship of a group of companies that they say meet this characteristic—above all, General Electric, but also Coca-Cola. Yet the prices of these companies' stocks fell substantially in the market decline that started in the spring of 2000. A similar fate can befall any company. Missing, of course, from the Dow 36,000 analysis are the companies, once included in the Dow Jones Average, that through bad luck or bad management, had gone out of existence or had disappeared, including twenty-nine of the thirty stocks that were in the Dow Jones Industrial Average in 1929.

On the day following the congressional testimony in which Greenspan said that the Glassman-Hassett argument could not be ignored, the Dow fell over 250 points. Still, it wasn't that one-day market drop that put the monkey on the back of the American Enterprise Institute's dynamic duo. It was, instead, a sharp critique of their analysis by the Wharton School's Jeremy Siegel that appeared in the *Wall Street Journal*. What gave the critique weight was that Glassman and Hassett based much of their argument on data derived from Siegel's book *Stocks for the Long Run*. Yet, Siegel argued that his data did not support Glassman and Hassett. "It is wrong to say that stocks are underpriced at current levels." And he argued that their implied assertion that the Dow was already worth 36,000 at the end of 1999 was patently ridiculous.

Turning a Deaf Ear to the Street's Gurus

A few days after the World Trade Center calamity, word on the financial cable shows from those on the Street was that the entire market had just been on the verge of turning upward. The intrinsic message was that the gurus would have ultimately been proven correct about their optimistic year-end forecasts if it hadn't been for those nasty terrorists. Out of the anger, sadness, and fear also emerged another strong emotion, in some ways the most powerful of all. It was "cover your ass" week for everyone on Wall Street who had been saying that the market was bottoming, even though earnings forecasts and economic statistics were pointing to continued economic weakness. Despite the circumstances, the rush to rationalize bad forecasts is a common phenomenon among the Street's economists and analysts. And for most, it works well. Few analysts or economists are ever fired, unless it is for consistently bearish forecasts.

But in virtually every era, there are a few gurus who rise to such prominence that they can't crawl off bad forecasts easily. These are the voices that rise above the cacophony and become famous, idols of the financial press, and objects of strong attachment for many investors. That was the role of Goldman Sachs's Abby Joseph Cohen in the 1990s, and of Henry Kaufman, then of Salomon Brothers, in the 1980s.

The danger to individual investors is that they will form a passionate attachment to one of these temporarily compelling figures. Yet the record of any one of them will show that their success comes not from any consistent ability to forecast the market, but rather from a talent for catching the particular temper of a particular time in the market. Kaufman was deemed a genius in the days when interest rates were rising and he continued to forecast higher rates long after they began to fall. Cohen was the apostle of sound economic fundamentals and rapidly rising earnings per share. But her star fell after the market reached its peak in early 2000.

When these market gods stumble, they fall hard. The press has a way of turning on them. This would do no damage to the individual investor in and of itself. But it is important for the investor to realize that the great gurus are the products of a particular era, not of a continuing ability to correctly forecast the market. Indeed, a good rule for the investor is to begin to suspect that the odds favor a market or markets that move in the opposite direction to which the guru is pointing.

Beware the "No Business" Meeting

Some of the most dangerous noises come out of what John Kenneth Galbraith has called "the no business meeting." In times of difficulty, government often calls on business leaders for what it calls "advice." There is no evidence that anything useful comes out of the conclaves of top business leaders that appear on the scene at those times.

On October 3, 2001, President George W. Bush flew to New York. He was scheduled to visit a school and to return to the site of the World Trade Center cataclysm. But the mission that received the most attention was a meeting with what the White House stressed was a group of the absolutely most important chief executive officers in the land, including the heads of Xerox, American Express, and AOL Time Warner. The White House announced that the purpose of the meeting was to seek input for the post–World Trade Center economic stimulus package to aid the economy.

But the real agenda was the classic "no business meeting" ploy, that is, to shore up business and consumer confidence by reinforcing the economic message emanating from Washington: "shop till bin Laden drops." It is not to deny the grave threats posed to the economy by the attack on the World Trade Center to say that the average investor should ignore the messages, subliminal or otherwise, that come out of these meetings. Again, the fallacy of composition applies. There is no doubt that the economy would have been better off if the American public as a whole had gone on a shopping spree. But for any individual family, it could have been disastrous advice. Emptying the family coffer is not exactly a smart thing to do when the unemployment rate is rising and the economic future is fraught with uncertainty.

The "no business meeting" was a feature of the crash of 1929. Leader after leader, from President Hoover to Secretary of the Treasury Mellon to the most famed economist of the day, Yale's Irving Fisher, repeated the same theme, over and over again: The fundamental condition of the American economy is sound. That message may have contributed to some stock market rallies in 1930, but it left the investor exposed to the disasters of 1931, when the stock market crashed once again and the nation's banks closed.

It is important that the average investor remember the real lesson of "no business" meetings. When they occur, something is really wrong with the economy and caution is the order of the day.

Chapter 10

Stillwater Investing:
The Positive Program

Bill Wolman spent six years at *BusinessWeek* before he attempted his first story on the stock market. Before that, he wrote strictly about economics. But in January 1966, the Dow Jones Industrial Average began flirting with the 1000 level. It was, in fact, a period that had very much the same feel as the opening months of the year 2000. The economy had grown very rapidly in the first half of the 1960s, just as it had between 1995 and 1999. It was the era of the "new economics"—the belief that during the Kennedy years, government had discovered something new: how to manage fiscal policy in a way that keeps the economy growing at a steady rate. In those days, the "new economics" played the same role in stock market thinking that the "new economy" played in the second half of the 1990s. And in those days, Bill was a "true believer" that John Fitzgerald Kennedy and Lyndon Baines Johnson had, indeed, found a new way to perpetuate prosperity.

Emboldened by his convictions, he wrote a story in the January 26, 1966, issue of *BusinessWeek,* entitled "Stocks Near Their Own Millennium." The Dow did crack the 1000 level on an intraday basis in July of that year, and moved slightly above it for a while in 1977. But it took sixteen years, until 1982, for the Dow to decisively move above 1000 and make Bill's 1966 prediction come true. And Bill has not forgotten that long-term lesson.

His mistake was a failure to block out the noise coming from Wall Street and concentrate instead on the history of stock prices itself. Had he done so, the story that he wrote in 1966 would have been genuinely useful to his readers. It would have pointed out that peaks in price-earnings ratios of the kind that was forming in 1966 would have been followed by long periods of market stagnation. It would then have gone on to argue that investment success in the coming years would require a radical change in strategy from the one that worked during the preceding market boom.

That recommendation for change, which would have worked so well in the mid-1960s, is even more pertinent in the opening decade of the new millennium. By the spring of 2001, price-earnings ratios had risen to even more extreme levels, and political, economic, and cultural trends had produced an environment in which Americans were even more prone to an exaggerated optimism about the economic future. For this reason, we, in fact, believe that the postmillennial decade is showing signs of sharing some critical characteristics with the 1930s: worldwide excess capacity; a dearth of truly profitable new investment opportunities; and the prospect of slow growth for all the major developed countries. This all requires an approach to investing that will put money decisions on more sober and realistic grounds.

Providing the best guide to the new investment terrain begins with answering this key question: What is the likely rate of return to stock market investment over the coming decade? And the best answer to that question comes from the record of the market during the earlier periods of stagnation: the decades following the 1901, 1929, and 1966 peaks in the market.

Fortunately, the strategies needed to apply the lessons of history to stock market decisions are neither complex nor fancy. They are, instead, simple and straightforward. Three things will really matter: Investors should buy stocks only when valuations fall to levels history suggests are safe; investors must aim at income as well as capital gains; and they must seek ways of keeping the amount of money that they hand over to Wall Street for its services to an absolute minimum. These three principles, and only these, will provide a reasonable chance for investment success.

Simple though these ideas may be, they represent a radical departure from the investment strategy recommended by Wall Street. The Street's gurus are hooked on the idea of asset allocation. They will almost never suggest that there are times when investors should totally ban stocks from their portfolios. It is always appropriate, they say, to keep a proportion of your money in stocks, usually more than 50 percent. That strategy works only during the relatively short periods when the market is in a sustained rise. It would not have worked well in the sixty years of the twentieth century that consisted of three long periods during which the market was stagnant.

In these periods of stagnation, which we believe will include the postmillennial decade, average investors must think of bonds or cash as the place to keep their money most of the time. They should depart from this rule only when p/e's are really low. Cash is not king only in very bad markets. Cash is also king in stagnant markets. That is the fundamental rule that should guide investments in the decade that lies ahead.

The Postmillennial Stock Market

The key to the longer term outlook for the postmillennial decade lies in the lessons drawn from the behavior of stock prices in the post-bubble markets of the past. It should first be stressed that king-sized bubbles in the economy are rare events. The bubble that burst in the early spring of 2000, as we saw in Chapter 2, was preceded by three earlier bubbles, the peaks of 1901, 1929, and 1966.

An outstanding characteristic of the major bubbles of the twentieth century is that they turned into clouds casting a very long and gloomy shadow, leading to subdued markets for years to come. As we saw in Chapter 2, the total inflation-adjusted return to stock investment including both dividends and capital gains was −.02 percent in the twenty years following the 1901 peak. It was .04 percent in the two decades following 1929, and 1.9 percent in the twenty years following 1966. We believe that returns that are in, or slightly above, that kind of zone are the best assumption that investors can make for the years ahead.

Our principal reasons for expecting a stillwater market in the postmillennial decade were made clear in this book in Part 2, "The Lessons of History." Our essential finding was that just as the 1990s resembled the

1920s, the postmillennial decade will represent the brave new world's version of the 1930s. In economic terms, this means that overall economic growth will be slow, inflation will be subdued, and profits will be under pressure. This is the fundamental economic outlook.

The noise coming out of Wall Street will seek to tell you that this is an antiquated point of view that ignores basic changes in America's "new economy." To begin with, they say, the information revolution has a dynamism that has never been seen before. To this we respond that the "new economy" of the 1980s and 1990s is but one of a series of "new economies" that have transformed the industrial world for centuries, going back to the origins of modern capitalism in the Netherlands in the fifteenth century. The high period of each of these technological revolutions has always led to rapid growth, particularly in the countries where they have been centered. But the history of these periods is that the rapid economic growth has always given way to a slowdown that lasts until technology regathers its momentum, creating profitable investment opportunities once again. And, as we showed in Part 2, the investment binge of the late 1990s shared many characteristics with the investment binge of the late 1920s. For these reasons, we find that there is nothing in the technology argument that warrants the belief that the stock market will put on a better long-term performance in the wake of the 2000 bubble than in the wake of other stock market bubbles of the twentieth century.

The possibility that economic policy officials have learned to better manage the economy must be taken more seriously as an argument that the post-2000 bubble stock market will perform better than it did following earlier bubbles. The record does show that rates of return in the post-1929 market were better than those following 1901 and that those following 1966 were better than those following 1929. And we grant that those modest improvements are a testament that, largely due to the work of John Maynard Keynes in the 1920s and 1930s on the capitalist left and of Milton Friedman in the 1950s and 1960s on the capitalist right, economic policy has been better able to contain the extremes of the business cycle.

Yet we nevertheless believe that there will be forces at work in the postmillennial decade that are likely to hold the real return to stocks close to the 1.9 percent figure that prevailed in the years following the 1966 bubble peak.

The demographic destiny of the United States is one of those forces. Most economists have attributed the superior growth record of the United States in the 1990s to technological leadership. We are not inclined to deny the validity of this argument. But it is also worth noting that demographics have also played a role. Compare the United States, the European Economic Community, and Japan. Thanks largely to immigration, the United States had the youngest population profile and grew the fastest. Japan, with the oldest population profile, grew the most slowly. The European community was in the middle, both in population age and economic growth. The evidence is that an aging population retards economic growth.

The impact of an aging population on growth is likely to be severe in the United States over the coming decade. The reason this is so lies in the findings on the history of social policy laid out in this book in Part 3, "The Elusive Search for Family Security." The failures of social policy in the past will require major changes in Social Security, private pension policies, and health-care policies in the United States in the coming decade, changes that will put extreme pressure on the budget. The events of September 11 focused Washington's attention on the war on terrorism and homeland defense, allowing Washington, particularly its Republican administration, to deflect attention from what ought to be called the demographic budget crisis. Yet as the costs of the war on terrorism became apparent and the surplus vanished in the federal budget, long-term interest rates, vital to the cost of housing and autos, actually rose in the second half of 2001. There is simply no way that the United States will be able to avoid the cost of past social neglect. And the implication is that the stock market will have to live with the negative effects of relatively high long-term interest rates in the post-millennial decades. It is therefore virtually inevitable that the need for social policy repair will be a drag on the stock market in the postmillennial decade.

An equally needed repair in accounting standards will also cause problems for the stock market. Accounting seems far away from Social Security and Medicare. But the boom years of the 1980s and 1990s led to a walk on the wild side in the way in which corporate earnings were reported. Enron was unquestionably an extreme case. Yet throughout corporate America, as we saw in Chapter 9, companies found new ways to use creative accounting to hype the earnings numbers that they reported to investors.

The extent to which creative accounting led to earnings hype in the boom years is as hard to understand as the reasons they were able to get away with it. The companies in the Standard & Poor's 500 Index, as it were, set the standard for the way in which Wall Street perceives the nation's corporate landscape. Figure 10.1 compares earnings growth in the 1990s as measured by total earnings per share of the companies included in the S&P 500 with the growth in economic profits as reported in the U.S. government's national income accounts. The first is a measure of accounting profits, subject to manipulation through the use of creative accounting techniques. The government's figures are sterner, much closer to the result that would have been achieved if the conservative Generally Accepted Accounting Principles (GAAP) had been used to report profits.

The difference between the growth of profits in the 1990s as reported in the S&P numbers and those reported in the government numbers are a decade-long testament to the power of creative accounting, the complicity of Wall Street security analysts, and the weakness of regulators, for as Figure 10.1 shows, accounting profits grew roughly twice as fast as economic profits in the 1990s.

Doubts about the validity of reported accounting profits began to have serious effects as soon as the market began its retreat from its early 2000 peak, just as questions about dubious financial practices surfaced soon after the 1929 crash. And unsurprisingly, the Enron debacle led to a swelling of the chorus of editorialists, politicians, and ordinary investors calling for reform.

What is important to the investor is that the impact of the Enron affair is likely to be long-lasting. Its effect, of course, will be to greatly impair the creativity of accountants. The implication is that the growth of accounting profits will come more in line with the growth of economic profits.

The restraining effect on stock prices is likely to be major. The result of the post-Enron furor will be to bring down the rate of growth of accounting profits, even if the economy and its corporate sector do relatively well. As accounting standards are tightened, reported profits of the

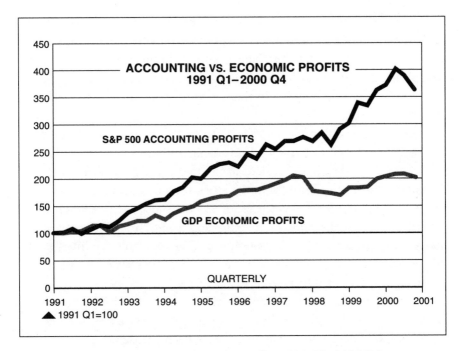

Figure 10.1   Accounting vs. Economic Profits 1991 Q1–2000 Q4.

kind embodied in data pertinent to the types of companies included in the S&P 500 are certain to be held back, even if the growth rate of the economy stays strong. For this reason, the long-term outlook for stock prices will be a victim of the changes that will come because an era of accounting laxity was brought to an end by the Enron affair.

The difference between our view of the long-term outlook for the market and Wall Street's view has profound implications. The noise coming from the Street readily grants that the glory days of the 1980s and the 1990s are over. But though Wall Street admits that the days of double-digit gains in the market have ended, the prevailing view expressed by the Street as 2001 came to an end was that the investor could count on a continuing revolution in the application of technology to bring real long-term inflation-adjusted gains in stock prices of about 7 percent in the postmillennial decade. That number represents a vastly more optimistic outlook than the one we believe is realistic.

A comparison of our view with the conventional view is shown in Table 10.1. The first column represents Wall Street's view of inflation-adjusted returns of 7 percent. That number, should it prove to be correct, would represent an investment comfort zone, especially for those who had begun their 401(k)s in the booming stock market years of the 1980s and 1990s.

The next three columns of Table 10.1 are far less sanguine. They represent the inflation-adjusted total return, including both dividends and capital appreciation, that prevailed in the two decades following each of the twentieth-century bubbles in the stock market. As can be seen from the table, investing $1,000 per year for ten years results in an investment worth $14,784 at the end of ten years and $43,873 after twenty years under Wall Street's 7 percent assumption. The worth of the investment drops to $11,103 after ten years and to $24,506 after twenty years if our expected 1.9 percent return is instead achieved.

If our expectations are approximately met, price-earnings ratios are fated to fall, and fall steeply, from the level that prevailed at the end of 2001. One way of gauging what would have been a reasonable p/e for that day is to look at the record of the market over the twentieth century as a whole. For the entire 100-year period, taking in both bad times and good, the average p/e ratio on the Dow Jones Industrial Average was 15. Any investor who believes, as we do, that the economy faces a difficult decade would conclude that the market was still grossly overvalued on that day.

A really cautious investor might have reached even grimmer conclusions. We came up with a 15 p/e ratio based on the average p/e for the post–World War II period. But a stern realist might instead argue that the relevant comparison would be with the average p/e of 12 for the entire twentieth century. None of this need prevent stock market rallies in which the prudent investor will stand a strong chance to make money over the next decade. There were some substantial rallies in the earlier stagnation decades, which would have represented relatively safe bets for the average investor.

Still, as we have seen, the p/e ratio that prevailed even after the World Trade Center debacle was too high. That meant that the stock market still faced an extended period of adjustment. We believe, in fact, that we face an extremely difficult period that will extend to the middle of the postmillennial decade as price-earnings come down to levels that are

	@7%	@7% cum	-.02%	-.02% cum	.04%	.04% cum	1.9%	1.9% cum
TABLE 10.1				Total Inflation-Adjusted Rates of Return to Stocks				
1.	1,070	1,070	999.8	999.8	1,004	1,004	1,019.00	1,019
2.	1,145	2,215	999.6	1,999.4	1,008	2,012	1,038.36	2,057
3.	1,225	3,440	999.4	2,998.8	1,012	3,024	1,058.09	3,115
4.	1,311	4,715	999.2	3,998.0	1,016	4,040	1,078.19	4,193
5.	1,403	6,154	999.0	4,997.0	1,020	5,060	1,098.68	5,291
6.	1,501	7,655	998.8	5,995.8	1,024	6,084	1,119.56	6,410
7.	1,606	9,261	998.6	6,994.4	1,028	7,112	1,140.83	7,550
8.	1,718	10,979	998.4	7,992.8	1,032	8,144	1,162.51	8,712
9.	1,838	12,817	998.2	8,991.0	1,037	9,181	1,184.60	9,896
10.	1,967	14,784	998.0	9,989.0	1,041	10,222	1,207.11	11,103
11.	2,105	16,889	997.8	10,986.8	1,045	11,267	1,230.05	12,333
12.	2,252	19,141	997.6	11,984.4	1,049	12,316	1,253.42	13,586
13.	2,410	21,551	997.4	12,981.8	1,053	13,369	1,277.23	14,863
14.	2,579	24,130	997.2	13,979.0	1,057	14,426	1,301.50	16,164
15.	2,760	26,890	997.0	14,976.0	1,062	15,488	1,326.23	17,490
16.	2,953	29,843	996.8	15,972.8	1,066	16,554	1,351.43	18,841
17.	3,160	33,803	996.6	16,969.4	1,070	17,624	1,377.11	20,218
18.	3,381	36,384	996.4	17,969.8	1,075	18,699	1,403.28	21,621
19.	3,618	40,002	996.2	18,966.0	1,079	19,778	1,429.74	23,050
20.	3,871	43,873	996.0	19,962.0	1,083	20,861	1,456.91	24,506

DATA: The table compares Wall Street's estimate of total returns of 7 percent per year with the actual rates of return archived in the wake of the great stock market bubbles of the twentieth century. In the wake of the 1901 peak, the inflation-adjusted return to stocks, including dividends, averaged -0.2 percent. It averaged 0.4 percent a year for the twenty years following 1929 and averaged 1.9 percent for the twenty years following 1966.

more in line with historical experience. That probability is reinforced, as we have seen, because accounting reform will reduce the growth rate of the profits that companies report.

The market never moves neatly and quietly along its trend line. Instead, it swings above and below its intrinsic value. One characteristic of the kind of market we foresee is that these swings will tend to be large, reflecting the basic maxim that bear markets are more volatile than bull markets.

This volatility is apparent both in the bear market of the 1930s and the sluggish market that began in 1966. In the first half of the 1930s, it fell more than 25 percent below its trend six times, while in the years between

1966 and 1970, it fell below its trend three times. Each of these down-swings provided a strong opportunity to make some money. The trick will be to avoid falling into the trap of believing that the long-term trend of stock prices will conform to Wall Street hype rather than to the more modest trend suggested by history. We believe that short- to intermediate-term stock market gains can be made when the market falls about 20 percent below its trend value. There will, of course, be the risk that it could fall somewhat farther than that. But it is a risk that is well worth taking.

So far, all our recommendations pertain to the market as a whole. To implement them, the investor can use index funds, a basket of stocks designed to move up and down at about the same rate as the broad stock market indexes themselves. One nice thing about index funds is that they tend to charge low management fees and therefore minimize the amount of your gain that you have to leave at Wall Street's table.

In long-term difficult markets, it is particularly important to keep the cost of your investments as low as possible. The beginning of wisdom is never to buy an investment like a mutual fund that has a "load"—a sales commission paid for the "privilege" of having some investment manager look after your money. The cost is alarming. Some funds have loads as high as 8 percent. That means that investors who buy the fund put only $9,200 to work for every $10,000 they invest. That means that the fund must return 8 percent before investors can even get their money back when they sell. Eight percent loads have become scarce because investors have caught on in recent years. But 4 percent loads are still quite common. Even at these lower rates, load funds should be avoided at all costs since they perform on average no better than no-load funds.

But even with no-load funds, the costs to the investor are high. This is a problem in all markets, but it is downright robbery in periods when it is tough to find stocks that go up. In 1998, Wall Street earned about $100 billion for the simple task of trading stocks and commodities. The average cost for even the most economical equity funds came to 0.98 percent of the money under management. And that was only the cost of operating the fund. It does not include the commissions paid for trading the stocks in the portfolio. In 1998, the best and most conservative equity funds traded their average stock about once every two years. Each time stocks are traded, brokers exact a fee.

In a study for the Century Fund, economist Dean Baker reports that the expense ratio for 401(k) plans holding mutual funds consisting mostly of stocks comes to about 1.44 percentage points. The cost of trading stocks adds half a percentage point to the cost that the owner of the 401(k) must bear. Add up the two numbers and it costs the beleaguered 401(k) owner about 2 percentage points per year. This sounds small, but is in fact, a huge number. Suppose for the moment that the value of the 401(k) is $100,000 and the dividend yield of the portfolio is 3 percent, a generous assumption. That means that of the $3,000 that 401(k) owners receive in dividends, they pay out $2,000 in fees and commissions. That may not be the end of the story. If the monies in 401(k)s are insured by the government's Pension Benefits Guaranty Corp., as many in post-Enron Washington are recommending, Baker estimates it would cost .15 percentage points. That's another $150 in costs to the 401(k) investor. Given the frequency with which pension monies have vanished in the past, this insurance fee is well worth paying. But it nevertheless means that the $3,000 in dividend income shrinks to a paltry $850. It is an incredible disappearing act, but it happens all the time.

In the fantasy land of rapid capital appreciation in the 1990s, the disappearance of dividend income into the hands of money managers was hardly noticed because the rise in stock prices to where they were wildly overvalued meant that the average investor was enjoying large capital gains. But capital gains are likely to be meager on average in the coming decade, and that means that high management fees are to be ruthlessly avoided.

John Bogle, founder of Vanguard, a money management group, deserves credit for finding ways in which the average investor can keep costs low without sacrificing solid investment results. Bogle's approach to the market mirrors a fundamental conclusion of this book: There is no evidence that any money manager can consistently beat the averages. It follows from that point of view that the most rational approach to the market is the wide diversification that is available in some index funds.

There is another set of index funds that is well worth the attention of investors. One of the most famous and successful investment organizations that was genuinely designed to serve its members was set up to provide retirement income to educators. That, of course, is TIAA-CREF. In 1999, that highly successful organization, with a long history of excellent service to its members, opened its doors to the public by setting up a series of index funds that anyone can buy. It has even lower management fees than the Vanguard index funds.

There is one, and only one, departure from our general diversification rule that is worth considering in the difficult markets that we see ahead. We've already seen that dividends will be important over the coming decade. In our review of the markets in difficult circumstances, particularly in the 1930s, we saw that dividends played a critical role in supporting retirees.

The same will be true in the coming decade. As a vivid example of the comfort that can be derived from dividends, consider what happened after the World Trade Center disaster. After the disaster intensified the plunge in the markets, some high-dividend stocks began to look good. On September 25, 2001, people close to the stock market began to notice that stocks had fallen so far as to make their dividend yield higher than that on long-term government bonds. And Wall Street began to notice the reemergence of dividends as something worth considering. We are not suggesting that investors go back to earlier decades and depend entirely on dividend yields for their retirement and other savings. We're not that retro in our views. What we are suggesting is that this is merely one of the ways—overlooked during the bull market of the 1990s—that you can make your money increase over the next decade, rather than have it dissipated by a myriad of administrative fees and other costs. There are mutual funds, called income funds, whose goal is to produce a high current yield. It is among these funds that investors will find a way of benefiting from stocks of companies that pay high dividends. Make sure that the income funds are no-load. You can find a ranking of these funds on the Web by tapping into Morningstar.com.

Employees who invest through their 401(k)s face special problems. They are not ordinarily free to choose the way in which they invest. Even in the most employee-friendly companies, the choices available for 401(k) investments are usually made by the employers. It is the corporations that make the choices. And that, of course, means that the choices are often made in the company's interest rather than purely on the basis of the investments that would be most beneficial to the employees themselves.

In selecting the financial institutions that they do business with, corporations have a large number of interests that they serve. And good management of 401(k) funds is only one objective. Companies usually put most of their thought into their investment-banking relationships. They often choose those investment bankers who they believe can make the best deals for them and who offer the most support for their stock, should it be needed when they bring new securities to market. In the wake of the Enron affair it is likely that Washington will make some changes that will seek to limit conflicts of interest between companies and their employees in how 401(k)s are administered. Changes that we believe will produce an "ideal" 401(k) are recommended in Chapter 11. But we are not confident of the legistlation to the average worker.

Employees who are unionized can sometimes bargain for 401(k) administration that is in their best interest. But in nonunion companies, employees are generally powerless to make sure that their interests are served. This is not an ideal circumstance. The most that can be said is that employees do have some power to complain about their 401(k)s and that they should individually pressure the human resources departments of their companies to represent their interests. The dissatisfied employee is obviously in a tricky situation. But that does not mean that individual efforts to improve the choices available are impossible.

The Case Against Stock Picking

To some investors, our stressing index funds and diversification will sound like total capitulation of the most craven kind. They know that there are many intelligent hardworking, highly educated people working on the Street. And they may legitimately wonder why this work simply will not pay off for the Street's customers in the form of superior investment results.

The answer may well be found in a famous quote from John Maynard Keynes: Americans are too prone, he said, to guess "what average opinion thinks average opinion is going to be; and this national weakness finds its nemesis in the stock market." Keynes, of course, knew that stock prices often diverge from the valuation levels that inhere in earnings growth and interest rates. That then makes stock picking a psychological game in which it is extremely difficult to win.

Keynes once wrote a book called *The Theory of Probability*. He was well aware that the economic and business world is fraught with uncertainty.

There is simply no way that any company can be certain that its strategy will succeed in an environment that is evolving in unpredictable ways. And being a well-trained economist, he knew that success breeds intense competition that tends to erode profits. To us, the implications for the stock market are best grasped by realizing that only one stock was in the Dow Jones Industrial Average in the market peaks of 1929 and 2000. That was, of course, General Electric, which was totally transformed over the intervening years.

Our positive advice to the average investor is simple and straightforward: Do not even try to pick stocks, because you are likely to fail in the long run unless you get luckier than you have any right to expect. Gerald M. Loeb, a journalist who became one of the most successful people on Wall Street in the 1950s and 1960s, wrote a book first published in 1983 called *The Battle for Investment Survival*. He vividly documented the quicksilver shifts in profitability; and for that reason, the worth of any stock—indeed, any portfolio of stocks—can change at a moment's notice. Even General Electric, the last survivor in the Dow Industrials, fell from 60 to 30 in the few short months between August 2000 and September 2001. It is a sobering reminder of the realities of a highly competitive economy.

We have already seen that profits grow at the same approximate rate as the economy as a whole in the long run. Positive profit surprises for some companies always come at the expense of bad news for other companies. The list of companies that stumble is long and sometimes includes the totally unexpected. In the late 1990s, 3M was widely perceived as one of the best-managed companies in the country. It could be counted on to grow and grow. Yet the company faltered, and its profits growth rate tumbled in the late 1990s. Even the vaunted Coca-Cola, which was widely held to have solved the problem of successful global marketing, ran into trouble as the 1990s came to a close. Cisco Systems was celebrated throughout the business press as the best-managed company of the late 1990s. It had, according to most stories, the top management information system and the most brilliant CEO in John Chambers. Yet the stock fell from 80 in March 2000 to 11 in September 2001.

Other companies celebrated for their management genius suffered an almost equivalent fate. Jeff Bezos, the CEO of Amazon.com was *Time* magazine's Man of the Year in January 2000. But his company's stock fell from 107 in December 1999 to 6 in September 2001. Other widely celebrated companies with management that was worshiped both on Wall Street and in the business press suffered similar fates. Sun Microsystems fell from 64 in September 2000 to 8 in September 2001. And as sickening as the plunge in these stock prices was for the average tech investor, it left the p/e ratios still above the level dictated by the standards of history.

Stocks as Gambling

Our stock market advice for the upcoming decade is obviously austere. We do not apologize for this. But we also recognize that many Americans will find that life is dull as a consequence.

For them, we recommend that stock investing be viewed as a form of gambling. There is no question that the stock market offers bets that are far superior to anything available in lotteries or Las Vegas. The reason is simple and straightforward. The house take in state lotteries is gigantic. The New York State lottery, for example, returns only 82 cents to the few winners for each dollar bet. The house take set by the Nevada Gaming Commission is some 9 cents out of each dollar bet. There is no way that gamblers can make money in the long run. Economists call lotteries and casinos negative-sum games in which no one but the house can possibly win.

The stock market, by contrast, provides a substantial advantage to bettors. Adjusted for inflation, stock prices have risen at about 7 percent per year. That means that over the very long run, stocks are a positive-sum game, returning more than the original stake to those who choose to bet on stocks.

The implication, of course, is that as gambling goes, the stock market is a very good deal indeed. And there are people who want to take a chance on bets that would really transform their lives. That is an argument for playing the market. It will work only a little bit better than the lottery for the vast majority of people. But there is a chance that the market will create a few big winners. And we respect the motivation of those who want to try to be among them.

Thinking of the market as a gambling casino immediately leads to betting through the use of options. A "call option" gives its owner the right to buy at a particular price. A "put option" gives the buyer the right to sell at a specific price. Options on particular stocks are called equity options. Options that give the right to bet on indexes are called index options. All options expire after a time. The longer the right to exercise them lasts, the more the options are likely to cost.

The beauty of options trading is that the losses are limited to the amount of money spent to buy them. If the stock moves against you, you do not lose more than you put up. It's a lot like stepping up to the table and putting your money on the line at an Atlantic City craps table.

Bold options gambles should focus on options that are cheap enough to give you a big bang for the bucks you put up. A call option is cheap if it gives you the right to buy a stock at a price that is well above the price that is quoted on the market, especially if it expires relatively quickly. It will only work out if you catch a sudden updraft in the demand for the underlying stock. In seeking this kind of opportunity on your own, you should focus on stocks in companies and industries that you know best that would maximize your chances of spotting a marketing or technological development that will pack an immediate wallop and suddenly get plenty of attention. Capitalizing on this kind of opportunity is a long shot. But remember that you are gambling here, hoping for a win big enough to have a real impact on the way that you live.

Put options are an exact analogy designed to work if the stock falls. Again, the big wins are scored from the money options, in this case giving you the right to sell at prices well below the price prevailing in the market. But this time, you are betting on a quick dive in the stock.

Options are obviously not for everybody. They are the way to go for those who crave the gambling experience and even those who want to take a flier once in a while. But options used in this way are nothing but a gamble. The odds are better than in Las Vegas, and average investors should keep their initial stake low. Perhaps no more than the cost of a trip to Vegas itself!

Bonds

Bonds play a crucial role in the investment strategy we recommend for the upcoming decade. Bonds and bond funds are less familiar than stocks to the average investor. The 1990s, for the most part, was not a decade in which people went around giving each other tips on the best bonds that were being issued. We think that for the whole generation of new investors who got into the market early in the decade and are now looking for a serious safety net, there is good reason to explain this market in simple detail. Everyone thinks of bonds as safer than stocks, and they are. Even the return on low-yielding Treasury bills beat the S&P 500 between mid-1998 and the end of 2001. That strongly suggests that there are times when bonds are the right investment for every family, not just older Americans who can't afford any risk at all. Bond investing can be fun, safe, and rewarding for all Americans.

But investors have to watch their step. You can take a shellacking if you have to cash in a bond when inflation drives up interest rates. And as with all investments, the returns on a bond can be drastically cut by the commissions and fees that buying and holding them can entail. The good news is that there are "do-it-yourself" ways to buy government bonds that involve no commissions. And what's really nifty is that you can play the bond market so that the income you get is programmed to come in at exactly the time you need it.

First of all, bonds are basically IOUs, issued by a government agency or company. A bond is a promise to repay borrowed money—which the government or private industry uses to finance its expenses. Governments, especially the federal government, often issue bonds to cover general expenses. Private companies, in contrast, issue bonds to cover the cost of making capital expenditures—setting up new factories or buying new equipment. In the private sector, issuing bonds to meet ordinary expenses is a no-no. Any company that does so is almost guaranteed that the ratings on its bonds will be reduced by the so-called rating agencies, Standard & Poor's and Moody's. When investors buy bonds, they are lending money to the issuer, who pays the investors a set interest rate, most often twice a year.

In the good old days, investors usually held bonds for ten to thirty years, until they matured. Bond investors, not stock players, were usually thought of as rich. They spent their time, as one could see in old *New Yorker* cartoons, clipping coupons. Today, trading in bonds has been modernized. Coupons have mostly disappeared because their duties have been turned over to computers. There is a much larger range of bonds available to investors. Especially in the new climate of the postmillennial decade, bonds must be the basic staple of the average American's portfolio. The reason? They provide a much-needed safety net that does not exist in many areas of today's life. If your bonds are Treasury bonds, issued by the U.S. government, they are the safest investment around.

No matter what happens to interest rates, the income you get from the bond stays the same, as does the face value of the bond on the day it matures. If a $10,000 bond yields 6 percent on the day that you buy it, it will continue to pay you $600 a year until it matures, no matter what happens to interest rates in the meantime.

But what happens to interest rates while you are holding a bond does make a difference to what a bond is worth if you want to sell it before it matures. Suppose the interest rate on the kind of bond you are holding goes up to 8 percent. That means that investors would get a check for $800 a year in interest for thirty years for their $10,000 investment if they bought a newly issued bond. So, if you want to sell your 6 percent bond, you would have to take a loss. How big a loss depends on how close your 6 percent bond is to maturity. But if the rise in rates occurs in the first year, your bond would be worth only $7,667 if you had to sell it on the open market. That, of course, means that a rise in inflation, which usually brings with it higher interest rates, is very dangerous for those who hold bonds. It's also the reason that big bond investors, like banks, hate inflation, whereas homeowners often enjoy seeing the value of their houses go up while the size of their mortgage debt stays the same. In contrast, deflation and falling interest rates benefit those who want to, or have to, sell their bonds before they mature. If the interest rate falls by 2 percentage points in the year that it is issued, the family that owns the $10,000 6 percent bond will be able to sell it for $12,500. Most bonds have a fixed rate of interest when you buy them.

Barring emergencies, the average family can protect itself from the impact of changes in the value of bonds before they mature. Bonds give comfort because they are more likely than any other investment to serve the exact goals that they are bought for. If you are planning to send your kids to college, you can buy bonds that mature at exactly the right time and are almost certain to give you the amount of money you need and have counted on. And the same is true about the certainty of meeting any other goal. Bonds held to maturity are safe and sound. You can't always buy a newly issued government bond that matures exactly when you need it. But you can always find bonds that come due at the exact time needed to meet your goal. If your daughter is in kindergarten and you want to have college tuition the summer before she enters college, you can buy an already issued thirty-year bond that will mature in thirteen years, exactly when you need it.

You may not get exactly the bond you need. But the cheapest and sometimes most convenient way to buy a government bond is from the U.S. Treasury itself, by just calling your local Federal Reserve Bank. Except for U.S. savings bonds, traditional bonds ordinarily come in denominations of $1,000, $5,000, or $10,000 each. U.S. savings bonds come in even smaller denominations. Savings bonds can be bought for as little as $25 and are among the best investments available for the person with very limited investment funds. You can just walk into a bank and buy savings bonds over the counter, and some companies even offer them through payroll savings plans.

Government agencies also issue securities. The best-known and most popular are Ginnie Maes, issued by the Government National Mortgage Association. Ginnie Maes are mortgage-backed securities, basically pools of mortgage loans. The bank that issues the mortgage sells it to Ginnie Mae, which bundles it up with many others. A certificate representing this bundle is issued in denominations of at least $1 million. This certificate is then sold to a broker, who will in turn slice it up and sell shares in minimum denominations of $25,000.

The bank that issues a mortgage-backed security collects the monthly loan payments from the homeowners and passes them on to the ultimate buyers of the security. Such certificates are always backed by some federal or state agency, which guarantees timely monthly payments to the ultimate investor. Thus, if the homeowner defaults, the bank must still make its monthly payment to the security holder.

Various government agencies provide these guarantees. Quasi-federal agencies (such as the Federal Home Loan Mortgage Corporation, popularly known as Freddie Mac) and private corporations (such as the Federal National Mortgage Association, popularly known as Fannie Mae) also guarantee mortgage-backed securities. But by far the most popular backer is the federal government, through Ginnie Mae. Its guarantee is backed by the "full faith and credit of the United States," as are Treasury securities. Ginnie Maes combine the security of government guarantees with high yields. Ginnie Mae yields tend to be higher than AAA-rated long-term industrial bonds and ten-year Treasury notes.

Ginnie Maes pay higher yields than other government-backed securities because they must make up for a few drawbacks. The biggest risk with Ginnie Maes is that the underlying mortgages can be prepaid. When interest rates fall, people tend to pay off their mortgages and refinance with lower-rate loans. When that happens, the Ginnie Mae investors receive their principal and interest sooner than expected. They must then reinvest the money at lower rates. Therefore, Ginnie Maes are not a surefire way of locking in high yields.

Buying a Ginnie Mae at a discount may be an advantage. Its yield is lower than the prevailing rate, so there is little chance of prepayment of the underlying mortgages because of refinancing. There's no liability if the certificate is paid off early, because the investor makes a profit on the difference between the purchase price and the par value he or she receives when mortgages are prepaid.

Agency bonds are a good deal most of the time. They don't quite have the safety of ordinary treasuries, but it's hard to believe that the federal government would renege on what people in the bond business call its "moral obligation" to protect the owners of these securities.

The investor will find that do-it-yourself bond investing only works well for Treasury bonds. Otherwise, the investor will have to deal with a brokerage firm or bank to buy corporate or municipal bonds. It isn't easy to buy them in lots of less than $250,000 for corporate bonds or $25,000 for agency and municipal bonds. If you want to invest smaller amounts, you will have to pay through the nose to get a broker to take your business. The transaction costs tend to be prohibitively high. At that price, achieving diversification—a must with municipal and corporate bonds, where default is always possible—is virtually impossible for all but the wealthiest investors.

Investors who nevertheless want to buy federal government agency, individual corporate, or municipal bonds directly should shop around, calling several brokers with their specifications—the amount of money available to invest, the grade of bond, the maturity date, the option of state and local tax breaks, the location of the municipality or agency issuing a bond—and then compare prices and yields. If a brokerage firm has large inventories of bonds at a particular time, it may offer them at a better price. Discount brokerage firms don't sell bonds at discounted prices, so their prices aren't necessarily lower.

Although investors generally don't pay a commission when they buy a bond that a broker or banker has on hand, they have to pay the difference between the "bid" and the "ask" price. The difference, which goes to the broker, is called the spread. Effectively, the spread is the broker's commission and can range from 0.75 to 5.0 percent of the purchase. That is a stiff fee indeed. And it is usually much greater for small lots than for large ones. Before buying any municipal or corporate bond, the investor should check whether comparable investments—such as a long-term certificate of deposit issued by a bank—might not give the same return or better, especially after counting in transaction costs.

For these reasons, the average investor with limited assets is often better off buying bonds through mutual funds or through unit investment trusts, which will be described in detail in the following section. Both bond mutual funds and unit investment trusts are diversified portfolios of bonds that can be purchased for as little as $1,000.

Bond Mutual Funds and Unit Trusts

Because average investors face high transaction costs in buying individual bonds, they are often better off investing in a bond mutual fund or a unit trust. Some have relatively low expense, and the vast majority are liquid and diversified.

Both funds and trusts pool money from many investors and buy a wide variety of bonds. In mutual funds, professional money managers buy and sell bonds actively. Trust portfolios stay the same until the trust dissolves. That happens when the bonds in it have matured. The interest a mutual fund pays moves up and down when interest rates change and bonds are bought and sold. But with its fixed portfolio, a trust will pay the same amount of interest until the bonds in it mature.

Because the bond fund's portfolio is constantly changing, the price of a share and the interest rate paid will fluctuate. With a trust, the interest earned annually remains stable because there is no trading activity, though default and the calling of bonds in the trust's portfolio can affect the annual yield.

The two approaches can lead to very different results. If you invest in a unit trust paying 8 percent annually, your rate will be locked in whether interest rates in general rise to 12 percent or fall to 5 percent. If your investment is in a bond fund, your yield will tend to reflect changes in interest rates. In addition, with a fund you can have interest payments automatically reinvested.

Trusts charge no management fee. Most funds charge about 1 percent, which can be a substantial burden on the average investor in the low interest rate environment that we foresee. Trusts may therefore be a better investment than funds in the decade ahead. But a trust incurs costs in record keeping and mailing out interest checks. It has to get the money somewhere, so it always involves a sales charge, whereas a no-load mutual fund does not. A trust is best suited to long-term investing, where the cost of the sales charge can be averaged out over several years. In either case, always read carefully the prospectus of any fund or trust you are considering.

Sometimes bonds are at their best when they are not whole. When younger people are saving to send their kids to college, what they really need is a piece of paper that grows in value as quickly as possible. And they are quite willing to give up any interest they may get from holding a whole bond. Others, perhaps older people, are quite willing to give up the appreciation and the value of the piece of paper if they can increase the amount of money that they get each year or each month.

To serve the differing needs of these groups, financial institutions have put on a striptease act. They have divided the bond in two. One part, the principal-only bond, pays no interest but gains in value as it approaches maturity. The other, the interest-only bond, pays out annual interest payments. On Wall Street, these bonds are called "POs" and "IOs," for rather obvious reasons. Wall Street creates these strips because they can make money from dividing the needs of two groups of investors and charging each group a bit extra for strips that serve their special needs.

Dial 529 for Education

Everyone is familiar with the 401(k), if only because of the tax advantages that it brings to the average investor who is saving for retirement. Equally important are the numbers "529," which can play an equivalent role in the financing of your child's college education. They refer to state-sponsored college savings plans that went into effect in January 2001 and are named for the section of the federal tax code that created them. For most people, the 529 is the best way to save for college.

The beauty of the 529 is that it is an even better tax break than the 401(k). In the retirement plan, the taxes don't disappear. They are deferred: You don't pay taxes on the earnings of a 401(k) while the money is left in the plan, but you must pay ordinary income taxes when you begin to take the money out. In the 529, by contrast, the ride is tax-free all the way. This is a big change from the past, when earnings were taxed at the student's income-tax rate when they were withdrawn. Several states have also rid these accounts of their own taxes, and more such breaks are expected to follow. One caveat: The money must be used for higher education or you will pay taxes and a penalty when the money is withdrawn, typically 10 percent of earnings.

Federal law allows you to choose to put your money in any state's 529 plan—not just in the one run by the state where you live—and you will still get tax advantages. It is, however, worth looking at your own state's plan first, since it's the one that's most likely to allow you to deduct contributions to its plan from state income taxes. Generally, deductions are hard to pass up, so calculate your tax savings before opting for an out-of-state plan.

Still, if your state's plan has high fees—1 percent of assets or more—or unappealing investment options, shop around. Going with an out-of-state plan is becoming easier. In the past, some states levied taxes on withdrawals from out-of-state plans while exempting money in their own.

Tax-free status makes a big difference. According to T. Rowe Price Associates, if you invest $5,000 a year in a 529 equity fund that earns an average annual return of 10 percent, you'll have $287,704 after eighteen years. In contrast, a taxpayer in the 28 percent bracket would have $224,527 after taxes in a regular brokerage account and $250,157 in a custodial account, which exempts only the first $750 in gains per year from taxes. T. Rowe Price's expected rate of return is unduly optimistic, but its insight into the advantages of tax saving is worth remembering.

There are other college savings options that are free from federal and possibly state income taxes: education individual retirement accounts and state-sponsored plans that let you prepay tuition. But neither allows you to save as much as the amount permitted by many 529s. With a prepaid plan, you can save only as much as it costs to attend a state school. And education IRA contributions are now capped at $2,000—not enough to pay for a state university eighteen years from the time you start, let alone Harvard.

With a 529, you should be able to save enough to cover four years at a private college if that's what you choose. The states don't manage your money. Instead, each has selected a professional to offer a handful of stock and bond funds. New Hampshire, for example, picked Fidelity Investments, while New York selected TIAA-CREF, our favorite money manager.

The 529 plans do have flaws: Some 529s offer only a few investment options. There are some rigid rules that can make it difficult to change a portfolio once it's been set up. Just get to know the rules for the state plan(s) that you choose. Despite some of these annoyances, if a parent starts putting money into a 529 early on and invests regularly, there's no better deal around. Eighteen years from now you will have a comfortable amount of money to pay for college.

The 401(k) De-Hoax Program

A total de-hoaxing of 401(k) plans requires new legislation and new corporate attitudes toward their employees. Our recommendations for fundamental structural change in the nation's retirement programs come in the next chapter. But first we will deal with the here-and-now question: how to make the best of 401(k) plans as they currently exist.

Some 401(k)s are obviously better than others. But we have never been able to find a company that gives its employees either the kind of guidance or the kind of investment options that employees need to make the 401(k) effective in meeting individual goals. Most of the problems this has caused can be overcome by following the investment advice implicit in this book, to the full extent allowed by the investment options that are available in the employer's 401(k). Because 401(k)s have sprung from the heads of managers, they are far from ideal for workers. Part of the problem is simply managerial arrogance. Most 401(k)s seek to encourage employees to copy the investment strategies followed by the wealthy. What is ignored is that the wealthy usually have less reason to worry about losing money in stock investments because their very wealth obviously gives them a greater cushion against the losses incurred in a sustained market decline.

The fundamental purpose of a pension plan is to replace as much of the purchasing power provided by a lost salary as possible. Although the salary replacement rate was low in the old-defined benefit plans, it was at least an intrinsic goal. As it evolved in practice, the 401(k), by contrast, became the icon of the equity culture of the 1990s. In that equity culture, participants in 401(k) pension plans were told, in effect, to choose their investments and take their chances. In many plans, employees are given a large number of choices, including many varieties of stock market investments, providing a not-so-subtle nudge in the direction of investing heavily in the stock market, particularly in the stock of the company that the employee works for. Employees who follow that advice assume every conceivable risk: the economic risks of inflation, deflation, recession, and stagnation. They also must take on the specific business risks of the companies whose stocks they buy. These risks are unacceptable for the average family under any circumstances. They are particularly high in the stagnant economic environment that we foresee. They are doubly dangerous in a stock market where dividend yields are so low that the hope of a decent return to stocks depends on finding new baby boomers who are willing to buy them at higher and higher prices.

It follows, of course, that the core of 401(k)s should be bonds. And we have saved our discussion of the best kind of bonds for retirement plans for last: inflation-indexed bonds issued by the U.S. Treasury.

Plans that offer the choice of investment in the government's inflation-indexed bonds are scarce, even though they have recently been yielding about 4 percent a year, adjusted for inflation, and most important, are totally riskless. These bonds are the best choice for people planning for retirement, considerably superior to a dangerous stock market. Employers have done nothing to encourage employees to shift their retirement funds into bonds. And even more disturbing, few 401(k) plans offer inflation-indexed bonds as an option. Government is also at fault. Virtually no one in Washington has urged employers to change their 401(k)s. That's why plans provide only the standard options, almost always stressing equities.

The threat of inflation has seemed remote in recent years. But retirement is a long-term proposition, and no one can be certain that the stagnation of the postmillennial decade will not turn into stagflation. Most of our experience with pension plans harks back to the days when defined benefit plans were the order of the day. One of their worst attributes was that they were almost never indexed to inflation. Those of our relatives who retired and lived a long time under defined benefit plans saw the purchasing power of their pensions wither as the price level rose. Even low rates of inflation hurt in a world where longevity is likely to increase. Over a decade, even a 2 percent inflation rate cuts the purchasing power of a fixed sum pension by 22 percent over a decade. Finally, it is naive to buy the argument that stocks are a good hedge against inflation. The late 1960s and the 1970s were high-inflation years, yet the stock market went absolutely nowhere.

The time for change has come. The average American family has a long way to go to adjust to a stagnant stock market. Enron and its aftermath have undermined trust in the U.S. markets and many of the companies whose stocks trade on them. But those families who now throw up their hands and become passive about investing would be making a grave mistake. Revelations of corruption and trading irregularities have, as we have seen, followed earlier stock market bubbles. But the historical record shows that investment success was nevertheless possible in these difficult periods. It is possible again.

Chapter 11

The Political Agenda:
De-Hoaxing the 401(k)

Throughout the great boom of the 1990s, the 401(k) plan was presented to the nation as a solution to providing income for older Americans. The picture painted by 401(k) advocates was of a system that for the first time in history would allow average Americans to benefit significantly from the growth of the economy and the success of the country's great corporations. But we have seen in this book that, in truth, the 401(k) was grafted onto a pension system that revealed serious flaws throughout its history. And we have presented evidence that instead of making the system better, the 401(k) has increased the risk that the average family faces in planning for its retirement. That is the great 401(k) hoax that threatens the American family and brings about a clear and urgent need for pension reform.

We've tried to offer up the best investing advice possible for difficult times. Investors will have to navigate in a stillwater market where the returns will be far lower than in the great stock market boom of the 1990s. We believe that our advice will make a difference. But families by themselves cannot overcome the obstacles to economic security that have been created in a pension system that often serves the interests of the corporation and Wall Street at the expense of the family. The political and regulatory environment in which the pension system functions must change. Beyond taking charge of their own portfolios, those who earn their living from work in the United States must become activists by speaking up at work and voting for politicians whose primary goal is to serve their interests, not just those of the employers and their allies on Wall Street.

The corporation and Wall Street, as we showed in Chapter 8, have succeeded in fighting off serious attempts at reform for decades. Successful corporate efforts to minimize federal involvement in private pension administration have left the American worker with private pensions that are paltry when compared with the size of the pension fund assets carried on corporate books. It is part of a pattern that has left American workers behind those in most other developed nations in basic health-care and unemployment benefits. Years of attack on the income-security plan that did pass—the Social Security Act of 1935—have resulted in a drive for privatization that would make the system vulnerable to the same risks that characterize 401(k)s. Long experience with private pension plans that disappeared with the plants that moved overseas have made homeland workers the victims of pension plan termination. Homeland security surely has an economic dimension.

The 401(k) may easily become part of that history of disappearing pension plans. We have already argued that the 401(k) came into existence because corporations during the difficult years of the early 1980s wanted to shed the responsibility for accumulating enough pension fund assets to actuarily guarantee their defined benefit plans. Similarly, the problems that have emerged in the opening years of the postmillennial decade imply that the 401(k) could end up as the latest chapter in a sad story that has already dragged on for over a century. Indeed, 401(k)s began to erode as soon as the economy slowed in the spring of 2000. Company 401(k) matching funds began to erode even before the Enron debacle. In 2000, according to the Profit Sharing/401(k) Council, the average 401(k) plan matched 2.5 percent of company payroll, down from 3.3 percent in both of the previous two years, and the lowest level in at least a decade.

But the pension story can still have a happy ending. What is needed is an FDR–style New Deal for the nation's pension system. A national dialogue must begin, one that involves all income groups in the United States, including those who invest in the stock market and those who cannot afford to do so. Should the United States have an expanded—not a partially privatized version—of the current Social Security system with reforms made particularly to end bias against working women? We believe it should. Is there a possibility that the Taft-Hartley Law should be examined and reformed so that workers will have much more direct control over what happens to their pension plans? We believe that it should be looked at closely. Should the nation reexamine ways to better protect those who do invest in 401(k) plans? We believe that it should. Indeed, 401(k) reform is our immediate agenda.

The "Ideal" 401(k)

What is clearly needed is an emancipation proclamation backed by new legislation which ensures that the nation's pension system is set up so that it serves the interests, and only the interests, of those who earn their living from work. Throughout its history, the American pension system has sacrificed the needs of average Americans to the gods of the corporate world and of Wall Street. That must now change. The American family that wishes to do so must be free to seize control of its own financial future. This means that those with 401(k)s must have unrestricted choice among alternative investments. And that freedom of choice should be available not only for the funds that the employee himself puts into the plan but also for the disposition of the match that the employer provides. This of course implies that a 401(k) looks like a standard brokerage account, although margin accounts and short selling should not be allowed.

Conflicts of interest between employees and their corporate employers must now be brought to a screeching halt. There are many instances where corporations have chosen a financial institution with which they do a wide range of business, including investment banking, as the administrators of their 401(k) programs. The effect is to diminish corporate incentives to get the best possible deal for their employees. The way in which a financial institution runs a 401(k) and the fees that employees pay for running it will not come into question when the financial institution running a company's 401(k) is also the company's lead investment banker. The law must be changed so as to make the interests of the manager of the 401(k) coincide closely with the interests of the employee.

Restrictions on when and how employees are able to buy and sell securities for their 401(k)s must also end. There are many companies that limit changes in 401(k) portfolios to once a month, or once a quarter, or even once a year. The ideal 401(k) would in contrast allow employees to shift their funds at any time they want to. That requires a system that allows employees virtually instant information. Participants must also be given constant telephone and Internet access to the financial institution that is responsible for administering the 401(k). Also, transaction fees must be kept low.

Ideally, company-matching contributions to 401(k)s should be made in cash, not in company stock. In addition to avoiding the disasters that befell the participants in the 401(k) plans of companies like Lucent and Enron in 2001, providing company matches in cash is the only effective way of allowing employees freedom of choice.

Weaning companies away from using their stock for matching contributions will not be easy. In defending stock matches, companies are fond of pious rhetoric about giving employees incentives to work hard and be loyal to their employers. The truth, however, is that using stock for matching contributions provides dollars and cents benefits to corporations, and is very much involved with the pumped-up, "creative accounting" aspects of the 1990s. According to Hewitt Associates, as of October 31, 2001, 29.6 percent of 401(k) assets held in 1.5 million pension plans were in the stock of the company sponsoring the plan. That was up from 28.4 percent the year before. Procter & Gamble, Sherwin-Williams, and Abbott Laboratories all contributed over 90 percent of their 401(k) match in the form of company stock; Pfizer, BB & T, Anheuser-Busch, and Coca-Cola over 80 percent; and General Electric, Texas Instruments, William Wrigley Jr., Williams Companies, and McDonald's over 70 percent.

Corporations use stock for matching contributions to take advantage of loose accounting rules that can make their books look better than they really are. When stock is used instead of cash, the value of the stock need not be deducted as a cost on their income statements. That, of course, ensures that reported profits will be higher than they would be if the payment is made in cash.

In the real world, however, Congress is unlikely to ban stock contributions, despite the Enron debacle. Companies are free to stop matching whenever they want to. If reported profits are threatened across a broad base of companies, as they are likely to be as more conservative accounting procedures are put into place, incentives to "match" are likely to wane. It's not unlikely that many companies could follow the lead of Ford Motor, *U.S. News & World Report,* and Daimler-Chrysler's Chrysler Group in suspending 401(k) matches through at least 2002. Congressional efforts to regulate the percentage of contributions made in company stock could well lead to significant reductions in company matches. This would not be surprising at all, since compensation paid out in the form of benefits to American workers dropped during the 1990s, despite huge corporate profits and a booming stock market. According to a 1999 study by the U.S. Chamber of Commerce, a survey of large firms showed a drop in the benefit share in compensation from 42 percent in 1989 to 37 percent in 1999, despite the widespread prosperity.

Banning stock contributions to 401(k)s could easily come at a cost to American families. As we have seen, companies began trimming their benefit programs even in the booming 1990s and the trend to more meager benefits will only intensify in the slow-growing economy that we believe will dominate at least part of the postmillennial decade. A shift from stock to cash contributions has a cost to the corporations. It could easily lead to a world in which employers greatly scale back their matches to 401(k) plans or abandon them entirely.

To prevent that from happening, Washington should consider enacting a new set of tax deductions for corporate 401(k) matches. The cost of that kind of change could be covered by substituting new 401(k) tax breaks for the tax cuts aimed at the upper-income brackets that were proposed by President Bush and enacted by Congress in 2001. Any tax change that benefits the average family at the expense of the rich would of course have been an act of political heroism in a world where legislation is the creature of money politics. There is now a strong chance that the fallout from the Enron debacle will force Washington to make cosmetic changes that will benefit the average family. But the forces in favor of leaving the 401(k) basically as is will continue to be powerful. So it is unlikely that the post-Enron momentum for campaign finance reform will increase the probability that the proponents of 401(k) reform will be on a more level playing field in the battle against corporate interests.

Though financial freedom is our goal, we do believe that there should be a legal limit on one asset choice for 401(k) plan participants: the stock of the sponsoring company itself. In our ideal world, a company's own stock would be banned from the 401(k)s that it sponsors. The average employee already has enough exposure to that company and the simple principle of diversification suggests that for most people, a decision to both work for and invest in the same company brings unneeded risk. But realizing that many employees want to show confidence in the companies that they work for, we recognize that they should be allowed to put as much as 10 percent into its stock. That 10 percent investment rule already applies to company funding of defined benefit plans under the rules of ERISA. Surely it should also apply to 401(k)s.

Even if all our recommendations are followed, there would still be a problem. As long as pension monies are run by typical financial houses, conflicts of interest will continue to produce a stream of decisions and actions that favor the corporation and Wall Street over the employee. To us, this creates the need to assemble and empower a group of professionals beholden neither to the employers nor to Wall Street nor to the union to which these employees may belong. Instead, it must be composed of people whose sole motivation is the interests of the workers themselves.

Finding and funding this kind of professional advice will not be easy in the current environment. Yet there may be a way to do so. The U.S. Department of Labor funds a national mediation service beholden only to the public to help in mediating industrial disputes. In a similar vein, the Labor Department could set up a service that certifies a group of pension counselors beholden only to the workers themselves. If such an elite group is created, the costs could be borne either by employers or the investment houses that would get the 401(k) business because it had these certified councilors on its staff. To believe that such a group could come into existence may seem idealistic. But it is possible to imagine that an aroused public, determined not to repeat the pension disasters of the past, could develop enough muscle to beat down the resistance of Wall Street and corporate interests. In the world of investment caveat emptor—let the buyer beware—is empty advice.

We recognize that many employees feel that they are not qualified to make their own investment decisions, and would therefore be more comfortable if the decisions were left to the "professionals." The needs and desires of this large group of workers must be recognized.

Finally, middle-class Americans should take a real look at the 50 percent of the nation who operate outside of any private pension plan at all. Revolutionary as the idea may seem in the environment of this postmillennial decade, is there any way to actually increase Social Security payments for the millions of Americans who will soon be retiring with little savings at all? Social Security, which was finally passed against violent opposition, was considered by many at the time to be revolutionary in the 1930s, decades after other developed countries had set up pension insurance programs. And when it was passed, initial payments were considered to be "paltry"—even by 1930s standards—when people were literally going hungry. To top it off, the first payments did not start going out until 1942. In the face of facts to the contrary, Social Security continues to be considered as a supplementary pension plan backed up by private plans, both company and union, to which most Americans supposedly have access. The truth is that both Washington and the American public tend to believe that the private pension system is more effective than it really is, an illusion that is carefully fostered by the huge advertising dollars spent by Wall Street.

The Enron disaster should serve as a useful reminder that private pension plans like the 401(k) have had a history of slipping away when Americans, like the Enron workers, least expect them to. Taft-Hartley, enacted in 1948, sets up a major legal roadblock so that workers cannot control their own pension funds. At a minimum, those provisions should be repealed. People have written endlessly about the "new new economy." We, by contrast, believe in a new New Deal. We need a period of deep reform in Washington early in the new millennium so that all Americans are in a position to benefit from another creative capitalist burst like the one we had in the 1990s. Equity and growth are not mutually exclusive.

Notes

Chapter 1: Introduction

PAGE 12. "Data compiled by . . . ," Edward N. Wolff, *Top Heavy: A Study of the Increasing Inequality of Wealth in America* (New York: Twentieth Century Fund Press, 1995).

PAGE 13. "Taken by themselves . . . ," Jeff Madrick, "A Bull Market Amid a Boom in 401(k)s Must Mean Fat Pensions? Think Again," *New York Times*, C2 February 21, 2002.

PAGE 14. "As Yale University . . . ," Robert J. Shiller, *Irrational Exuberance* (Princeton, N.J.: Princeton University Press, 2000), pp. 44, 217–219.

PAGE 14. "'One page of history . . . ,'" Louis D. Brandeis, *Other People's Money* (New York: St. Martin's Press, 1995).

Chapter 2: The Anatomy of a Hoax

PAGE 25. "That warning . . . ," Jeremy Siegel, *Stocks for the Long Run* (Chicago: Irwin Publishing, 1994; 2d ed., New York: McGraw-Hill, 1998).

PAGE 25. "However, the long run that . . . ," John Maynard Keynes, *A Tract on Monetary Reform* (London: Macmillan, 1923), chap. 3.

PAGE 25. "Samuelson's comment . . . ," Paul A. Samuelson, *Economics* (New York: McGraw-Hill, 2001).

PAGE 31. "Again, research by . . . ," Edward N. Wolff, *Top Heavy: A Study of the Increasing Inequality of Wealth in America* (New York: Twentieth Century Fund Press, 1995).

Chapter 3: "Family Values": How the Hoax Was Perpetrated

PAGE 39. "On April 14, 1998 . . . ," David Coulter appeared on CNBC on that date to comment on the merger between Bank of America and Nation's Bank.

PAGE 41. "The well-known academics . . . ," Sylvia Ann Hewlett and Cornel West, *The War Against Parents* (New York: Houghton Mifflin, 1998).

PAGE   42. "'It's kind of a cultural . . . ,'" Joseph Weber and Amy Barrett, "The New Era of Lifestyle Drugs," *BusinessWeek,* May 11, 1998.

PAGE   48. "It is perhaps fitting . . . ," Teresa Ghilarducci, *Labor's Capital* (Cambridge: MIT Press, 1992), p. 14.

PAGE   48. "A great burst . . . ," ibid., p. 14.

PAGE   49. "'The bull market . . . ,'" Siegel, *Stocks for the Long Run.*

PAGE   50. "'Long, long ago . . . ,'" Joanna Cole, "The Old Woman Who Lost Her Dumplings," in *Best-Loved Folk-Tales of the World* (New York: Doubleday, 1983), pp. 506–509.

PAGE   51. "It was not a book . . . ," Don Underwood and Paul B. Brown, *Grow Rich Slowly: The Merrill Lynch Guide to Retirement Planning* (New York: Penguin, 1993).

PAGE   51. "Nor was it a . . . ," David Elias, *Dow 40,000: Strategies for Profiting from the Greatest Bull Market in History* (New York: McGraw-Hill Companies, 2001).

PAGE   52. "'It is rare . . . ,'" Siegel, *Stocks for the Long Run.*

PAGE   52. "As has been . . . ," R. H. Tawney, *Religion and the Rise of Capitalism* (Piscataway, N.J.: Transaction Publishers, 1998), and Max Weber, *The Protestant Ethic and the Spirit of Capitalism* (London: Guernsey Press, 1997).

PAGE   53. "There was a best-selling . . . ," Thomas J. Stanley and William D. Danko, *The Millionaire Next Door* (New York: Simon and Schuster, 1998).

PAGE   53. "Data from NYU's Wolff . . . ," Jeff Madrick, *Unconventional Wisdom* (New York: Century Foundation Press, 2000), pp. 114–115.

PAGE   53. "And for much of the . . . ," Barbara Ehrenreich, *Nickel and Dimed: On (Not) Getting By in America* (New York: Metropolitan Books, 2001).

PAGE   54. "The folk tale . . . ," Cole, *Best-Loved Folk-Tales of the World.*

PAGE   55. "At the time that . . . ," authors' interview with an Italian banker in Rome, 1997.

PAGE   56. "There are signs . . . ," Walter Bagehot, "Essay on Edward Gibbon," in Charles Kindleberger, *Manias, Panics, and Crashes* (New York: John Wiley and Sons, 1996).

Chapter 4: Rhyming the 1990s with the 1920s: Politics and Culture

PAGE   61. "'I am amazed at myself . . . ,'" David Denby, "The Quarter of Living Dangerously," *New Yorker*, April 24, 2000.

PAGE   62. "'The culture of money . . . ,'" Elizabeth Drew, *The Corruption of American Politics* (Secaucus, NJ: Birch Lane Press, 1999), p. 61.

PAGE   62. "'It was the ultimate in . . . ,'" Stephen Labaton, "Now Who, Exactly, Got Us into This?" *New York Times* Section 3, February 3, 2002.

PAGE   62. "The phrasing of Francis Fukuyama's . . . ," Francis Fukuyama, *The End of History* (New York: William Morrow and Co., 1993).

PAGE 63. "The war that ended . . . ," William Wolman and Anne Colamosca, *The Judas Economy* (Boston: Addison-Wesley, 1997).

PAGE 63. "'The 1920s were . . . ,'" Arthur S. Link, "What Happened to the Progressive Movement in the 1920s?" *American Historical Review* 64 October 1958–July 1959: 833–852.

PAGE 64. "'Deficit, deficit, deficit . . . ,'" David Halberstam, *War in a Time of Peace* (New York: Scribner, 2001), p. 222.

PAGE 64. "The symbolic apogee . . . ," Jonathan Chait and Stephen Glass, "Praised Be Greenspan," *New Republic*, March 30, 1998.

PAGE 64. "Former Fed governor . . . ," Justin Martin, *The Man Behind Money* (Cambridge: Perseus Books, 2001), p. 204.

PAGE 64. "Harding was the most . . . ," Carl Sferrazza Anthony, *Florence Harding* (New York: William Morrow, 1998).

PAGE 65. "'All steelmen . . . ,'" Theodore C. Sorenson, *Kennedy* (New York: Harper & Row, 1965), p. 461.

PAGE 65. "'The chief business . . . ,'" Donald R. McCoy, *Calvin Coolidge: The Quiet President* (Lawrence: University Press of Kansas, 1988), p. 156.

PAGE 65. "'By . . . statement and inaction . . . ,'" ibid., pp. 320–321.

PAGE 65. "Newspapers snidely reported . . . ," ibid., p. 272.

PAGE 66. "The Vermont native . . . ," ibid., p. 389.

PAGE 66. "As Yale economist . . . ," Shiller, *Irrational Exuberance*, p. 217.

PAGE 67. "Investing in the hinterlands . . . ." Anne Colamosca was the editor of *Insight*, an international investment letter for CNBC, which reported on investments in developing countries, along with those in the developed world.

PAGE 68. "'It was Europe . . . ,'" Alfred Kazin, *On Native Grounds* (New York: Harcourt Brace & Co., 1982), p. 190.

PAGE 69. "The integration of the world . . . ," Wolman and Colamosca, *The Judas Economy* (Boston: Addison-Wesley, 1997).

PAGE 70. "'America was going . . . ,'" David Minter, *A Cultural History of the American Novel: Henry James to William Faulkner* (Boston: Cambridge University Press, 1996), p. 107.

PAGE 70. "As Frank Rich wrote . . . ," Frank Rich, "Love that Bill," *New York Times*, March 7, 1998.

PAGE 71. "'As a Certain Age . . . ,'" Henry Alford, "Slaves of the Hamptons," *New York Times Book Review*, August 8, 1999.

PAGE 71. "Social critic David Brooks . . . ," David Brooks, *Bobos in Paradise: The New Upper Class and How They Got There* (New York: Simon & Schuster, 2000), p. 39.

PAGE 71. "Yet Brooks falls short . . . ," ibid., p. 269.

PAGE 71. "Similarly, H. L. Mencken . . . ," H. L. Mencken, *My Life as Author and Editor* (New York: Vintage Books, 1995).

PAGE   72. "'Are the banking system . . . ,'" Alfred Kazin, *On Native Grounds*, p. 256.

PAGE   72. "As literary critic . . . ," Elizabeth Hardwick, *American Fictions* (New York: Modern Library, 1999), p. xvii.

PAGE   74. "As Alfred Kazin . . . ," Alfred Kazin and Charles Shapiro, eds., *The Stature of Theodore Dreiser* (Bloomington: Indiana University Press, 1955), pp. 3–12.

PAGE   74. "But William Finnegan . . . ," William Finnegan, *Cold New World: Growing Up in a Harder Country* (New York: Random House, 1998).

PAGE   74. "Finnegan asserts . . . ," ibid., p. xiii.

PAGE   75. "In 2001 . . . ," Ehrenreich, *Nickel and Dimed*, p. 216.

PAGE   75. "'The whole upper tenth . . . ,'" Herbert G. Gutman and Stephen Brier, *Who Built America: Working People and the Nation's Economy, Politics, Culture, and Society*, vol. 2 (New York: Pantheon Books, 1992), p. 269.

PAGE   76. "Many 'enlightened corporations' . . . ," Lynn Dumenil, *Modern Temper: American Culture and Society in the 1920s* (Hill and Wang: New York, 1995).

PAGE   78. "'His formidable . . . ,'" Drew, *Corruption of American Politics*, p. 152.

PAGE   78. "That anger showed . . . ," Richard B. Freeman and Joel Rogers, *What Workers Want*, (Ithaca, N.Y.: Cornell University Press, 1999).

Chapter 5: Rhyming the 1990s with the 1920s: Economic Comparisons

PAGE   82. "In each case . . . ," John Kenneth Galbraith, *The Great Crash* (New York: Houghton Mifflin, 1988), p. 3.

PAGE   83. "The problems occur . . . ," Shiller, *Irrational Exuberance*, pp. 44–68.

PAGE   85. "'It was a golden age . . . ,'" Galbraith, *Great Crash*, p. 55.

PAGE   86. "In July of 1997 . . . ," Dean Foust, "Alan Greenspan's Brave New World," *BusinessWeek*, July 14, 1997.

PAGE   86. "According to Yale's . . . ," Shiller, *Irrational Exuberance*, p. 97.

PAGE   86. "Despite the determined hosannas . . . ," John Maynard Keynes, *The Economic Consequences of the Peace* (London: Macmillan, 1919; New York: Harcourt Brace, 1920).

PAGE   88. "In a brilliant analysis . . . ," "Bubble Trouble: The U.S. Bubble and How It Will Burst," *HSBC Economics and Investment Strategy* (London, July 1999).

PAGE   89. "As John E. Schwarz . . . ," John E. Schwarz, "The Hidden Side of the Clinton Economy," *Atlantic Monthly*, October 1998.

PAGE   89. "The final years of the 1990s . . . ," Center on Budget and Policy Priorities, an analysis of "The Congressional Budget Office: Study of Historical Effective Tax Rates," May 2001.

PAGE   90. "After the crash . . . ," Gutman and Brier, *Who Built America*, p. 270.

PAGE   90. "Historian Lynn Dumenil . . . ," Dumenil, *Modern Temper*, p. 306.

PAGE   91. "'The new consumerism . . . ,'" Juliet B. Schor, *The Overspent Consumer* (New York: HarperCollins, 1998), pp. 5–6.

PAGE   91. "Today, in contrast . . . ," ibid., p. 4.

PAGE   94. "Advertisers planned elaborate . . . ," Frederick Lewis Allen, *Only Yesterday* (New York: John Wiley & Sons, 1997), pp. 78–82, 128–129.

PAGE   94. "Installment buying became . . . ," ibid., pp. 127–130.

PAGE   94. "In spite of the country's . . . ," Gutman and Brier, *Who Built America*, pp. 277–287.

PAGE   95. "By the end of the 1920s . . . ," Lendol Calder, *Financing the American Dream* (Princeton, N.J.: Princeton University Press, 1999) pp. 234, 265.

PAGE   95. "These forms of . . . ," ibid.

PAGE   95. "Only those unions . . . ," ibid.

PAGE   96. "And just as in the Netherlands . . . ," Angus Maddison, *Dynamic Forces in Capitalist Development* (New York: Oxford University Press, 1991).

PAGE   98. "Paul Samuelson once . . . ," said in an interview with Bill Wolman in the early 1960s.

PAGE   98. "[B]etween John Maynard Keynes . . . ," Paul Krugman, *The Return of Depression Economics* (New York: W. W. Norton, 1999), p. iv.

PAGE   99. "Perhaps the most widely . . . ," Peter Temin, *Lessons from the Great Depression* (Cambridge: MIT Press, 1996), p. 83.

PAGE 101. "Movement of capital to . . . ," Walter Bagehot, *A Description of the Money Market* (London: John Murray, 1917), pp. 32–34.

Chapter 6: The Postmillennial "Hangover": Why the 2000s Will Feel Like the Brave New World's Version of the 1930s

PAGE 107. "In a cover story . . . ," Michael J. Mandel, "The Next Downturn," *BusinessWeek*, October 9, 2000.

PAGE 108. "And that is particularly . . . ," Paul Krugman, "A Defining Issue," *New York Times*, December 4, 2001.

PAGE 109. "In a research study . . . ," Robert Gordon, "Productivity on Stilts: Has America Entered a Golden Age of Economic Growth?" *Economics Focus*, June 2000.

PAGE 111. "More recently . . . ," Michael A. Bernstein, "Why the Great Depression Was Great: Toward a New Understanding of the Interwar Economic Crisis in the United States," Steve Fraser and Gary Gerstle, eds., in *The Rise and Fall of the New Deal Order, 1930–1980* (Princeton, N.J.: Princeton University Press, 1989), pp. 32–54.

PAGE 116. "But even before . . . ," Wynne Godley and William Martin, "How Negative Can U.S. Savings Get?" (Levy Economics Institute, 1999).

PAGE 117. "'It was,' as Luc Soete . . . ," Michael J. Mandel, "The Internet Economy: The World's Next Growth Engine," *BusinessWeek*, October 4, 1999.

PAGE 118. "Back in the 1920s . . . ," Lendol Calder, *Financing the American Dream* (Princeton, N.J.: Princeton University Press, 1999), pp. 71–73.

PAGE 119. "Edward Hyman Jr., . . . ," see *Money and Stocks*, a weekly publication of International Strategy and Investment, New York, N.Y.

PAGE 120. "Fine, the public . . . ," Gary Weiss, "Tiger Is Licking Its Wounds," *BusinessWeek*, March 13, 2000.

PAGE 122. "Charles E. Mitchell . . . ," Galbraith, *Great Crash*, pp. 153–154.

PAGE 122. "'The cumulative impact . . . ,'" Drew, *Corruption of American Politics*, p. 259.

PAGE 122. "Carl Bernstein remarked . . . ," Carl Bernstein appeared on Chris Matthews's *Hardball*, September 8, 1999.

PAGE 123. "William Greider . . . ," William Greider, *One World, Ready or Not* (New York: Simon & Schuster, 1997).

PAGE 125. "Although relatively powerless . . . ," Eric Hobsbawm, *The Age of Extremes* (New York: Pantheon Books, 1994), pp. 213–214.

PAGE 125. "Students rioted in Cairo . . . ," ibid., pp. 199–222.

PAGE 127. "'History teaches . . . ,'" editorial, *BusinessWeek*, February 8, 1999, p. 130.

Chapter 7: Power Play: The Attack on Social Security

PAGE 131. "In a rave review . . . ," Bruce Weber, "Shavian Artillery Levels Hypocrisy," *New York Times*, July 13, 2001.

PAGE 131. "He slyly tells . . . ," George Bernard Shaw, *Pygmalion* and *Major Barbara* (New York: Bantam Books, 1992).

PAGE 133. "Those in between . . . ," Theda Skocpol, *The Missing Middle* (New York: W. W. Norton, 2000).

PAGE 134. "Shaw understood . . . ," Shaw, *Pygmalion* and *Major Barbara*.

PAGE 136. "The prevailing ideology . . . ," Richard Cloward and Frances Fox Piven, *Regulating the Poor: The Functions of Public Welfare* (New York: Vintage Books, 1993), p. 46.

PAGE 136. "The famed lawyer . . . ," Brandeis, *Other People's Money*.

PAGE 137. "The result was . . . ," Teresa Ghilarducci, *Labor's Capital* (Cambridge: MIT Press, 1992), p. 10.

PAGE 137. "Ann Shola Orloff . . . ," Ann Shola Orloff, "The Political Origins of America's Belated Welfare State," in Margaret Weir, Ann Shola Orloff, and Theda Skocpol, eds., *The Politics of Social Policy in the United States* (Princeton, N.J.: Princeton University Press, 1988), p. 53.

PAGE 137. "'Thus,' adds Orloff . . . ," ibid.

PAGE 138. "The belief in self-help . . . ," Ehrenreich, *Nickel and Dimed*, pp. 193–221.

PAGE 139. "As a result . . . ," Ann Shola Orloff, *The Politics of Pensions* (Madison: University of Wisconsin Press, 1993), pp. 308–312.

PAGE 139. "The assault on radical reform . . . ," Frederick J. Hoffman, *The Twenties: American Writing in the Post-War Decade* (New York: Collier Books, 1961), p. 396.

PAGE 140. "God forbid that . . . ," Ghilarducci, *Labor's Capital*, p. 17.

PAGE 142. "There were also . . . ," John Myles, "Postwar Capitalism and the Extension of Social Security into a Retirement Wage," in Weir, Orloff, and Skocpol, eds., *Politics of Social Policy in the United States*, p. 273.

PAGE 143. "It is usually said . . . ," Cloward and Piven, *Regulating the Poor*, pp. 258–260.

PAGE 143. "Yet even with . . . ," Helene Slessarev, "Racial Tensions and Institutional Support: Social Programs During a Period of Retrenchment," in Weir, Orloff and Skocpol, eds., *Politics of Social Policy in the United States*, p. 373.

PAGE 144. "John Myles has argued . . . ," ibid., pp. 265–284.

PAGE 144. "Prior to the outburst . . . ," Bill Wolman and team, "The Reindustrialization of America," *BusinessWeek*, June 30, 1980.

PAGE 145. "As we have already seen . . . ," John Myles, "Postwar Capitalism," in Weir, Orloff and Skocpol, eds., *Politics of Social Policy in the United States*, pp. 178, 274–284.

PAGE 145. "Nixon's decision . . . ," Myles, "Postwar Capitalism," pp. 274–284.

PAGE 146. "Ronald Reagan . . . ," Thomas Byrne Edsall, *The New Politics of Inequality* (New York: W. W. Norton, 1984), pp. 17–19.

PAGE 147. "Thomas Byrne Edsall dates . . . ," ibid., pp. 107–140.

PAGE 148. "One notorious example . . . ," *BusinessWeek*, Economics Notes, December 11, 1978.

PAGE 148. "One reason . . . ," Myles, "Postwar Capitalism," p. 278.

PAGE 148. "By 1981 . . . ," ibid., p. 278.

Chapter 8: Pension Power: Who Has It, How They Got It, and How It's Used Against the Family

PAGE 151. "But after the terrorist . . . ," Josh Friedman, "First the Market Slump, Now Some Savers Losing 401(k) Match Funds," *Los Angeles Times*, November 11, 2001.

PAGE 152. "Walter Reuther . . . ," Nelson Lichtenstein, *The Most Dangerous Man in Detroit* (New York: Basic Books, 1995), pp. 282–284.

PAGE 152. "This was because . . . ," ibid., pp. 282–284.

PAGE 152. "The reason, of course . . . ," Edsall, *New Politics of Inequality*.

PAGE 152. "And to make matters . . . ," Ghilarducci, *Labor's Capital*, p. x.

PAGE 154. "In 1875, American Express . . . ," ibid., p. 14.

PAGE 154. "That's true even though . . . ," Teresa Ghilarducci, "Small Benefits, Big Pension Funds, and How Governance Reforms Can Close the Gap," in Archon Fung, Tessa Hebb, and Joel Rogers, eds., *Working Capital: The Power of Labor's Pensions* (Ithaca, N.Y.: Cornell University Press, 2001), pp. 159–166.

PAGE 155. "Ghilarducci asks, . . . ," ibid., pp. 158–180.

PAGE 156. "Ghilarducci argues, . . . ," Ghilarducci, *Labor's Capital*, p. 89.

PAGE 157. "Despite the passage of ERISA . . . ," Ghilarducci, *Labor's Capital*, pp. 55, 105.

PAGE 158. "From that point on . . . ," Orloff, *Politics of Pensions*, pp. 4, 13.

PAGE 158. "Although many American companies . . . ," Ghilarducci, *Labor's Capital*, pp. 32–35.

PAGE 158. "Ghilarducci argues . . . ," Ghilarducci, *Labor's Capital*, pp. 32–35.

PAGE 160. "Women received 34 percent . . . ," Ghilarducci, *Labor's Capital*, pp. 68–69.

PAGE 161. "Unions have a good record . . . ," ibid., pp. 111–159.

PAGE 161. "In 1957 and again . . . ," ibid., pp. 46–49. For a further discussion of the Teamsters' Pension funds, see Ghilarducci's *Labor's Capital*.

PAGE 162. "The result was . . . ," ibid., p. 153.

Chapter 9: Stillwater Investing: Drowning Out the Noise

PAGE 170. "Yet the pros . . . ," Edward Hyman, Jr., *International Strategy and Investment Daily Economic Report*, September 18, 2001.

PAGE 171. "If thought corrupts . . . ," George Orwell, "Politics and the English Language," in Rovere, ed., *The Orwell Reader: Fiction, Essays, and Reportage* (New York: Harcourt Brace, 1984), p. 364.

PAGE 171. "In his book . . . ," John Kenneth Galbraith, *Great Crash*, pp. 144–167.

PAGE 174. "In the last five . . . ," Jeffrey M. Laderman, *BusinessWeek*, January 24, 2000.

PAGE 175. "The original and most famous . . . ," The early history of "random walk" theory is described in Burton G. Malkiel, *A Random Walk down Wall Street* (New York: W. W. Norton, 1996). It accurately summarized the work of Fisher Black and Eugene Fama.

PAGE 175. "Random walks have . . . ," Anthony Lo and A. Craig Mackinlay, *A Non-Random Walk down Wall Street* (Princeton, N.J.: Princeton University Press, 1999).

PAGE 176. "Its reasoning points . . . ," Malkiel, *Random Walk*.

PAGE 177. "In early spring . . . ," Anne Colamosca, "The Options Option," *Columbia Journalism Review,* May–June 2000.

PAGE 177. "'If you look . . . ,'" ibid.

PAGE 177. "'A handful of editors . . . ,'" ibid.

PAGE 179. "A real clue . . . ," Jennifer Reingold, "Executive Pay," *BusinessWeek*, April 19, 1999.

PAGE 179. "In a story for *Forbes* . . . ," Gretchen Morgensen, "Stock Options Are Not a Free Lunch," *Forbes*, May 18, 1998.

PAGE 180. "According to Hewitt Associates . . . ," Hewitt Associates, "2001–2002 Salary Increase Survey Report," Fall 2001.

PAGE 182. "These stock buybacks . . . ," Charles Parlato, "The Profits Illusion Game," *American Outlook* (Summer 1999).

PAGE 185. "*Dow 36,000* . . . ," James K. Glassman and Kevin A. Hassett, *Dow 36,000* (New York: Crown Publishing, 1999).

PAGE 186. "It was, instead, . . . ," Jeremy Siegel, Letter to the Editor, *Wall Street Journal*, A23, April 14, 1998.

PAGE 187. "Some of the most . . . ," Galbraith, *Great Crash*.

PAGE 188. "Leader after leader . . . ," ibid.

Chapter 10: Stillwater Investing: The Positive Program

PAGE 189. "Emboldened by his . . . ," Bill Wolman, "Stocks Near Their Own Millennium," *BusinessWeek*, January 26, 1966.

PAGE 199. "Economist Dean Baker . . . ," Dean Baker, "Saving Social Security with Stocks: The Promises Don't Add Up," Twentieth Century Fund/Economic Policy Institute Report, 1997.

PAGE 201. "Keynes once wrote . . . ," Edward Chancellor, *Devil Take the Hindmost* (New York: Farrar, Straus and Giroux, 1999), p. 155.

PAGE 202. "Gerald M. Loeb . . . ," Gerald M. Loeb, *The Battle for Investment Survival* (New York: John Wiley & Sons, 1995).

Chapter 11: The Political Agenda: De-Hoaxing the 401(k)

PAGE 218. "According to Hewitt Associates . . . ," Steven Greenhouse, "Response to 401(k) Proposals Follows Party Lines," *New York Times,* February 2, 2002.

Index